About Th

Thomas Stone gives truth to the saying that "Necessity is the Mother of Invention." He suffered from depression, panic attacks, chronic headaches, insomnia, marital problems, and a dozen other symptoms. He tried the normal solutions, marriage counselling, group therapy, psychotherapy, but his symptoms wouldn't go away.

At the age of 30 he admitted to himself that he was **neurotic,** the mildest form of mental illness. The professional therapists had not cured him, so he set out on a personal mission to cure himself. He had no university research grant, no laboratory full of electronic equipment. The library was his source of information. His living room became his laboratory, and his family became his test subjects.

Working for 20 years, he explored 250 different therapies. He combined ideas ranging from Freud to Primal Therapy and added many discoveries of his own. Gradually he developed a **DO-IT-YOURSELF THERAPY** that is more effective and more permanent than going to a professional therapist.

His method is based on two basic assumptions: **First,** that depression, headaches, panic attacks, insomnia, marital problems, addictions and hallucinations all have the same cause, *blocked traumatic memories from early childhood.* **Second,** that if you can recall these traumatic events, and *drain away the pain by crying,* your brain will gradually repair itself and your symptoms will disappear.

Using the therapy on himself, he found 25 traumatic memories, and he cried about each one. His depression and headaches disappeared. He started sleeping better. His coldness turned into warmth. His marriage improved. His reading speed quadrupled. His energy doubled.

His wife Nancy saw the changes, and asked him to use the therapy on her, with similar results. Then his daughter Beth and her husband, then son David, and several friends and neighbors wanted to do it.

Cure By Crying is both a revealing personal story and a step-by-step do-it-yourself manual. If you decide to try this method, we promise that you won't be sorry. You are about to embark on the most fascinating journey you will ever take…

…the journey into your own hidden past.

I

Cure By Crying

How To Cure Your Own • Depression
• Nervousness • Headaches • Violent Temper
• Insomnia • Marital Problems • Addictions
by Uncovering Your Repressed Memories

By Thomas A. Stone

PUBLISHED BY CURE BY CRYING INCORPORATED

DES MOINES, IOWA, USA

PRINTED IN USA

III

ISBN: 0-9647674-0-6

Library of Congress Catalog Card Number: 95-92448

Copyright ©1995 Cure By Crying, Inc.
4316½ S.W. 9th, Des Moines, Iowa 50315
To order books and tapes from publisher: 1-800-410-2873
Quantity discounts available.

CURE BY CRYING trademark registration pending in U.S. Patent office.

First Printing, August 1995, 5M

Printed in the United States of America

CAUTION!

Re-experiencing your blocked traumatic memories from childhood can be a physical strain on your body. At times you may experience bawling, screaming, and faster heart beat. If you have any kind of pre-existing health problems, especially heart problems, stroke, diabetes, and sleep apnea, you should consult your physician before attempting The Therapy.

CAUTION!

Street drugs, alcohol and even prescription drugs may cause you to experience much more bawling, heavy breathing and fear than the patient who does therapy without drugs. They can also interfere with your natural brain chemistry so the therapy will not work at all. Consult your physician about your prescription drugs before you attempt The Therapy. If you try The Therapy while using drugs or alcohol, be sure to read pages 41-44, and 193-201.

CAUTION!

If you have pre-existing schizophrenia, paranoia, manic depression or suicidal tenencies, and you are using prescribed medications, consult your psychiatrist before attempting The Therapy. You should continue to take your medication and do not reduce dosage without supervision of your psychiatrist.

Also we believe that your condition is a combination of blocked traumatic memories, plus a vitamin mineral deficiency. You should not attempt The Therapy until you start a complete vitamin and mineral supplement program.

The safest way for you to do The Therapy would be to ask your professional therapist to read the book and use the method. If your therapist is not willing to use this method, only then should you consider trying the therapy without a professional. Read pages 173-178, and 193-201.

How The Book Is Organized

I have written this book for three groups of readers: 1) the non-professional general reader who wants to cure his/her own symptoms, 2) the professional therapist who wants to use the method in his/her practice, and 3) the scientific researcher.

The earlier chapters (1-9) are written in non-technical language for the general reader. Later chapters (10-11) and appendixes are of special interest to professional therapists and researchers.

- Chapter 1 is a simplified overview, some important basics and some warnings.

- Chapters 2 through 8 explain the method in detail. Note that the list of questions (Appendix A) is essential to the method. We decided to put them in an appendix because it is reference material like a dictionary, and would have interrupted the flow of the book.

- Chapter 9 will give you reassurance if you have hallucinations, voices, panic attacks or other strange experiences.

- Chapter 10 is mostly for the serious researcher who wants to know how the method evolved. However, we encourage everyone to read the part about brain chemistry, page 193.

- Chapter 11, again for the serious researcher, talks about my credentials and experiments. Also Nancy, Beth and David give their testimony that the method does work.

- The appendixes discuss issues that are not relevant to the general reader.

    Appendix A is only for people who actually do The Therapy seriously.

    Appendix B is my personal sub-conscious symbolism for serious researchers.

    Appendix C is a message to people who may follow in my footsteps in the distant future.

Contents

DEDICATION

About 10% of the population is mentally healthy. They are confident and full of energy. They don't understand why the rest of us have so much trouble.

Another 20% is *almost* mentally healthy. They may have a few bad habits, but they can overcome them by making a firm decision, "Just do it."

The remaining 70% struggle with low energy, shyness, headaches, addictions, bad tempers, sleep problems, failed love, sex problems, difficulty reading, talking and selling. They attempt to solve their problems by positive thinking, astrology, pills, support groups, subliminal learning, and religion, but their lives always stay the same because **they never find the real cause of the problem, blocked traumatic memories.**

This book is dedicated to the 70%, and to their children.

THANK YOU

To Nancy for being my first "test patient." To Beth, David and Chris for being "test children" and proving that this book works. To Ada and Julie for helping me get started toward my own cure. To Chuck for believing in the book even though he is too mentally healthy to really understand. To Sue Burt for retyping the book at least fifty times. To Jan and Tanya for valuable marketing suggestions. To Ed for many useful technical suggestions. To Carl Mazzie for legal common sense. To Nancy, again, for many hours of crying together. And to James E. Tolleson for being the only person in the whole world who ever convinced me to follow my instincts while it seemed that everyone was telling me I was wrong.

1

Curing Yourself

I'd like to tell you a story of a little boy named Tommy. His mom has a bad temper. Before he reached the age of 2 she had knocked him unconscious 3 times. Twice he was hospitalized. As you can imagine, his feelings about girls and affection are already confused.

One day when Tommy is about 4-years-old, he sees his mom and dad fighting. Suddenly mom is yelling in his face, "Do you want to live with mom or dad? Make up your mind!" Can you imagine a 4-year-old making that kind of decision?

Tommy sucks his thumb and pushes the question out of his mind. About an hour later a taxi arrives. Tommy sees his older brothers climb into the taxi while the driver throws suitcases into the trunk. Suddenly he knows that he must get into the taxi.

As he tries to climb in, his mom picks him up and carries him back to the house. Her face is cold and angry. Tommy clings desperately to her neck as she pushes him into the front door. Dad holds him and latches the screen door.

For a moment, mom stoops down to the little boy's level and looks at him through the screen. Her face is not angry now. She is sad and full of pain. Tommy looks into her eyes one last time. His little hands reach up and try to touch her through the screen. He wants to say, "Mommy, why can't I go? I want to go with you."...but he never says it.

Moments later, she is climbing into the cab. Tommy desperately runs to the back door, but dad latches that door too. After the taxi is gone, dad unlocks the doors. Tommy

1

walks to the curb where the taxi had been. He sucks his thumb and stares down the empty street. Dad sits in the grass beside him. They stay there together for two hours. Tommy is hoping the taxi will turn around and come back, but dad knows that it won't.

Dad is not a very good cook. For the next week, they eat hot dogs every meal. Dad has to make a business trip and he can't find a baby-sitter, so he decides to take Tommy with him and leave him with Uncle George who lives in Chicago.

Uncle George lives in a big apartment. Next to the apartment is a little yellow house. George is not accustomed to baby-sitting. At about 12:00 noon, he lets Tommy play outside without close supervision. About 12:30 George looks outside and realizes Tommy is nowhere in sight. Desperately he phones all his neighbors. He searches two blocks in every direction. Finally he calls the police. George is in a panic. How will he ever explain this to Tommy's dad?

At about sundown, a police woman appears at George's door holding Tommy by the hand. The little boy seems dazed. She tells George that the man who lives in the yellow house had taken Tommy and locked him in the attic. She asks if he wishes to press charges. Please come down to the police station and sign some papers.

Try to imagine what is happening inside Tommy's mind. Within one week his mom left him, his dad left him with a stranger in a strange town and then he was kidnapped and sexually abused.

You have probably guessed that the little boy's name was Tommy Stone. The story is true. It really happened to me, but I didn't know about it until I was 45 years old. **It was a totally blocked memory.**

Please don't misunderstand me. This book is not about blaming parents or feeling sorry for Tom. The book is about healing the mind. **The point is that my blocked memories were causing my symptoms. When I uncovered them and cried about them, my symptoms disappeared.**

I didn't know I had been mistreated. No one had ever told me. But I did have plenty of symptoms. I had headaches,

I was terribly shy, I was a slow reader, and I was tired all the time. I figured I was normal.

My most destructive symptom was about girls. I would fall in love with a girl I knew only from a distance. I would be so obsessed that I would think about her every minute of the day. And when I had a chance to talk to her, I would be physically unable to speak. Some people think this kind of love is beautiful, but I can tell you it is not. It is miserable! It destroys marriages with jealousy, and interferes with productive work.

I'm writing this book to tell you how I cured my own headaches, depression and a dozen other symptoms without the help of a professional therapist…and without drugs. The method requires the help of another person, roommate, spouse or friend, but you can also make enormous progress by yourself, working alone in a quiet room.

If you have ever experienced depression, shyness, lack of energy, sleep problems, nightmares, headaches, addictions, problems with the opposite sex, violent temper, difficulty in reading, talking or selling, and especially if you have failed to solve these problems by other methods, this book contains answers you have been looking for all of your life.

The method is based on two assumptions: first, that your symptoms were caused by painful events in early childhood that you have blocked from memory; and second that if you remember these events and, more importantly, cry about them, your symptoms will gradually fade away.

The crying is more important than the remembering, though both are essential in the long run. I'm convinced that even when you cry at a sad movie, you are improving your mental health ever so slightly.

THERAPY PRINCIPLE NO. **1**

The First and Most Important Principle In This Book Is: The More You Cry, The More Your Mind Will Heal Itself

---

I myself have spent hundreds of hours digging out blocked memories, remembering, crying, weeping, bawling. All the time I was using this method, my friends, relatives and several professional therapists were telling me I was wasting my time, that my pursuit was hopeless, endless and self-indulgent. But a voice inside told me to keep going.

With my wife, Nancy, helping me, I began to find memories that shocked me: twice I was near death; I almost drowned at age $1^1/2$; my favorite playmate died of pneumonia when I was 3. Mom left when I was 4. I found a total of 25 blocked memories and spent hours crying about each one. I had difficulty believing they had really happened. But as I felt my whole body shaking and the tears gushing from my eyes, I asked the obvious question: "If it never happened, then why am I crying?"

At times I became discouraged. The therapy seemed endless. Sometimes I'd have several sessions in a row with no progress, and I'd wonder, "Am I fooling myself? Are my friends right? Am I being self-indulgent? Is my mind making up fantasies?"

Eventually I began to see the light at the end of the tunnel. One by one my symptoms faded away. My headaches and nightmares disappeared. I began to have more energy. For the first time in my life, I woke up in the morning feeling alive and cheerful. It was as though a great fog had lifted and I was seeing the daylight for the first time in my life.

At last I knew without doubt that I had been doing the right thing. My wife Nancy saw the changes in me and decided to use the method on herself. My daughter and her husband wanted to do it. As I told more and more people about it, I began to receive more calls and inquiries about therapy than about my regular business. It seemed that every family had at least one person with a serious emotional problem that could not be helped by the normal medical community. Not only had I freed myself from a crippling illness, but I may have found something that could help thousands or perhaps millions of other people.

If you make the decision to do this therapy, I promise that you won't be sorry. You are about to embark on the most fascinating journey you will ever take, the journey into your own hidden past. Don't be afraid. It won't hurt very much. The therapist watching you will be more uncomfortable than you. The crying and bawling will never be more than you can handle. It will be almost a pleasure compared to the misery you've endured all of your life. The Therapy is a lot of work, but if you are anything like me, pretty soon you'll look forward to therapy sessions, and you'll be fascinated by the memories you find, even while the tears are running down your cheeks.

DEFINITION OF NEUROSIS

The condition of having traumatic memories stuck in your head is called **"NEUROSIS."** This neurotic condition is physical in the sense that there is a physical change in the brain, as though "wires" have been cut or "switches" have been turned to the off position.

The traumatic scene is blocked but not erased. It continues to exist in the form of electrical/chemical energy locked in the brain. It continues to exert a force which the neurotic will experience as nervousness, depression or irritation, and since he is unaware of its source, he tends to blame the feeling on his current life. He may think "My job makes me nervous," or "I'm depressed about my girlfriend," or "My roommate irritates me."

Neurotics lack energy because most of their energy is used to suppress the old pains. Their lack of energy is in direct proportion to the size of the pile of pain. As the pain is "discharged" by bawling, the energy improves dramatically.

It's no wonder that neurotics don't know they are neurotic. The memory of trauma is blocked. They literally do not know they were mistreated. And not knowing is the single biggest stumbling block that prevents them from getting cured.

Since a very large percentage of our population is neurotic, (My guess is 70%) most of their symptoms are socially acceptable. They are told by parents, teachers and TV commercials that everyone has stress and headaches. (For the record, I haven't had a headache for 5 years. Before therapy I averaged 2 or 3 headaches per week.)

The concept of curing neurosis by crying is childishly simple. The real difficulty is how to uncover the blocked memories. Frustrated by the problem, the professionals have looked for short-cuts such as drug therapy. No doubt drugs do a lot of good, but they leave the blocked memories in tact, stuck somewhere in the nervous system, interfering with efficient thought, distorting normal brain chemistry and the weakening immune system.

I don't like treating symptoms. I much prefer to find and eliminate the cause. Mental health people today are fond of saying that "Your emotional problem is caused by a chemical imbalance in the brain." But I have to ask, "What causes the chemical imbalance?" Isn't is possible that blocked memories cause the imbalance?

My purpose in writing this book is to present a method that eliminates the cause of neurosis, the blocked memories. The method is so simple that it does not require professional training. It can be done by two friends, husband and wife, roommates, or even cellmates in a prison. Of course, I do not object if professional therapists wish to use this method.

I am not a professional therapist. I did not invent this method. Most of it was discovered between 1903 and 1960. The method which we in our family call simply "The Therapy" is a combination of 13 discoveries by other scientists and 7 discoveries of my own.

A neurotic treated by most other therapies or by drugs may improve his life slightly. He'll be able to "cope" or "function better" but he'll never reach his full potential. He remains neurotic, but manageable.

By contrast, a neurotic treated by "The Therapy" will mature and blossom. He'll learn to listen and perceive reality better, to persuade and inspire people. His reading speed will double. His sleep problems will improve. His energy will quadruple. He'll get into action instead of putting things off. In short, he'll grow toward his full potential...without drugs.

The Method. . .In A Nutshell

The method is explained in detail in the next four chapters, but here is a simplified view of how it works.

In the early 1990s there was a popular TV series called *Star Trek, The Next Generation*. My favorite character was Data, the robot. In one episode, Data was malfunctioning. Captain Piccard approached him and said, "Data, you've been acting strangely lately. **What's wrong with you?**" Data answered, "Just a moment, I'll do a diagnostic check." Then Data would close his eyes and look internally at all of his wiring and programming. That, in a nutshell, is how The Therapy works. One person, playing the role of the therapist, asks the most obvious of questions, for example, **"What's wrong with you?"** The other person, the patient, closes his eyes and looks at his internal wiring and programming.

There are lots of obvious questions you can ask: **"What's wrong with you?"**..."Why are you depressed?" ..."What happened when you were little?"...just to list a few.

The big difference between robots and humans is their reaction to pain. Ask Data "What happened when you were little?" and you would expect him to remember every detail. But you ask a human the same question, he's likely to say, "I don't remember."

But why would a human not remember? Why do we assume that he can't. After all, many humans have a photographic memory. Do they have a bigger brain, more connections? No! The neurotic has the same size brain as the genius with the photographic memory.

In "The Therapy" we don't accept the answer "I don't remember." Instead, we ask the question again...and again... and again. If you ask the same question often enough, eventually the brain will give you an answer. It may not be the whole answer, but just a small piece of the puzzle, and as the brain lets go of one small piece, it also lets go of some pain, just a few tears at first, then crying, then an explosion of bawling.

As the small amount of pain is discharged, the pile of pain is reduced in size ever so slightly, and the mind is more willing to let go of another piece of the puzzle, followed by more bawling, then another piece, and so on.

...and that, in a nutshell, is how The Therapy works.

THERAPY PRINCIPLE NO. **2**

If You Ask A Question Over and Over, Your Brain Will Eventually Answer It.

The method is simple enough that it does not require a professional therapist. What makes the whole process simple is that the patient does most of the work by following his intuition. Neurotics are highly intelligent and perfectly capable of understanding this book. Except for the first few sessions, the patient runs the show. For the best results, both the therapist and the patient should read the book thoroughly. We have the book available on cassette for patients who are slow readers.

You may find a professional therapist willing to use this method, but there are some definite advantages to using an amateur. The most obvious advantage is cost. With an amateur therapist, you pay by trading time. You can be the therapist one day, and your friend can be therapist the next.

Another problem is that the professional therapist is often motivated to prescribe drugs. He knows that long hours of talk therapy are not cost effective. Drug treatment promises faster results, and insurance companies will pay for it.

A more subtle danger with the professional is that you may view him as an authority figure. The danger is that you might believe his suggestions, when he is only guessing. We call it "planting" when the therapist plants an idea into your head instead of pulling it out of your head. Planting is a serious mistake. If the professional says, "Perhaps you were jealous of your sister," you might think, "I'm not aware of that, but maybe I was." If the amateur says it, you are more likely to have the healthier thought, "I know more about my thoughts than you do, so stop interrupting."

Is It Dangerous To Dig Out Blocked Memories?

Whenever I put on a seminar, someone always asks if The Therapy is dangerous. Could the remembering cause a person to commit suicide? Could The Therapy cause a heart attack?

My personal view is that The Therapy would have the exact opposite affect. A suicidal patient will be much, much more likely to commit suicide if he doesn't do The Therapy. As soon as he discovers his first blocked memory, his feeling of depression will be replaced by a feeling of hope. Removing the pain from the nervous system will make the entire body healthier, and take pressure off of the heart.

The nervous system has a marvelous self-defense mechanism which I call the "governor." The subconscious mind is very clever about which blocked memories are allowed to come to the surface, and which ones remain blocked a while longer. Believe me there is an intelligent power at work in The Therapy, almost as though the subconscious mind is a separate living person.

THERAPY PRINCIPLE NO. **3**

Your Own Nervous System Has A
Built-In "Governor" That Protects You
From Feeling Too Much Pain

Even as I write this book, my own therapy is not 100% finished. There is one traumatic scene that has not yet been discharged. I know approximately what happened because many details have come up during The Therapy. But I have not yet felt all of the pain. I have not finished crying about it. (The scene was about being kidnapped in Chicago). The reason I have not been allowed to finish this scene is because I have recently developed a minor heart ailment (atrial fibrillation) and my *governor* has decided that it is too dangerous for me to feel the pain at this time.

I tell you this as an example of how the nervous system has a very intelligent self-defense mechanism. In fact, neurosis is essentially a self-protection mechanism. At the moment of trauma, your nervous system chose to block the memory, rather than to die.

One possible danger, in my opinion, is drugs. A nervous system without any drugs is capable of regulating its own therapy, but drugs (both prescribed drugs and street drugs) might change the brain's ability to self-regulate. If you are on drugs, alcohol, or prescribed medications, be sure to read pages 41-43 at the end of this chapter before you try The Therapy. Also read pages 193-200 about brain chemistry.

Although I personally believe that your own nervous system will do a wonderful job of protecting you, for legal reasons, I must make this very clear: I am not a doctor, or a psychiatrist. This book represents my personal experiments and discoveries among my own family and friends. Our method has **not** been tested on hundreds of mice, rats or patients at any hospital or university. If you chose to try this method, you do so at your own risk, (though I can think of nothing more risky than to continue your life as a neurotic).

WARNING! There is such a thing as physical neural damage from accident, disease or chemicals and of course, this therapy might not undo that damage. If you have drugs in your system, The Therapy might work and it might not work. There are many different kinds of drugs and each one has a different effect. If you try The Therapy with drugs in your body, you do so at your own risk. To reduce your risk, read pages 41-43. Also read pages 193-200 about brain chemistry.

WARNING! If you have a pre-existing heart condition, you should definitely consult your doctor before you try the therapy. Also, read pages 221-223, Chapter 10, about heart attacks in the middle of the night.

When Do The Symptoms Disappear?

Some symptoms disappear instantly! Some will fade gradually, and some will stay with you until the end of therapy.

■ **HEADACHES, LACK OF ENERGY,** and **NERVOUSNESS** go away fairly quickly, as soon as you reduce the pile of pain. I used to have headaches 2 and 3 times a week, but since therapy, I haven't had a headache in 5 years.

■ **DEPRESSION:** The feeling that most people call "depression" will change in quality. Before therapy, depression feels like, "There is no hope. Life has no meaning." After you have experienced some blocked memories and the bawling that comes with them, the same feeling will become, "I feel like another blocked memory is trying to come up." My definition of depression is the feeling you have when a blocked memory is trying to come to the surface. You may still have the feeling, but you'll know it is temporary, and you won't think "There is no hope."

■ **SLEEP PROBLEMS:** Most sleep problems are caused by blocked memories. Nightmares are old feelings trying to come up during sleep. If you ever experience the intensity of a terrifying nightmare, it should give you some idea of the amount of pain that is stored inside of you.

In the beginning, therapy can cause nightmares to be more frequent, because the questioning will throw your defenses off balance. But the more you cry and remember, gradually your nightmares will be less frequent and much less intense. My early nightmares were so terrifying that I had to wake up, turn on the light, and wake up Nancy to protect me. It felt like I was being electrocuted. The last time I had a nightmare, it was so mild that I just laid in bed and looked at it calmly to see if I could find an old feeling.

Difficulty falling asleep will improve quickly. Difficulty waking up can seem to get worse temporarily. Much of the work of therapy is done during sleep. Your brain is rewiring millions of switches that have been disconnected for years. It's very hard work, and you may experience what we call "heavy sleep." You will feel as if you were drugged. Your body will need to sleep until the rewiring is done, and you should give in to the urge to sleep late if you can afford to. Believe me, it's not laziness. You are actually working very hard.

WHAT IS A SYMPTOM?

It is not always easy to distinguish between a symptom and a normal activity. One person may become a movie star because he loves the theater. Another may do it because he has a neurotic need for constant attention.

Love can be neurotic or healthy. A healthy person might fall in love once or twice in a lifetime. A neurotic can "fall in love" twenty times and he may fall for self-destructive losers.

Food, drink, sex, love, and even joking around can be sick or healthy. The real issue is compulsion. If you can choose to eat or not to eat, you're healthy. If you have an uncontrollable compulsion to eat, if you can't stop or slow down, it's probably a symptom of neurosis.

Divorce can be healthy or sick. Arguing can be healthy or sick. Relationships can fall apart because people have different interests, and there is nothing sick about that. But most arguments result from old feelings. Neurotics in general are very poor communicators. They can be totally inept at conversation, easily irritated, quick tempered. They don't listen, they twist what you say, have to be right all the time, or at the other extreme they are dull, quiet, passive and never show any feelings. These problems are caused by blocked traumatic memories.

Some "symptoms" are just bad habits. You may cuss like a truck driver before therapy, and then after therapy you may continue to talk rudely. The ability to talk graciously has to be learned. The therapy may clean the junk out of your mind and leave your mind open to learn new information. But you have to fill in the blanks by studying and thinking and by finding someone to imitate. Whether you learn to talk at age four or 40 (like me) you have to learn it from someone else.

PROGRAMMED OR HYPNOTIC SYMPTOMS

There is another kind of symptom that is not only important but fascinating. I could not decide whether to call it a "programmed symptom" or a "hypnotic symptom," so I decided to use them both. We call it the *programmed symptom* because it's like a faulty command in a computer. We also call it a *hypnotic symptom* because it's like a hypnotic command stuck in your head. Programmed symptoms are fascinating because they can go away instantly after a blocked memory is discharged.

Here is an example from Nancy's therapy. When our children were little, they would interrupt Nancy and she would get very upset. Now every mother knows that children interrupting can be frustrating. But with Nancy it was more than frustration. She would get much more upset than the situation deserved.

As her therapy progressed, we came across a scene which we call the "Dinner Table Scene." Nancy was about 3 years old, and she came to the dinner table with something exciting to talk about. As little Nancy tried to tell her story, her father interrupted with "What do you know about the price of beans?"

She tried to say it again, and again her father interrupted. She tried again...and again...and again. No matter how often she tried to talk, her father continued to shut her up. It went on for years. Nancy was not allowed to talk. At some point it became unbearable for her little mind and it became a blocked memory.

When Nancy finally recalled this event, she discharged it as *lethargy* (see pages 115-116) instead of bawling. Her body became stiff and heavy and she could not move. Her arms and legs were like weights. It went on for at least a half hour, and when she finished, she was breathing heavily as though she had run a race. The heavy breathing is a very dependable sign that there has been a successful discharge.

After Nancy discharged this *Dinner Table Scene,* her reaction to being interrupted changed. The kids continued to interrupt, of course, and she was still frustrated, but it was in more reasonable proportion. She would admonish the child with one or two words and go back to her conversation. I call this a *programmed symptom* because the *Dinner Table Scene* had programmed her reaction, and discharging the scene had the affect of repairing the programming.

Another example: Before my therapy, I had a subtle stiffness to my walk. I noticed it especially in public or at a party. If I would stand up and walk across the room, my legs would feel stiff as though my programming was saying "hold still" or "don't move."

In my very first week of therapy, I found a traumatic scene in which my father was using those exact words, "hold still" and "don't move." After discharging the scene, the stiffness disappeared from my walk instantly. Suddenly I was loose, I could mosey, I could slink, I could slither, I could strut across the floor. The stiffness was gone forever. The phrase "hold still" had been a *programmed command* that programmed my body.

There is something else I want to tell you about symptoms. The stiffness in my legs was subtle and invisible to anyone but me, and when the stiffness went away, no one could see the change except me. If I had a truckload of university scientists and laboratory instruments, it could never be documented or proven. It was wonderful and exciting for me, but totally irrelevant to anyone else. Achieving a loose walk was not a major event. It did not get me a better job, nor save my marriage. It was a minor improvement, one of thousands, but seen together, the thousands of little improvements add up to a big jump in my joy of living. For the first time in my whole life, I feel good, I have energy, I'm loose, I'm comfortable, and I can't imagine going back to the way I used to be.

MEASURABLE SYMPTOMS

Loosening the stiffness in my walk would be invisible to a scientist. If I say I went from 2 headaches a week to no headaches at all, I really can't prove it. The fact that I multiplied my reading speed four times can't be proven. It could result from practice rather than removing blocked memories.

I would like to tell you about two of my symptoms I consider visible and measurable.

All of my life I have had a rash on my face below my eyes and on the left and right sides of my nose. It was always

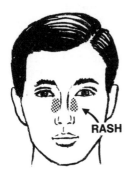

RASH

tender and on days when I was especially nervous, it would be red and raw like an open wound. I had tried cleaning and moisture creams and medications, but nothing seemed to work. It really hurt badly and believe me it was very visible.

During the year when I went to a professional psychiatrist, the rash continued just as it had my whole life. When I finally tried the method in this book, I found blocked memories the very first day, and tears gushed from my eyes. They poured like a waterfall down, onto the area of the rash. The rash area was like the "river bed" for all of the blocked up tears that I had held back for 40 years. The tears continued to gush day after day as more and more blocked memories came to the surface. Within weeks, the rash was gone forever.

I know a young man who has the same rash. He works at a store where I shop. His rash is as red and raw as mine and in exactly the same spot. When I think of him, I know what causes his rash, and I am anxious to finish this book so I can give him a copy.

Another measurable symptom is my absent-mindedness. It's measurable, but I still can't prove it to a scientist. I am a little absent-minded today, but before therapy I was much worse. I would typically drive a half hour to work and arrive at my office only to discover that I had left my wallet, or tie, or brief case, at home. I always forgot something. The only way I could solve it was to have a written checklist, and even then I would forget something.

As The Therapy progressed, I continued to forget things, but the time lapse (the time from when I left home until I realized I had forgotten something) shortened, in a surprisingly measurable way. Before therapy it took at least a half-hour to remember the item. Later it took 20 minutes, then 15 minutes, then 10 minutes, then 5 minutes. The more I did The Therapy and the more I cried, the shorter the time lapse. I actually measured my therapy progress by how far I drove before I had to turn the car around and go home to get my wallet. Today, the time lapse is consistently about 10 seconds. I'll walk out my front door and just as I'm opening the car door, my mind will say "Oops, you forgot your wallet."

TEMPORARY CURE VS PERMANENT CURE

It is possible to remove symptoms without curing the neurosis. Some therapies appear to remove symptoms, but if the pain isn't felt, the symptom can reoccur. The most obvious example is pills. If you take a pill to overcome depression, it seems obvious to me that the cure is temporary.

Many therapies work on your present day situation and make no attempt to dig out the past. This can be very effective on people who are 90% mentally healthy to start with. Once the patient recognizes his own bad habit, he can change his life with a decision, and the therapist will rightfully say that the symptom went away within a few days. But the issue here is how much pain is stored in the nervous system. A patient with only a little pain can make quick progress by working on current problems, but a patient who has 30 or 40 traumatic scenes will make no progress until he cries about his blocked memories.

Sometimes just attention and the hope of attention can relieve symptoms. A neurotic who is depressed may suddenly feel better when he finds a new girl friend, or a job that makes him feel important, or a counselor who seems to really care. But when the girl friend or job or counselor is gone, the depression will return because the blocked memories are still there.

The "faith healing effect" or the "placebo effect" can remove symptoms. Medical research is full of examples of people being cured by sugar pills because they believed the pills would work.

The placebo affect is much like hypnotism. Dr. Ernest Hilgard of the Stanford Laboratory of Hypnotism Research tells us that there is a certain kind of person who responds well to hypnotism. They want to believe in a magic cure, but their logic will not allow them to believe in magic. So when they are given a "magic with a scientific basis," only then can they believe it. Hypnotism, acupuncture, transcendental meditation, astrology, can actually remove symptoms because of belief. In fact, the symptoms can go away permanently.[1]

Symptoms can be removed by pills, by personal attention, by faith, by force, and by your own decisions, and if these things work for you, why not stay with what works. Everyone does not need to remove their blocked memories. But fixing a symptom without fixing the cause is a little like remodeling a house with a bad foundation. You can patch the cracks in the wall, only to find another crack a week later.

I believe it is important to remove the underlying pain because of the damage it does to your body. There is no absolute proof, but many studies suggest that blocked pain may be the cause of backaches, migraines, allergies, digestion problems, immune problems and possibly even cancer.

OTHER SYMPTOMS:

Most of my symptoms are just like yours, so you might enjoy knowing how long it takes to cure some typical symptoms using The Therapy:

Face rash ....went away instantly

Stiff walking......................went away instantly

Sleepless nights.................enormous improvement in
6 months

Headaches........................enormous improvement in
2 months

Nightmares......................gradual reduction in intensity

Nervousness ....enormous improvement in
3 months

Depression.......................the meaning of the word
depression changed almost
immediately from "Nothing
to live for" to "Here comes
another old memory."

Slow reading....................Quadrupled speed in 2 years

Insane compulsive crushes
on the opposite sex ......went away completely in
4 months. I still like girls, but
it is no longer a compulsion.

Lack of energy ....enormous improvement in first
month, but it does reoccur when
a new memory comes up.

Procrastination.................gradually improved in one year

Irregular bowels ....went away in 2 years, but does
reoccur from time to time.

Narrow mindedness.........went away almost instantly

Closed mindedness..........went away almost instantly

Immaturity......................gradually went away in 3 years

Nasal voice......................voice became full within a year
but nasal voice reoccurs when
I face a new challenge

Lack of intuition...............improved gradually

Irritable, unfriendliness,
violent temper..............improved gradually

Selfishness.......................improved gradually

Absent-mindedness ....improved gradually

Inability to sell.................improved gradually

Doing Therapy Alone

Discovering your blocked memories is fascinating for you, but for your therapist (roommate, husband, wife), it can be enormously boring. You might be searching for just the right word that can open the door to your feelings, while your therapist will want to push you, draw conclusions for you, and of course he'll be interrupting instead of helping.

This is one danger of using an amateur therapist, and yet he's not so different from the professionals. Ever since the time of Freud, therapists have longed for short-cuts. This is why they get off track. They offer drugs instead of trying to find the cause. The premise of this book is that if you want a cure, you must dig out the old scenes and cry about them. Anything less is just a temporary bandaid.

If you want to keep digging out blocked memories and your therapist doesn't, you may have to eventually get away from him and go it alone. You definitely need another person at the beginning, perhaps the first month, or the first year, but once you learn to recognize your own *brain feelings,* once you have seen *programmed commands* in action, once you have discharged a *similar story* and found the real scene that is hidden under it, once you have learned to use *dreams* to find blocked memories, and once you discover your own *doorways,* you might be ready to go it alone.

When I started my own therapy, I originally started with a professional therapist named Julie. From the beginning, I had a knack for finding blocked memories. Julie said I was the easiest patient she had ever worked with. I was finding scene after scene and bawling my eyes out, and feeling better every day. But she became bored very quickly, and started looking for shortcuts.

At first I assumed that she knew something that I didn't know, but later I began to suspect that she was getting me off track. One day when I was just about to explode from a new scene, she kept trying to change the subject. Eventually she said it out loud what she honestly felt, "You can't expect me to sit here and listen to every detail of your whole life story. It would take forever." And of course she was right. It was a lot to ask from anyone.

I wanted to dig out all of my blocked memories, but Julie tried to convince me that it was hopeless and endless, and I almost bought it. It was natural to assume that she knew more than me.

Eventually I stopped going to Julie. My wife Nancy became my therapist, and I became hers. Against Julie's advice, we continued to work on the blocked memories. I must admit there were moments when I had my doubts and I started to think Julie was right. Sometimes we would have several sessions in a row with no progress. During one part of my therapy, I became obsessed with death because I was reliving a time when I had almost died. But eventually our decision to work on blocked scenes proved to be valid.

Gradually our symptoms faded away. Our minds started to open up. We became interested in more things. Nancy went back to school to work on a second degree. My reading speed exploded and I began to study subjects that I never cared about before: history, economics, sports, self-defense, selling, politics, religion. My piles of books filled every room in the house.

We got involved in new activities, and suddenly our schedules were so busy that **we stopped doing therapy because there was no time to do it.** I was for all practical purposes cured, in the sense that my headaches and nightmares were gone, I had plenty of energy, I was happy and positive, and I was taking responsibility instead of blaming everything on others. Nothing irritated me. I was a warmer, friendlier person. I wasn't perfect, but I was much, much better.

I reached a point where I decided, "No more therapy! Let's get on with our lives!" But about a month after this big decision, I was driving to my office, and something on the radio got me thinking, and suddenly I found myself weeping. I entered my office, turned the lights down low, closed my eyes and asked myself the question that Nancy would have asked. "What's the feeling!" I played both roles, therapist and patient. I started to weep, then cry, then I bawled for about 20 minutes. **A part of a blocked scene came to the surface, without a therapist, all by myself. It was much more efficient than using a therapist. It only took 20 minutes, and I didn't have to waste Nancy's time.**

Since that day I have done many hours of therapy alone, and my mind has continued to mature. We have learned some tricks and methods to speed the process of doing therapy alone, which I would now like to share with you.

THERAPY BY GOING TO THE MOVIES

The easiest way to do therapy alone is with a video movie. I remember one day Nancy was at home and phoned me at my office. She said that she had been bawling for two hours by watching the end of the movie *Wuthering Heights.* She had drained off so much pain that she was exhausted and out of breath. She literally had to crawl on her hands and knees to the phone. She had watched the last scene over 20 times.

Through the years she has discharged many hours of bawling by watching the movies *Always, West Side Story, Thelma & Louise.* She cries in movies about saying good-bye and someone leaving.

I stayed home from work one morning and bawled 3 hours by watching the last scene of *Ice Castles,* 23 times. I've also used *West Side Story, Spartacus, Xanado* and many others.

By far the easiest way to discharge old pain by yourself is to find a movie that makes you cry, then don't fight it. Sink into it. Get a VCR, rent the movie, lock yourself in a room away from interruptions, and watch the part that makes you cry over and over.

This is obviously a *similar story* reliving explained on pages 29-31. You may not know why you are crying. But trust me when I say it is a valid discharge. It is reducing your pile of pain, and it is moving you closer to mental health. Remember the first law: The more you cry, the more your brain will heal itself…even if you are crying in a movie.

You might be tempted to just use movies instead of therapy, but that won't work. Many of the movies that have made me cry had absolutely no affect when I originally saw them before starting therapy. Apparently the therapy sessions push old feelings closer to the surface and then the movie gives you an indirect outlet. The movie is the perfect indirect outlet for the pain. You can explode with feeling without viewing your scene directly.

Your old feelings come to the surface in a definite sequence, though the sequence may not be logical. It's a lot like a log jam. You cannot remove a log from the middle of the jam. You have to start at the edge, remove one log, then one more. Eventually you can clean out the whole pile of logs, one log at a time.

The point is that old feelings come up in sequence. The movie you watch today may have no affect on you today, because that particular feeling is not ready to discharge. A month or a year from now that same movie could make your cry for 3 hours because it is similar to a scene that is now ready to come up. Without the therapy sessions, a sad movie will give you only a little discharge.

You're therapist may not be with you when you watch the movie, but it will be useful to tell him about it later. Tell him why the movie makes you cry, and as you tell him, you'll explode in tears again and you'll gain a better understanding of your feeling. It's an efficient way to do therapy, because you might work 3 hours alone, and your therapist only has to work a few minutes.

I wish everyone would cry in the same movies. I could just give everyone a copy of *West Side Story* and we'd all be cured. Unfortunately, my favorite movie is likely to bore you to death, and vise-versa. I'm listing here some specific movies that Nancy and I have used for therapy, on the chance that they might have the same effect on you. But most likely, you'll want to pick your own movies.

NANCY'S MOVIES: *Wuthering Heights*   *Always*
                   West Side Story   *The Alamo*
                   Thelma & Louise

TOM'S MOVIES: *Spartacus* *King and I*
Ice Castles *Miracle Worker*
Godfather *Platoon*
Xanado *Camelot*

DOING A THERAPY SESSION BY YOURSELF

Doing therapy with a movie is by far the easiest way to discharge, but it is not enough. There will be times when you have to do a formal therapy session by yourself. When I do therapy alone, I go into my bedroom or office, I lock the door and I play both roles, patient and therapist. I use the same routine as if I had a therapist (See Chapter 2). I take the phone off the hook, close my eyes, put on a blindfold, I ask myself a question out loud, and I look inside my mind for pieces of the answer.

The biggest problem is that it is sometimes difficult to pay attention, to stay focused. It is easy to get dopey and drift off to sleep. I'd like to share with you some tricks to help you stay awake and focused:

■ **MORNING IS BEST.** Morning for you may be 6:00 am or noon. My point is that you should do therapy at a time when you are normally awake. Don't try it just before your normal bed time.

■ **LET YOUR EMOTIONS TELL YOU WHEN TO DO IT.** I never attempt self-therapy unless I have old pain pushing to the surface. Your feelings will give you clues when something is coming up on its own. If you feel *tears,* if you feel *irritable, impatient, depressed, dull, lacking enthusiasm,* your body may be telling you that an old feeling is coming up. I personally know that I need therapy whenever I *can't decide* something. I never try therapy alone unless I feel one of these clues.

■ **LISTEN TO MUSIC DURING THE SESSION.** If you ever cry in movies, it's the music that makes you cry. Music is the most amazing of all human creations. Most of our other inventions can be explained logically, but music makes no logical sense at all. **Music is feeling reproduced outside of the body.** Every single human emotion can be portrayed in music: love, loss of love, loneliness, hopelessness, joy, majesty, patriotism, hope, fear, silliness, playfulness. Each feeling can be portrayed in a thousands shades of gray. Music is the most wonderful tool for self-therapy because when you play the right song, you'll feel the feeling.

It takes some effort to find the right music. You're looking for music that matches your pain. If you're feeling loneliness, you need loneliness music. If you're feeling hopelessness, you need hopelessness music. When I was little I was near death twice, and I have gone to great lengths to find a collection of *death music*. I've recorded them on one cassette and have used it for over a hundred hours of self therapy. I've cried buckets of tears from that music, and have totally cleaned all death feelings out of my brain.

As with movies, I wish that every neurotic would react to the same music, but we all seem to react to different songs. I prefer music without words, because words interfere with my thoughts. Nancy usually picks songs with words. Some of you will find old feelings with country music or christian music. As we learn more from our readers, we hope to develop a set of music tapes that will affect the majority of neurotics, and make them available to you.

THERAPY PRINCIPLE NO. **4**

Music Will Help You Find Old Feelings.
You Need Music That Matches Your Old Pain.

■ **DREAMS AND OTHER DOORWAYS.** You will want to get into your pain quickly to keep awake and focused. It may take 20 minutes to get your mind off of your daily work and on to your internal world, but beyond 20 minutes, you want to find feelings quickly, and the best way is to be familiar with your own *doorways*. (See pages 54-56).

Each patient has to discover his own doorways. Whenever Nancy finds a color on her viewing screen, she can find a feeling. Whenever I find a famous movie star in my dreams, I can find enough pain for several sessions. Your doorway may not be colors or movie stars. Only you can find your own unique doorways. But believe me when I tell you that you do have a doorway. Your subconscious mind wants to give you an indirect way to let the pain out. The dam does have a leak, and once you find it, you can go back to the same leak again and again.

Whenever I feel the need for self-therapy, the first place I look for pain is in my dreams (see Chapter 4). Sigmund Freud told us in 1900 that "Dreams are the royal road to the subconscious." It was one of his greatest contributions to The Therapy. Every dream has some reference to a blocked scene, but you may not be able to find it. Even if you don't recognize the blocked scene in your dream, you accomplish a lot just by saying the dream out loud several times. Running through the dream stimulates the pain and puts pressure on the leak in your dam. It's like shaking a piggy-bank upside down. Something is likely to fall out.

■ **TELL YOUR THERAPIST AFTERWARDS.** Once you have done your work alone, phone your therapist or go see him in person and tell him about your session. This will be time well spent because you will have done 90% of the work without wasting the therapist's time. If you have found some valuable connections, you can summarize it for him and crystallize it for yourself. If you have found pain, you'll probably explode in tears in the first sentence out of your mouth. There is something about telling it to another living person that really opens the floodgates. No matter how impatient your therapist, he'll gladly listen to five minutes of pure discharge.

These are my tricks for doing therapy alone. I hope they work for you. Everyone is different. You may find your own shortcuts and doorways, and I hope you'll write and tell us.

Three Kinds of "Reliving"
and Fool's Reliving

There are many "mental-problem" movies like *Heroes, Sybil,* and *Three Faces of Eve,* that end with a scene where the patient re-lives the one traumatic event that caused the illness. This is very good movie making, but I'm afraid that it misleads the public about this subject of reliving a scene.

Some professional therapists add to the confusion. They feel they have accomplished something with one reliving after 5 years of seeing a patient. Sometimes they claim to have witnessed reliving when in reality, there was no reliving at all. I'd like to try to clear up the confusion.

In the first place, 99% of us did not become neurotic as a result of one traumatic event, but rather from an accumulation of day after day after day of mistreatment, no love, no touching, no one to talk to. Even the "primal scene" in Janov's writings (See page 36) is not so much a traumatic event as it is a day of totaling, the last straw, a moment of realization, "Mommy really doesn't care about me!"

In the second place, there are 3 kinds of reliving...or I might say 4 kinds, if I include fool's reliving. There are 3 kinds that are valid in the sense that they really do discharge old pain and they really do lead to a cure, and there is a 4th kind that is not a reliving at all. I believe the confusion comes from the fact that writers and psychologists lump them all together, either to make a more exciting story, or because they honestly are not aware of the difference.

Let's look at them one at a time.

COMPLETE RELIVING

Complete reliving is 3-D, stereo, totally vivid in every detail, every sound, every smell, and texture. The patient is so immersed in the scene that he feels he is actually there with mom or dad, in the front yard, with blood on his lip. In Primal Therapy, it is called "primalling," and it happens frequently with most patients. It is the fastest, most complete, cure, taking from 6-months to 2 years to discharge all the pain.

Complete reliving occurs rarely in Psycho-analysis and normal counseling...perhaps once in a therapist's lifetime, and then it is an accident, unexpected and uncontrolled.

I have experienced complete reliving only once, and it was very brief. I was there, and as fast as it started, it suddenly ended. I assume my Super Conscious was saying, "Oops! That was close!" (see Super Conscious, pages 61-63).

I've often wondered how a complete reliving is really possible. Why is the traumatic event replayed in 3-dimensional stereo? Our other memories are not like that? The very fact that a complete reliving does exist, is evidence in favor of the temporary file theory (see pages 81-84). The temporary file theory would explain why the traumatic event is stored with every detail in tact...because the child never lived it yet...he hasn't felt it yet...and when sleep came, he never processed the scene to file the usable information.

FRAGMENTED RELIVING

Fragmented reliving might also be called "reconstructed reliving." This kind of reliving is much more common. In normal Psychoanalysis and Psychiatry, each patient might experience it once every two years. In The Therapy it can happen continuously, depending on the patient. Nancy has discharged perhaps 5 scenes by fragmented reliving, while I have discharged about 24 scenes this way.

In *fragmented reliving,* it is as though the patient is look-ing at the scene through a key hole. The patient can't see the entire event. He sees just a small detail, a hand, a pink dress, a funny black hat, and the patient may discharge as he discov-ers each detail, perhaps just a few details in a session. It may take a month to put all the pieces together, the whole story... and then the patient feels unsure. "Did that really happen to me?" he'll say in disbelief. "I feel like I'm making this up." A wise therapist will encourage him by saying something like,

"Go ahead. Make a guess. What do you think might have happened." This is perfectly safe to say as long as the patient is crying. It is possible that the patient might guess wrong about what happened, but the therapy will work anyway. If he is bawling, he is bawling either about what really happened, or about something similar.

Fragmented reliving does lead to health, but more slowly than total reliving. In my opinion, any therapy that makes you cry, will eventually make you healthier.

I call it "fragmented" because the patient sees only little pieces of the scene. I call it "re-constructed" because in a sense, the patient really is reconstructing how the pieces of the puzzle go together. The Super Conscious (see pages 61-63) is giving you one small part of the story, just enough so you can cry without exploding.

I recall this experience often in my therapy. I would recognize a detail. Suddenly I'd have a hunch of what might have happened. I would think "It feels like a guess, but what if it is true?"…and just the possibility that it might have happened would make me explode in tears.

The patient really is guessing. He is reconstructing a story that is intentionally hidden by the Super Conscious. The patient is **not**…let me repeat, the patient is **not** viewing an actual recording of the event. There is a vivid "tape" some place in his mind, but it is hidden from his view, for his own protection.

In my experience of reconstructing scenes, I have noticed on my viewing screen, that one day the little boy (me) might be wearing a white T-shirt, and in the next session, while working on the same scene, the little boy would be wearing a blue and white striped shirt. This is why I'm convinced it is a reconstruction and not an actual recording. It might occur to you that this difference only proves the patient is making it up. But I'll say it again, if the patient is bawling, he has to be bawling about something.

In my experience, the most painful scenes will be discharged by a *symbolic* reliving first, to reduce the pile of pain to a manageable level, before the patient even begins to see the *fragmented reliving*. So now let's look at *symbolic* reliving:

SYMBOLIC RELIVING

Also called "similar story" reliving. Suppose your mother died when you were 6 years old. Then many years later, you go to a movie about a little child whose mother dies. You may not even remember your own Mother's death, but the movie might cause you to bawl heavily. This is *similar-story* or *symbolic* reliving. You are experiencing something similar to what happened to you, and yet you don't remember what happened. You don't remember it clearly, you don't even remember it vaguely, nor in a fragmented way. It is a blank. And yet the movie makes you cry for 15 minutes. You play the movie 5 times, and you cry 5 times.

The most vivid example of symbolic reliving from my therapy is also a good demonstration of how symbolic reliving and fragmented reliving are related to each other: One day, as I was driving to the office, I listened to a cassette about Abraham Lincoln. Lincoln was so heart broken by the death of his childhood sweetheart, that he disappeared for several days. When his friends finally found him, he was laying on her grave. The story caused me to discharge buckets of tears, and the feeling was overwhelming. That evening in a therapy session, I told Nancy about Abe Lincoln, and again I bawled so much I could hardly breath. There was so much feeling for me in that story that I discharged again and again over 3 sessions. And yet it did not make any sense. Why was I crying so much. It hadn't happened to me. I was never a great student of history. Why was I crying about something that had happened to someone else over a hundred years ago? I was not even aware that I might have witnessed death in my childhood.

About a month later, the story of what had happened to me began to unfold as *fragmented reliving,* and it was several months later that I pieced the whole story together. Briefly, I was about 3 and lonely for motherly attention.

There was an 8 year old girl named Amy who lived 2 houses away, who used to come over to play with me, and apparently I loved her. My memory of her is like a puzzle that I pieced together out of pieces from dreams. Here is what I have pieced together: one day she caught pneumonia, and within a week she died. I remember a neighbor lady standing at our front door telling my Mom "It happened so fast! I can't believe it." (potential programmed command).

Mom did not have enough sense to sit me down and explain it. She tried to hide it, but I kept begging "Can I go see Amy?" Finally, with some irritation, she blurted out, "Your little girl friend is dead. You're never going to see her again." Dad approached us as though he was aware that I was hurting. He stood behind me and put his hands on my shoulders. Mom was just mad. "He's old enough to learn a few things." They took me to the wake, and to the funeral. I burst into tears when I told Nancy about Amy's "little freckled nose sticking out of the casket."

I tell you the story because it clearly demonstrates the important relationship between *symbolic* reliving (Abe Lincoln story) and *fragmented* reliving (story of Amy). **The symbolic discharge comes first, and it is easy**…happening almost accidentally sometimes without a session. **The symbolic discharge has to be first** because we need to drain away a lot of pain before we can even start to look at what really happened.

THERAPY PRINCIPLE NO. **5**

Symbolic Reliving Is The Fastest,
Easiest Way To Discharge Old Pain.

Fragmented Reliving Comes Only After
A Scene Is Discharged Symbolically

The fragmented reliving is slow, it takes diligent effort by the patient, and the therapist can be bored to death. It can only happen after symbolic reliving has reduced the pile of pain. Symbolic reliving happens in a flash...fragmented reliving may take weeks or months.

Symbolic reliving is fairly common to life, because it is the easiest. You experience it every time you cry in a movie. It is a safe bet that it is usually the same type of scene that makes you cry...I recall several movies where a child lost his mother...and they all made me cry. (Amy was like a mother to me).

There is also some confusion about *symbolic* reliving that throws other therapists off track. A real event can be a *symbolic* reliving. For example, a 30-year old man may break up with his wife and be devastated, unable to get over it. He may go to a therapist who doesn't believe in going back into childhood pain. The therapist may encourage the man to "Get it off his chest." They might see some improvement after a few sessions. The therapist and the patient may attribute the improvement to "talking it out," "improved self-image," or advice from the therapist. But I'm here to tell you what really happened.

In reality, whatever the man was feeling about his wife was very similar to something that happened to him earlier, perhaps at the age of 1 or 3 or 7...something that is totally blocked. He has no memory of it at all. If he cried in the therapist's office, he was discharging symbolically. He really was draining away pain, but he and his therapist believe they have handled most of the pain, when in reality, they have hardly scratched the surface. The patient may feel better, partly from reducing the pile of pain, partially from the attention. He may over the course of several sessions simply meet a new girlfriend and start the "game" all over again. But there will be no cure, no real permanent change, until the whole pile of pain is greatly reduced. Whatever went wrong in his first marriage will just happen again.

The point is this: The pain he felt about his wife leaving

him was real. She really did leave. But his pain is also symbolic because there is a blocked childhood trauma hidden under the problem with his wife. A mentally healthy man might get over the loss in a month. The neurotic may feel the pain for years, because there is a gigantic pile of pain that is not getting discharged. He doesn't even know it is there. He is totally convinced that his feelings are present day.

Psychoanalysis uses symbolic reliving when the patient "transfers" parent feelings to the doctor. This is valid therapy because the analyst knows it is symbolic, and he is attempting to get to the childhood memories, but it is too slow. It digs for memories, but that misses the target slightly. The real target is to cry, to bawl, to discharge the pile of pain, then memory follows after the tears.

In summary, there are 3 kinds of reliving that lead to health. Complete reliving (primalling) is the fastest. Fragmented and symbolic reliving are slower, and they work together in a sequence: first we reduce the pain by symbolic discharge, then the scene can be viewed and discharged in a fragmented way.

There is a 4th kind of reliving that is not useful, *fool's reliving.*

FOOL'S RELIVING...NOT A RELIVING AT ALL

Several of my friends have told me about traumatic events from their childhood, as though they were saying "This is the event that messed up my mind." Then I ask a few questions that seem obvious to me. "How did you come to remember this event?" I ask. "Oh, I've always been able to remember it," they say.

They are missing the obvious, and I hope you have spotted it. If they have always remembered it, then it wasn't traumatic...at least it was not traumatic enough to cause symptoms. **If it was really traumatic, then they would not remember it at all. It would be total blank, or in some cases, there would be one minor piece of the story that is not blocked.**

Sometimes my friends tell me that the memory came during a session with a counselor, or even a hypnotist. So I question them further, "Did you cry when you remembered it?"..."No!" "Were you surprised when you remembered it?" ..."No, I've always known about it, I just hadn't thought about it for years."

That is not how a blocked memory comes to the surface. Memories that are truly blocked, will discharge symbolically first, then will come to the surface in pieces, and with tears, and the patient will feel some surprise and disbelief.

The most common example is "I was molested." It seems like just about everyone I know has told me that they were molested when they were young. And I have 4 friends who have told me they were raped, without me even asking.

I'm not trying to make light of child molesting, but I do question it's role in neurosis. **If you can remember it easily, then the memory is not blocked. It may have been unpleasant, humiliating, painful, confusing, but if the memory is not blocked, then it cannot cause symptoms. More likely there are other earlier traumas that are blocked.**

It is just like the man who could not get over his wife leaving him earlier (see page 31). A mentally healthy man might get over it in 1 or 2 months, a neurotic would suffer for years because of the hidden event. I suspect child molesting could be the same. A mentally healthy child who is molested, might get over it quickly, but a neurotic child might feel anguish about it for years because it may be connected to an earlier event (perhaps an earlier molesting) that really was traumatic and was hidden from view.

On this issue of rape and molesting, the movies and talk shows may have us confused. The truth is that most of us were not made neurotic by one big event. Most of us were damaged by an accumulation of day after day mistreatment.

What "Traumatic" Really Means

I remember talking with a young woman, let's call her Kathy, who remembered being molested at a very young age. As I was curious about therapy methods, I asked her how she was able to recall this event. She said, "I was talking to my therapist and suddenly the memory popped into my mind. I've always known it, but I haven't thought about it for a long time."

This was not a blocked memory. If she can recall it easily, and if she knows for sure that it happened, it's not blocked. It may have been awful, but it may not have been awful enough to damage Kathy's mind.

It is popular today to believe that emotional problems are caused by "traumatic events," but what does that mean? The death of a parent, rape, beating, molesting, these events seem like obvious traumas. They make great news stories, exciting movies, dramatic TV shows. But these seemingly obvious traumatic events obscure the true picture of what really causes mental illness: a lack of love and attention from mom and dad.

THERAPY PRINCIPLE NO. **6**

The Trauma That Causes Neurosis Is:
Lack of Love and Attention from Parents

In a sense, the child becomes neurotic because the parents are neurotic. The parents may have good intentions, and in their own way, they may love the child. But if they are neurotic, they will not be able to give the child enough attention. The child is mentally healthy (at least for a while). She is quicker, more alive, and more self-confident than her parents. They won't have enough energy or patience to

34

handle her. Their own compulsive needs and addictions consume so much energy, that there is little left for the child.

Violent events can certainly play a part in the illness, but one violent event by itself is unlikely to damage the mind of a child who is loved and wanted. The real significance of traumatic events is that they are the "last straw" or the "final proof" that no one cares. The child realizes that they have never loved her, and they never will.

Let's imagine for a moment that there are two Kathys (Kathy A and Kathy B). Both girls are molested at an early age. The word "molested" invites misunderstanding. It can mean anything from rape, to seduction, to mere touching. For the sake of clear illustration, let's be specific. Imagine that Kathy's Uncle Fred tries to touch her under her dress. Imagine that the first Kathy (Kathy A) was showered with love and attention from the day of her birth. Her parents thought she was adorable, and spent hours playing with her, talking to her, answering her questions, and challenging her mind.

Now let's imagine another Kathy (Kathy B). From the day of her birth, she wasn't wanted. Mom left her with a baby-sitter as often as she could so she could party with her friends. When they were together, she was not allowed to talk and ask questions. She was told constantly to "Stay in your room! Stop bothering me! Go watch TV." She is told that she is ugly, stupid, and "can't do anything right."

Finally, let us imagine the effect on the two Kathys if they are molested by Uncle Fred. Kathy A might be self-confident enough to say "No thanks!" and she would probably tell her parents immediately because she knows they will understand. The event would be unpleasant, but it would not become a blocked memory.

The effect on Kathy B would be much more destructive. She might put up with the molesting because she is starved for attention, or because she is afraid of adults (because she is afraid of Mom and Dad). She might keep it a secret from her parents because she knows that they would not listen, or would blame her, or they wouldn't believe her. **And the**

real trauma of the molesting would be the realization that no one cares. The molesting is not the cause, but it could be the "last straw," and it could become the "similar story" that is covering the real pain of *no parental love.*

The real trauma that causes emotional problems is the lack of love and attention. Kathy is ignored, not listened to, not played with, not taught, not challenged, day after day, year after year. No smiles, no encouragement, no fun, no answers, no help. Her neurosis is an accumulation of all those meaningless days, like logs in a log jam.

As the days go by, the child tries to explain to herself that "They really do love me, they just have to work," or "They'll love me if I do everything right." The child tries to find a substitute parent, a nurse, a sister, a teacher, a pet, but when the substitute has to leave, the pain of not being wanted returns.

Finally, one day, in an icy moment of truth, the child suddenly knows what she has tried to deny, "They don't love me and they never will." Janov calls this moment the "primal scene." For a 5-year-old, that truth is horribly painful. It is so traumatic that the nervous system will block the thought to prevent an overload of pain.

The moment of truth might be divorce, a beating, or being molested, but as often as not, the moment is insignificant to outside observers. A little girl falls out of a swing and she cries, "Mommy, help me," and suddenly she realizes, "Mommy isn't coming! She never comes, because she really doesn't care about me." It can be a moment when her drunk father gets angry for the 500th time, or the death of a pet, or a neighbor (substitute mom) moving away...or it can be an accumulation of several of these events.

Janov tells us that during the primal scene, the child will **"split,"**[2] and the word is descriptive of what happens. The split is spiritual and physical and it may involve several parts of the brain, but the most obvious split is between the left and right sides of the brain. Before the split, the child has the potential to use talents from both sides, a full range of creativity, language, music, logic. After the split, the child will live more in one side, and less in the other. This is why we find people who have great mechanical skill, but can't express their thoughts, or people with musical genius and no common sense. There are even retarded people with incredible mathematical skill. One part of the brain is blocked, the other side gets double use.

After the split, the child is no longer real. The real self has been hidden away because she knows that her parents cannot accept her as she really is. What is left is an actress. Instead of an original personality, she has a learned performance: the sweet little "angel," or the "brat," or the "scholar," or she pretends to be "stupid." Whatever the parents can accept becomes the performance. In the beginning, the child may know she is acting, but 20 years later, she is unaware of her own acting. Her real personality is forgotten and out of reach.

THE AGE OF THE SPLIT

The split usually happens between the ages of 5 and 8, but it can happen much earlier. The earlier the split, the more likely the child will be psychotic instead of just neurotic. I personally believe (but cannot prove) that all mental illnesses are pretty much the same. They are all caused by blocked painful events, and they can be cured by crying and remembering. Obviously, there are exceptions: brain damage from accidents, drugs, or disease, and perhaps some genetic disorders that I can't pronounce.

I suspect that schizophrenia, paranoia, manic-depression, depression, and most of the other official 230[3] mental illnesses are variations on a central theme. The cause is always blocked pain, but there are differences in how our symptoms are formed. For example, an 8-year-old will "split" differently than a 2-year-old simply because some parts of the 2-year-old's brain aren't functioning yet. The neurotic child may learn different performances, and different programmed commands, depending on culture, education, economic level of the family, and the age of the split. I suspect that a multiple personality happens when the child splits more than once.

The question of age is interesting. Some people think it is amazing if a patient remembers birth during therapy. In my experience, even though I was very neurotic, it was easy for me to remember birth. In fact I remember my thoughts just before I was born, and I remember being carried to my Mom's bed just after birth. **These memories were not blocked. I could have remembered them without therapy, but I had no reason to think of them.**

I did have some blocked memories in my first year, but they surfaced early and were relatively easy to find. When I found them, I bawled easily.

For me, the most difficult scenes to dig out were between the ages of 2 and 5. I call them the "middle years." I'm sure that the *middle years* would vary from patient to patient. For you it might be ages 3 to 8 or ages 5 to 9, but the principle remains consistent: the memories surrounding the time of the split will be the most blocked and the most difficult to dig out. I split when I was 4, so that time was the most blocked for me, in fact, there is a part of that time that is still blocked.

You might logically expect the very early years to be the most blocked and hardest to find, but in reality the first year is fairly unblocked because the infant is so strong and mentally healthy. He had all of his marbles. He was a tough little guy.

After age 8 the memory is good simply because the child is big enough to have some control of his life. He can fill his own needs. If he is ignored, he can watch TV or get attention from his friends at school.

But the middle years are tough digging. Much of the pain must be drained off by a similar story (see pages 29-31) before the actual scenes come into view. When you finally find the scenes, you'll piece them together from small fragments on your viewing screen or from pieces of dreams. Even when you understand what happened, you may not shed a tear. You may continue to discharge from similar stories before you find another fragment.

Don't! Don't!
Don't Confront Parents!

A friend of mine went to a psychiatrist and was able to remember being beaten up by his Dad. When he confronted his Dad about it, his father denied that it had ever happened and the conversation turned into an argument.

People frequently ask me if it is wise to talk to their parents about the bad things that happened when they were little. My answer is **No! No! No! Definitely No!** Confronting parents accomplishes nothing. It can lead to hurt feelings, or an argument, and it can confuse your therapy.

What possible good can come from confronting them? How would you expect them to react when you say, "I remember when you molested me when I was six." Do you expect them to admit it and apologize? Remember, they're neurotic too. They undoubtedly did the very best they were capable of. Do you expect that one conversation with you will cure their neurosis, when you've been working on your neurosis for years?

Confronting your parents can be very confusing for you. If you are working on a truly blocked memory, it will come to you in fragmented pieces, and you will feel your own doubts that it ever happened. What do you expect will happen inside your mind if your parents say; "No! It never happened. Your therapist has filled your head with lies. That book you read is a bunch of hog wash!"

There are several reasons why they might not tell you what you're looking for. They might honestly not remember ...and they might be lying.

An event that was traumatic for you could have been so unimportant to them that they didn't even notice. It was just another day to them. At the other extreme, it could have been very unpleasant for them, perhaps not traumatic, but unpleasant enough that they don't want to think about it. They may have worked very hard to forget that it ever happened. If they are embarrassed and ashamed about the event, they might lie about it, and no amount of arguing will get them to admit it.

It's important to keep your target clear. **Your goal in therapy is to reduce your pile of pain by crying.** You can do this by yourself and without any contact with your parents. By the time you see a fragmented scene come into view, you may have already discharged most of the pain. Remember, a truly blocked scene will discharge first as a similar story before you see it on your viewing screen.

You don't need someone else to tell you what happened. You will know, when your own nervous system decides that you're ready to know. Don't you understand? **You are being protected from pain by not knowing.** If you knew for sure, the overload of pain could damage your nervous system. That's why the pain is given to you in small portions. It's all you can handle safely. Not being sure is one of the ways your nervous system is protecting you. Trust me, keep doing The Therapy, and when the time is right, you'll know what happened.

I recall in my own therapy one evening I was struggling to put together several pieces of a scene. The pieces fit together so perfectly that **suddenly I knew!** I was no longer guessing, and I started to scream "MY GOD, IT'S TRUE! IT'S ALL TRUE! IT'S ALL TRUE!" Recognizing that it had really happened was in itself a trauma, a pain, and a discharge.

As I write this chapter, I still have a few scenes that I'm not sure about. I have never asked my parents what happened and I never will. The important thing to me is that my symptoms have gone away and I feel great for the first time in my life. The headaches are gone, the rash is gone, the nightmares are gone, and I'm full of energy. If my memories are fabrications, then why would the symptoms go away?

The therapy has improved my relationship with both parents. I feel no resentment and no anger. As much as I am capable of it, I love them. I love them more than I did before The Therapy.

If You Are On Drugs Or Alcohol

Addicts who go through Primal Therapy don't go back to their addictions. It is a complete cure because the blocked memories are gone. Former addicts have no desire to go back. In fact, smokers who go through Primal Therapy cannot smoke because it burns their mouth.

Their method is superior to the 12 step program and drug support groups. **The only reason you need a support group is because you're still addicted, because you still have blocked memories.**

Unfortunately, Primal Therapy is expensive and it cannot be done at home. The method in this book offers you a way to uncover your blocked memories and cure your addiction at home at no cost.

The problem of drugs is a viscious circle. You should get the drugs out of your body before you start The Therapy, and yet you may have difficulty giving up the drugs until after you get rid of your blocked memories.

Nancy and I have never used drugs or alcohol and that's why we were excellent test cases for The Therapy. My daughter Beth used marijuana continuously for 8 years, and she used it during therapy. She experienced a lot of terror during therapy, and I suspect that the drugs had a lot to do with that. Nancy and I have not experienced any terror during sessions.

There are many kinds of street drugs and prescribed drugs. Each one will affect the brain differently. Cocaine, crack, speed, crank and amphetamines deplete brain chemicals.[4] Morphine, codeine and heroin block old memories and make therapy impossible until you stop taking the drug, and then the old memories may come up with too much force.[5] Barbiturates interfere with therapy because they prevent dreaming.[6]

LSD and marijuana actually stimulate the blocked memories and then the brain must create hallucinations to stop the memories. LSD can damage your normal ability to maintain your blockage, resulting in "LSD-induced schizophrenia."[7] There have been several recorded cases of curing LSD-induced schizophrenia by uncovering blocked memories at other clinics. So far, we have no experience of curing it with The Therapy.

There are so many different drugs that it would take a billion dollars in research to know how each one affects The Therapy. For legal reasons and for your protection I must clarify that my advice on drugs is an "educated opinion."

My opinion is that The Therapy will help you get off of your addiction, and that your governor will protect you from overload. My opinion is that the only way your governor will fail is if the drugs have depleted your natural brain chemicals, or if you have a pre-existing health problem. My opinion is that given the right amount of vitamins and minerals, your body will rebuild whatever damage the drugs have done. Obviously, taking vitamins for one day will not overcome eight years of drugs, but a complete supplement program for four to six months could give your body time to do some repairs. This is my opinion. I am not a doctor. You are invited to go to your library, ask a doctor, and form your own opinion. Also read pages 193-200 about brain chemistry.

The bottom line is this: You should give up the drugs before you try The Therapy. But if you do The Therapy while drugs are in your system, you must take full responsibility for what happens, good or bad. I cannot be responsible for your decision. I was not the parent who caused your neurosis. I was not responsible for your decision to start taking drugs.

CAUTION! If you use drugs during therapy, the therapy might work, it might not. If there were any danger, the drugs that you decided to use would be the cause. The Therapy by itself is completely natural. It involves talking and crying, nothing more.

CAUTION. If you do The Therapy while you are using drugs, you and you alone are responsible for what happens.

If you decide to try The Therapy, in spite of these warnings, I'd like to suggest a few precautions. Get a physical check-up to be sure there is no physical damage. Talk to a professional psychiatrist, show him this book, let him read it and ask his opinion. If there are any members of your family who might object to The Therapy, let them read the book, and ask them for their opinion.

Read pages 351-356 in *Primal Scream*. They have some experience with how drugs might affect therapy.

Start taking a complete vitamin and mineral program as described in Chapter 10. Stay on it for at least a month before you try the therapy. Try to get off of your street drugs at least a month before you try it. You should continue your medical prescription, but ask your doctor's opinion on how the drug might affect your therapy. Ask your doctor to consider gradually reducing the dosage and let the vitamins replace the drug.

If you are addicted to heroin, morphine or meperidine, call our office to learn about a Vitamin C Based Rehabilitation Kit that will help you kick your habit without withdrawal symptoms.

Don't be surprised if your doctor, psychiatrist, and family members give you negative opinions about The Therapy. They are just people. They are not smarter than you. In the end you must make your decision alone. I'd love to help you but I can't.

I have an opinion about Beth's terror that might be useful to you. In normal therapy without drugs, the pile of pain is held under control. The nervous system will let go of small, manageable portions of pain, and then seal up the dam. I believe that in Beth's therapy, because of her drugs, the nervous system could not control the pile of pain, and **Beth came very near to a complete reliving.** That could be good if she could have gone all the way to a complete reliving, but

43

she never did. Instead, her nervous system gave her hallucinations as a defense. She saw monsters under the bed, so she could avoid feeling the monster inside of her head. A total reliving is a good thing. But coming near to a total reliving, without completing it is a waste of energy.

If you find yourself in Beth's situation, and you want to go for a total reliving, I suggest you read Chapter 10, and then read the *Primal Scream,* by Arthur Janov.

If you try The Therapy while on drugs, and if you have some success with it, please write and tell us your experiences so we can share it with other people who have a drug problem.

FOOTNOTES CHAPTER 1

1. Ernest R. Hilgard, Stanford Laboratory of Hypnosis Research, "A Study in Hypnosis," *Psychology Today,* Jan. '86, pp. 23-27.

2. Arthur Janov, *Primal Scream,* pp. 22-37.

3. The American Psychiatric Association publishes a *Diagnostic and Statistical Manual of Mental Disorders.* In 1952 it listed 60 types and subtypes of mental illnesses. By 1968 the list had grown to 145, and by 1985 it reached 230 separate conditions.

4. Durk Pearson and Sandy Shaw, *Life Extension,* p. 171.

5. Arthur Janov, *Primal Scream,* pp. 351-371.

6. Durk Pearson and Sandy Shaw, *Life Extension,* p. 193.

7. Arthur Janov, *Primal Scream,* pp. 351-371.

2

How The Therapy Works

The Method

A typical session can last anywhere from a half hour up to two or even three hours. In early therapy, it is ideal to do The Therapy every day or once every two days. Here is a brief outline of the routine that we use in every therapy session.

1. ISOLATE: If you can afford the time, the patient should isolate for 20 minutes before the session starts. He sits alone, wears the blindfold. No TV. No radio. Nothing to read. Nothing to eat. If your schedule is very busy, you can skip the isolation completely and The Therapy will still work.

2. THE BLIND FOLD: The patient wears a blindfold to block out light so he can see pictures in his mind. The place where he sees pictures is called his *viewing screen* or his *picture screen*. He lays in a comfortable position on a couch, bed or floor.

3. CURRENT PROBLEMS: The patient may spend the first 20 minutes of the session talking about *current problems*, for example, an arguement with his boss. We want to get his current problems off of his mind before we start the real therapy. Also, the current problems are often connected to his childhood, so talking about them will stimulate the old feeling.

4. QUESTIONS: The therapist then asks questions to the patient. He may ask the same question many times. He asks it once, waits about ten seconds, asks it again, waits another ten seconds, and so on. He may ask each question five, ten, or even twenty times. The patient watches his viewing screen and reports whatever pictures appear on the screen. **These pictures are the number one tool of therapy. The picture screen is our only link with the part of the brain that is blocked.** When we find a picture on our viewing screen, it is as though we are looking into our pile of pain through a key-hole, or through a small pariscope. We cannot see the whole picture of what happened. All we can see is one little piece.

As the patient looks at the picture, he tries to put into words what it reminds him of. It's like looking at one piece of a puzzle and trying to recreate the whole picture from just one piece. He concentrates on his feelings to help him find the whole picture.

THERAPY PRINCIPLE NO. **7**

Pictures on the Viewing Screen Are the Number One Tool of Therapy.

The viewing screen is our only link with the part of the brain that is blocked.

---

5. FREE ASSOCIATE: Starting with this one picture, the patient is encouraged to *free-associate*, which means he should say everything that goes through his mind, no matter how silly or disgusting, and especially he should say any surprising or interrupting thoughts. The more he free associates, the more pieces of blocked memories will "pop" into his viewing screen.

6. DISCHARGE BY CRYING: The patient concentrates on his viewing screen and on his subtle feelings. Gradually he pieces together *scenes* that happened when he was little, and **as he discovers each piece of the puzzle, he cries away the pain.** As he discharges the pain by crying, the brain begins to "re-wire" itself and his symptoms disappear.

7. **THE PATIENT TAKES CONTROL:** Eventually, the patient learns how the therapy works and begins to take more control of the sessions. The patient even decides which questions to ask. Later he learns to do therapy completely alone.

THE IMPORTANCE OF THE BLINDFOLD:

The blindfold does several things: First, it forces the patient to look inside of his head and not at the room. It helps the patient to become aware of his viewing screen. It's like the TV screen of the mind. Many times the first clue that a blocked memory is surfacing will be a picture on the viewing screen. We call it a "pop-in."

DEFINITION

A "POP-IN" is a small piece of a blocked memory, usually a picture, that *pops* into the viewing screen unexpectedly. It can also be a word, a phrase, maybe even a familiar smell.

When the picture comes on the patient's viewing screen, it can be fuzzy, fragmented, and difficult to grab hold of. The blindfold will help the patient focus on the fuzzy, fragmented pop-in which might have otherwise gone unnoticed.

Once we get a hold of a pop-in and ask several questions about it, we can frequently uncover a painful event, a scene when "Mommy died," or "Johnny left me." The pop-in will not immediately seem traumatic. It might be a childhood toy, or room, or a pet, or just a color. But it is the first piece of a traumatic puzzle. The patient will get more pieces over a period of an hour or a week or in some very painful scenes, several months, and as each piece of the puzzle is recognized, the patient will burst into tears.

Most people are embarrassed to cry in front of others. The blindfold allows the patient to cry with a little bit of privacy, with his eyes hidden behind the cloth.

Another purpose of the blindfold is that it allows the patient to feel and believe he is being listened to, even though the therapist may actually be doing homework or reading a book. I am not saying that the therapist should not listen. Of course, he should listen. Sincere listening helps the cure. But in real life, the patient and therapist might be holding down two jobs, and going to college. They may be doing therapy after a 12 hour work day. Time is precious, and therapy consumes a lot of time. It might be a good thing if the therapist can do his homework while the patient is talking and believing that he is being listened to.

In actual practice, the patient will talk about a lot of things that are not traumatic. **For every 20 minutes of crying, there may be an hour or more of digging and chattering that is not very exciting to the therapist.** But as soon as the patient starts to cry, the therapist will become interested and will want to stop his homework.

FREE ASSOCIATION and "FLOW"

Free association is one of the most basic concepts of psychoanalysis. It is important enough that it deserves some explanation. It is very different from your usual way of talking.

Psychoanalysts have used free association for almost a hundred years, and they have intuitively discovered what we call "pop-ins." In my very first session with Dr. Dunner, she said, "The only rule of therapy is that you must try to say everything that goes through your mind, *especially any interrupting thoughts.*" She wanted me to bring to her attention any thoughts that were *new* and *surprising* to me, thoughts that were out of the ordinary. These *interrupting* thoughts, as Dr. Dunner called them, are pieces of blocked memories or blocked feelings. We call them "pop-ins."

Normally, you are very careful to control what you say. You won't allow yourself to say things that are silly, childish, rude, disgusting or stupid. **The trouble is that when you hide negative ideas from your listener, you are also hiding them from yourself.**

48

When the patient learns to free associate, he starts talking faster and more freely because he is not constantly judging and deciding what to say. He just says everything! When the patient is talking fast and freely, I like to say he is having "good flow," like water flowing out of a faucet.

Talking is the ultimate human skill. Thoughts and feelings from a million nerve cells in a dozen parts of your brain are connected and organized and come flying out of your mouth in a split second. This wonderful process of talking fast and freely, of talking without judging, seems to loosen up blocked feelings, it lubricates the brain and causes pop-ins. **It's as though when you drop your guard on your words, you also drop your guard on your blocked memories.** This is what we call free association.

THERAPY PRINCIPLE NO. **8**

FREE ASSOCIATION and FLOW:
Talking Fast and Freely Without Judging
Creates a Sort of Trance, Loosens Blocked
Memories, and Causes "Pop-Ins"

THE PATIENT DOES MOST OF THE WORK

As the therapy progresses, the patient and the therapist have a lot to learn. The patient will do 85% of the work because only the patient has a front row seat. He watches his picture screen and looks for vague, fuzzy clues to his hidden past. It's a little like being in a dark room and he has to develop his sense of touch to find his way around.

He gradually learns to recognize his own *brain feelings*. When he sees a new picture on his viewing screen, he'll feel *surprise* and *curiosity*. As the blocked memory unfolds, he'll feel like he's *guessing*. Later, he'll have *hunches* and he'll sense *familiarity*. These are what I call *brain feelings*. It's a new skill that the patient must learn.

At the same time the therapist has to learn his 15% of the job. He'll learn which question to ask, when to ask it, and when to say nothing. This is very much an art. It requires sensitivity and compassion. Probably the best way to learn it is to be a patient for a while, and to experience the comforting effect of hearing the right questions, and the interruptive effect of hearing the wrong question at the wrong time.

I cannot emphasize enough why the patient must eventually be in charge of the therapy. When a little child has an overload of pain, he must block off whole sections of the brain that become un-usable. Different people will block off different sections, so each person will have different brain skills to work with. One patient may find old feelings by key words. Another may find old feelings by cold calculating logic. A third may find feelings by looking at dreams or songs that get stuck in his head. We all have different parts of our brain blocked, and we have to work with what's left. This may be why some people cannot do Dianetics which depends on key words.

THERAPY PRINCIPLE NO. **9**

The Patient Is In Charge of the Therapy

So let's give the patient 85% control, but not 100%. The patient does need some very special help. The most important thing the therapist must learn is which questions to ask, and when to ask them.

Why the Method is so Simple

Sometimes when Nancy and I did therapy late at night, Nancy (the therapist) would fall asleep while I was talking 100 miles per hour with the blind fold on. I have often started bawling by myself, thinking all the while that Nancy was listening.

That's how simple this method is. It even works when the therapist falls asleep...although I don't recommend doing it that way.

Even if you ignore everything else in the book, just talking will move your patient toward mental health. I remember a time before I knew anything about therapy, Nancy wanted to talk about her problems. If I would just shut up and listen for a half hour, she would eventually slip into the past and start talking about things her dad had done 20 years earlier. Her past was exerting it's own force, trying to come up by itself, even though neither of us knew anything about therapy at that time.

If you can just be quiet and listen without judging and without interrupting, you create an environment in which the patient can heal herself. The more you listen, the more easily she'll talk and the more quickly she'll slip into the past. While she seems to be talking endlessly on irrelevant subjects, have faith that she will eventually slip into an old feeling.

THERAPY PRINCIPLE NO. **10**

If You Can Listen Without Judging, The Patient Will Eventually Find an Old Feeling.

Your patient has an amazing amount of intuition that helps the therapy. You may be overwhelmed by our list of questions, but you can solve it quickly by asking the patient. "What question would you like to use?"

You will experience this intuition when you are the patient. You will experience feelings of *surprise, hunches, curiosity* and *familiarity.*

Sometimes when an old memory comes to the surface, you will wonder, "Did this really happen? Is it a memory or was it a dream? Did I just make up the story?" Your intuition will tell you the difference between a real memory and a made-up story by the way it *feels.* And your intuition will improve as you get more experience.

The only part of therapy that is really tricky is *hypnotic commands,* also called *programmed commands.* But they will eventually resolve themselves even if you never find the command. For several years of therapy Nancy had trouble digging out specific scenes. She would say "My therapy is different than yours (Tom's). You had a lot of violent traumas, but nothing big ever happened to me."

Then one day, all by herself, she said "I've been telling myself that nothing bad ever happened and so I've never really looked. Now I think maybe something *did* happen." Ever since that day it has been easier for her to find blocked scenes. It's as though she had a *hypnotic command* telling her *"Don't Look."* And she got past it by herself, by following her own intuition. For more about hypnotic commands, see pages 103-109.

YOUR QUESTION DOESN'T HAVE TO BE PERFECT

Old feelings are like a log jam. The logs are piled up and tangled in a big mess that started with perhaps one small twig. Pretty soon you have 1000 logs jammed in a pile. The log jam seems like a disorganized mess, and yet it has it's own built in sequence. Log number 1 has to be removed first, then log number 2, then log number 3 and so on. The first log may not be the biggest, nor the most important log, it is however, the only one that can be removed first.

Therapy is like clearing out the log jam. The one feeling that is ready to come up at the beginning of therapy is already predetermined. There is only one feeling that will come up, the first one in the pile of pain.

That's why the question doesn't have to be perfect. If you ask the patient, "What's the feeling" or "What would you like to talk about?" or "What happened when you were little?" eventually he'll uncover the same feeling, the one that's coming up on it's own.

I had this proven to me about 8 years ago. After studying Primal Therapy, I decided to attempt it by myself, by isolating for two days and closing my eyes and trying to remember blocked scenes. The experiment was a near failure.

I didn't primal. The only thing that happened was that I spent two days thinking about when Karen had left, when I was age 12. I did weep a few tears but not enough to make a dent in my pile of pain.

Four years later I went to a professional therapist named Julie. She started out by asking me a list of approximately 130 questions...scientifically chosen, very super-duper questions. One of the questions was, "Did someone leave you?" As I told her about Karen leaving, I burst into tears. After the questioning was over, Julie announced, "I think we ought to start the therapy by working on this memory of Karen leaving."

I hope you get the point: the painful memory of Karen leaving was the first feeling ready to come up. It was there on the surface when Julie found it with her scientifically chosen list of questions, and it was there 4 years earlier, presenting itself to me while I isolated, with no training, and no question list.

The feeling was coming up by itself. That's why the question "What's the feeling" is so powerful. It is a short way of asking "What is the one feeling that is trying to come up by itself."

The old feeling, the one that is ready, is exerting its own force, trying to reach the surface. The question does not cause the feeling to come up but rather it opens the door.

The old feeling has its own force, and the presence of another person seems to amplify that force. The attention of another person is extremely stimulating. When I isolated, Karen's memory caused only weeping. When I told the therapist, I exploded...simply because someone was listening when I said it.

THERAPY PRINCIPLE NO. **11**

Your Question Doesn't Have To Be Perfect, Because Only One Feeling Is Trying To Come Up By Itself, The One That Is Next in Line.

DOORWAYS

Now I want to give you a way to simplify still further. I call it "doorways," because it is like an easy entrance into the mind, or a *doorway* into the subconscious. Let me give you an example.

In Nancy's therapy, colors sometimes pop-in to her viewing screen. The first time it happened, she was talking normally and suddenly her viewing screen was white. A few minutes later it was white again, so we tried the question, "What is it about white?" She talked 5 minutes about several things that "white" reminded her of, and then she felt slight tears. The scene began to emerge. Very quickly she was bawling.

Her own parents had not given her any love. But in the summers, she would stay with Aunt Tilly. Aunt Tilly was kind and loving. Every Saturday, she would buy Nancy a North Pole candy bar, with a *white* wrapper, and take her into town to watch a movie which was in those days shown outside on a big *white* wall of one of the stores. Nancy cried as she remembered how much she loved her Aunt Tilly.

A few weeks later, we found *yellow* popping into Nancy's viewing screen, and another scene and more tears. Weeks later, it happened with *green* and *orange*. We had found a *doorway* with consistent results. Of course, we had to wait for the pop-in, but when it came, we were ready.

Once, during a stalled session, on a hunch, I took a chance and I started without a pop-in. I asked Nancy for her favorite color. She said it was *blue*. Then I asked her why she liked *blue*...moments later she was in tears. The doorway worked even without a pop-in.

Doorways are related to *pop-ins* but not identical. The *pop-in* seems to come out of nowhere. The patient is a little surprised. You might hear him stop in the middle of a sentence and say "What was that?" The therapy has been putting pressure on the pain, and an old feeling is being pushed to the surface.

The *pop-in* is the first clue that a scene is coming up. If it appears once, ignore it, but if it appears 2 or 3 times, assume there is something coming up, and try to form a question around it. I call it a *pop-in* because it seems to pop into the viewing screen from out of nowhere.

> **DEFINITION**
>
> A "DOORWAY" is a re-usable pop-in that is unique to each patient. It is as though the Super-Conscious is giving you an easy entrance into the old pain. He has opened a hole in the dam and if you go back to the same spot next week. He will open it again... and again.

Once you become aware of your patient's doorways, you can find old feelings more quickly. You can use this unique doorway over and over with this one patient. And of course, you can use your own doorways to help your own therapy.

My doorway is movie stars (pretty weird, right?) Once I had a dream about Gene Kelly. The next day, in therapy, I started talking about the dream, and I remembered a movie starring Gene Kelly. The movie stirred some painful feelings in me. I bawled for a half hour. During the next 4 sessions I found more and more pain about that same movie.

Since then I have discharged buckets of tears about Gene Kelly, Kirk Douglas, Michael Douglas, Al Pacino, Ann Bancroft, William Shatner, Leonard Nimoy, Richard Krenna, Steve McQueen and Tonto...and whenever I have a movie star in a dream, I know there is some easy discharge near the surface.

Another doorway for me is U.S. presidents. I have bawled buckets about Presidents Lincoln, Roosevelt, and Truman because of their terrible responsibility in the Civil War and World War II.

It is interesting to note that Nancy's doorways lead her fairly directly to real scenes. Aunt Tilly was a real person. My doorways are *indirect*. I cry about movie scenes that are *similar* to my blocked scenes. I suspect the difference is that I have a bigger pile of pain than Nancy. She has come closer to total reliving than I have, even though she has had about half as much therapy.

THERAPY PRINCIPLE NO. **12**

DOORWAYS:
After You Have Done Therapy For Several Months, Your Super-Conscious Will Give You An Easy Entrance, a Reusable Doorway Into Your Pain.

Doing Therapy With Just One Question

In Appendix A, pages 245-253, we will give you a list of 76 questions to help you get started. This may seem like a lot to learn, and yet I believe you will learn them naturally as you understand the logic behind each question.

We have developed specific questions for starting a session, for finding blocked memories, for finding memories in dreams, and for helping the patient focus on the pain. Some questions are direct and some are indirect. The most important questions are called "core" questions because they get to the core of the problem. An example of a core question is "What was the most unhappy day of your life?"

The core question you will use the most is "What's the feeling?" It is a shortened way of asking "What is the one feeling that is trying to come up by itself?"

If you can understand why the questions are asked, you'll learn them easily, and you may find yourself rewording them so they feel more natural for you. You will even create new questions of your own...and that's what I want you to do. We are all different, and sometimes changing one subtle word can make an enormous difference in the effect of a question. If you do therapy in another language, you'll have to create your own questions.

To make things even simpler, you don't have to use all of the 76 questions. **You can do therapy for weeks and months, using just one or two questions.** The questions are sort of like a checklist. You need a lot of questions at the beginning with a new patient, because you don't know which questions will affect him, but after several months both you and the patient will settle on just a few favorite questions.

It's sort of like starting an old car. When you don't know what's wrong with it, you might run through a checklist of 76 possibilities. After you become familiar with your old car, you may narrow it down to one or two things that usually go wrong.

Once the therapy is started, it will take on a life of it's own. You might nudge the patient every few minutes with his one favorite question. The patient may talk for an hour while you sit and say nothing. In fact, after the session is over, the therapy process will continue with no therapist at all. The patient may be driving to work or walking through a shopping mall and suddenly start crying and remembering.

During the later stages of my therapy, I went for months with one question, "Why can't you finish the therapy ?"

Nancy has gone many months with her 3 favorite questions: "What is the feeling?", "Why did you have to split?", and "Why can't you finish the therapy?" Whenever her session gets stalled for several hours, I usually try the *indirect questions list* (see pages 247-249), and while we have found feelings that way, she seems reluctant to use them. She prefers her 3 questions and they work for her.

I recall many times when I had asked, "What is the feeling," again and again for two hours, and I was ready to scream because I was sick of asking it. Just as I was ready to give-up the session, she would start to weep…5 minutes later she was crying…then bawling heavily for 20 or 30 minutes…all from one question. It is a very big example of why the patient should be in charge of the therapy.

The question **"What is the feeling?"** originally came from Janov's therapy. We use it constantly. It is an all-purpose question. It is a *starting* question, a *core* question, an *indirect* question, and a *probing* question (See Appendix A). You can do many hours of therapy with that one question.

Be sure to read the questions in Appendix A. We decided to put them in an appendix instead of in this chapter because we want you to understand the *principles* before you get bogged down with details. When you are ready to do The Therapy, it will be absolutely essential to study the questions in Appendix A.

CREATING YOUR OWN QUESTIONS:

Before therapy, I had the habit of saying things twice. I would sometimes repeat whole sentences. "Good morning! Good morning!" "Pass the salt. Pass the salt." It was very wearing on my listeners, but I didn't know I was doing it.

I first became aware of it by listening to a tape recording of my voice. I was embarrassed to death when I realized how bad it sounded. It was as though the number "2" was stuck somewhere in my mind. My mind would literally double numbers. If I memorized a phone number 981-1111, a few days later, I would recall it as 982-2222.

It was the subject of a pretty obvious question, so during one session we asked, "Why do you say things twice?" and "What is it about the number 2?" The answer did not come immediately. I hope you've learned by now that your mind must work on any question you ask, even if it takes a week or a month. The more traumatic the answer, the longer you will have to wait for it.

About a month later, we found the scene that had pro- grammed the "2" into my head. The scene would take many pages to describe, but the essence was that when I was 3, two different people abandoned me within a single week. As the scene came up, I can still remember screaming, "I found my two!…I found my two!…" I could feel the electricity discharging out of me as I screamed the words. Since that day, I no longer say things twice. Since that day, I no longer say things twice. (A little joke! I couldn't resist.)

There will be times when you will have to create your own questions, especially later in therapy when you are in the maturity stage (see Chapter 8). The questions will be obvious once you remind yourself that you were created perfect. Anything about you that falls short of perfection is subject to questioning.

In my favorite TV show, *Star Trek Next Generation,* we always expect Data, the robot, to have a perfect memory, a sense of responsibility, to talk at a reasonable speed, not too fast, not too slow, to have plenty of energy, to be honest, and to have self-confidence. But Data is just a robot. Why would you expect a man-made robot to be better than you? If Data said everything twice, you would know there is something wrong, and the same is true of a human. I don't really expect you to reach perfection, and yet you should question anything that is not perfect.

When you are the therapist, it is usually better to let the patient create his own questions. If you create the question, you might insult the patient and he might become defensive. I can just hear the conversation:

> THERAPIST: "Why do you say everything twice?"
> PATIENT: "I don't say everything twice!"
> THERAPIST: "Yes, you do!"

He'll be mad at you, and you'll doubt your skill as a therapist. So generally, it is better to let the patient come up with the question.

Eventually, you and your patient may both grow in mental health, and you will both be more open-minded and less irritable. You may reach a day when you can suggest a question and your patient may accept it without insult.

If you feel you must suggest the question to your patient, here is a safe and gentle way to approach him: "Are you aware that you *sometimes* say things twice?" You're asking him instead of telling him. The word "sometimes" softens the insult much better than saying "You always say things twice." Also, it is sometimes useful to talk to your patient outside of a formal session about what questions to use.

Most of the questions you create will start with the word "Why," for example:

> "Why do you swear so much?"
> "Why are you afraid to phone people?"
> "Why are you afraid of heights?"
> "Why are you so negative?"

I also like the question, "What is it about _____?" (you fill in the blank) because it is open-ended and allows the mind to search many possibilities.

> "What is it about the number two?"
> "What is it about the color white?"

Asking obvious questions may lead to a pop-in, or at the very least, it will "shake the wires." Use the same procedure as with all therapy: Ask the question again and again, watch your picture screen, free associate from any pictures that you find.

QUESTION PHYSICAL SYMPTOMS

A physical symptom can be part of a blocked feeling coming up. It may be so obvious that you'll overlook it. I remember one day I felt so tired I didn't want to get out of my chair. I decided to do self-therapy, so I asked the question that Nancy had asked me a thousand times, "What's the feeling?" The obvious answer was "I'm tired," and as I said those words out loud, I started to cry. I was tired of having a slow, groping mind, tired of being shy and scared, tired of letting people with half of my IQ push me around because they could talk faster. I was tired of carrying the weight of my miserable childhood for 40 years. Crying that day lifted some of the weight.

A *physical symptom* can be a doorway into blocked pain, so it is important to create a question around that symptom.

For example, if you have a backache or a rash, you can ask the question:

> Why does your back hurt?
> What is it about the rash?

Any physical symptom can be your nervous system screaming a message at you, a headache, stomach cramps, even farting can be a message. One of Janov's patients experienced a buzzing in his mouth. When he finally relived the scene, he discovered that the buzzing was the need to suck milk from his mother's breast. So whenever you have a physical symptom, you should ask the obvious question, "Why..."

Keep in mind that you can have a backache from lifting rocks, and you can have a rash from poisen ivy. As Freud would say, "Sometimes a cigar is just a cigar."

The Enormous Quantity of Pain

Finding problems in the human brain is similar to finding problems in Data the robot, with one big difference. The robot answers all questions without pain. The human, on the other hand, may explode into tears while answering the questions.

Probably the biggest mistake that other therapies make is that they grossly under-estimate the amount of childhood pain that is stored in the nervous system. The quantity is enormous. If we could capture the pain and hook it up to a generator, one neurotic could power a whole city. Once you start *discharging* your blocked memories, you'll know what we mean.

We use the word *discharge* to suggest that when the patient cries, he is *discharging* or reducing the electrical pile of pain. In reality, the activity of the brain is partly chemical and partly electrical, but I find the word *discharge* to be useful even though it may not be perfectly scientific. It is useful to imagine the overload of old pain is stored as electrical energy, and that every time the patient cries, he *discharges* a little of that overload.

When we ask the obvious question "What happened to you when you were little," the question may not get answered at first. It is useful to ask the question because it stimulates the pile of pain. It "shakes all the wires" and loosens up the log jam. But still, direct answers are so rare that we don't count on them to make the therapy work.

Direct questions may cause the patient to say nothing, or he may say something that seems irrelevant, or it may cause him to yawn, or get a headache, or feel sleepy or "dopy" (a feeling like being drugged). The painful events we are asking for were unbearable when they happened at age 2 or 3, and they are still unbearable today at age 20 or 40.

Janov would say that the patient is putting up "defenses" when he yawns or dozes off, as though he wants to avoid the pain and the cure. But I'm convinced that the patient is doing something else. He's trying to maintain a balance.

THE IMPORTANCE OF BALANCE

The patient wants to feel all the pain because that would cure the neurosis. But there is another part of him that seems to interfere with the therapy, and prevent discharge. It is popular to call that other part the "subconscious." I prefer to call it the "Super-Conscious," because whatever or whoever it is, it is intelligent and it is in charge of the therapy. It has more control than the patient. The patient may say "I really want to feel all the old pain," but the Super-Conscious knows better. The patient has forgotten how unbearable the pain was, but the Super-Conscious hasn't forgotten.

The distinction between your subconscious and your Super-Conscious is important. Your subconscious is like a big stupid filing cabinet, full of blocked scenes. It must be stupid because a hypnotist can easily plant a command there and make you walk like a duck.

The person that you call "I" is really only a small part of your self. Your Super-Conscious is much bigger and more intelligent than you are. Consider this: Who pumps your heart? Who runs your liver, your kidneys and your adrenal glands? Who controls over 75 trillion cells and over 50,000 chemical reactions in your body? Who creates your dreams? It's a bigger part of you that I call your Super-Conscious. Sometimes we call it "your nervous system."

I am not the first to talk about the Super-Conscious. Jung called it "archtypical self." Chiropractors would call it "innate intelligence." Robert Monroe called it "Super-Conscious." And Joseph Campbell talked about it without giving it a specific name.

It's amazing to consider the paradox of your Super-Conscious. You may have struggled with chemistry in high school, and simultaneously there was another part of you creating 50,000 chemicals, without ever reading a book.

I have no scientific explanation for the Super-Conscious. It could be just another part of your brain. It could be the "life force" of your body. It could be your soul. I don't know what it is. But trust me, He does exist. You may meet Him during your therapy. Whoever or whatever He is, He knows more about The Therapy than either you or I do, and we can't do therapy without His help. The Super-Conscious creates your dreams, and He sends you the pop-ins on your viewing screen.

If we could talk directly to the Super-Conscious and ask Him "Why is our progress so slow? Why won't you let the patient discharge all the pain?" I believe this is what He would say:

"I am willing to discharge the pain but I must give it to the patient in small, controlled "spoonfuls." Try to understand that I am right now and at every moment running and balancing trillions of cells, thousands of chemicals, hundreds of glands and muscles, 10 billion brain cells and a lifetime of old pain stored up behind a dam. Just like a dam in a river, I cannot allow a crack in the dam because it would explode out of control. I spent years constructing that dam. It's a wonderful dam. Without it we would have died.

I will not destroy the dam, but I will make a small hole in it, give you a controlled *spoonful* of pain and then re-seal the hole so we can stay balanced long enough to get through tomorrow's responsibilities. Every time I give the patient a spoonful of pain, he becomes a little healthier. Then I must rebalance the entire body and nervous system to adjust to the new health. I do this while we sleep".

When you ask a question, the Super-Conscious is the one who gives you an answer. Sometimes you will get a direct answer to an obvious question, but more often, the answers will come indirectly. Most of the cure will result from indirect questions that lead to discharge of small "spoonfuls" of pain, usually in the form of crying.

THERAPY PRINCIPLE NO. **13**

THE SPOONFUL PRINCIPLE.
Your Nervous System (The Super-Conscious)
Will Allow You to Feel Old Pain in Very Small
Pieces (Spoonfuls) Because Protecting and
Balancing the Whole Body Is More Important
Than Finding Blocked Memories.

3

Questions For Digging Out A Blocked Memory

When I was in grade school, I fell in love with a little girl named Karen. She had golden hair and she wore glasses. To me she was the most beautiful girl in the whole world. I hardly knew her.

I thought about Karen every waking moment. Sometimes I would follow her home from school. As we grew older, I eventually worked up courage to talk to her.

One day when she was 11 and I was 12, she told me that she had to go away forever. Her dad had found a new job in another city. It was a warm autumn day. There was a light breeze. We were standing in the grass and there were dry leaves all around our feet.

When she said she was leaving, I didn't know what to do. I jumped on my bike and peddled as fast as my feet would go. I never went back. I never said goodbye. I never told her how much I loved her. I always thought there would be more time.

After she was gone, I peddled over to her neighborhood. I sat alone in a swing in the lot next to her house. I sat there for hours waiting for her to come out. I couldn't believe that she had really gone.

Some people make light of "puppy love" but I never do. It was the most devastating day that I could remember. Twenty years after she left, I would drive by her house, I'd stop and sit alone in my car. I'd pretend she was still inside. I still couldn't believe she was gone.

So far in this book we've talked about blocked memories. The important thing about the story of Karen leaving is that **it was NOT a blocked memory. But it was the first scene that came up when I started therapy, and this first scene helped me to find the memories that were blocked.**

Have you ever looked at how rivers are formed? Take a look at the great Mississippi River. The mouth of the river is 4 miles wide where it flows into the Gulf of Mexico. 2000 miles up stream, rain  is falling on a hillside forming small creeks. Several creeks form rivers and the rivers run into the great Mississippi.

The pain in your brain is like the Mississippi River. Your pain may be physically stored in 50 scenes, in 50 different parts of the brain. But these scenes are all *physically connected by nerve paths,* so that if you find one scene, you can find another and another.

THERAPY PRINCIPLE NO. **14**

THE RIVER PRINCIPLE:
All Of Your Traumatic Scenes Are Physically
Wired Together By Nerve Paths

We call this discovery "the river principle," or "the river of pain." Just like a physical river, the *river of pain* has a bigger, wider part. This *mouth of the river of pain* is a traumatic scene so big and obvious that it is easy to find. Once you find it, you can find other scenes by going *up-stream,* by going into the past. In my therapy, Karen leaving was the *mouth of my river.*

The *mouth of the river of pain* will be easy to recognize, because it will be a recent scene that makes you cry. It could be anything after age 8. Sorry I can't be more specific. Mine was at age 12, Nancy's was at age 23. The important things to look for is that this scene is **not blocked,** it is **easy to recall,** and it is **easy to get tears** when you talk about it.

Compare this with a blocked scene. The blocked scene will come in pieces. And you will likely be thinking, "I'm not sure this ever happened. I feel like I'm making it up."

But when you find the *mouth of the river,* you know it really happened. The details may be forgotten, but not blocked. And when you recall the details you will explode with tears because you have found a scene that is physically wired into all of your other blocked scenes. You are draining away pain from all the other scenes, just as the mouth of the Mississippi is draining water from the little creeks upstream.

Can you think of a question to find the *mouth of the river?* Think about it for a few moments. If you have read this far, I'm hoping that you can develop an instinct for this whole process. There will be times when the obvious question is not in the book, and you will have to create your own. The important message of this book is not that you have to do it Tom's way, but rather you get the principles right, then you can create your own questions.

The obvious question to find the recent scene that forms the *mouth of the river* is, "Can you remember the most unhappy day in your life?"

A USEFUL QUESTION

The basic question to find the "Mouth of the River" is:

"CAN YOU REMEMBER THE MOST UNHAPPY DAY IN YOUR LIFE?"

There are other ways to ask the same thing: "Tell me about the most miserable day in your life?" "What is the worst thing that ever happened to you?" It is possible to have more than one river, so you might try, "Make a list of the 10 most miserable days you can remember."

In my therapy, the mouth of the river was the scene when Karen left. When I started to tell the therapist, I exploded in tears. The therapist told me to go to the beginning of the scene and tell the story again...and again...and again. Each time I told the story, I found *new details,* and I exploded again.

At the time, I was sure that all the tears were from the one scene, but now after finding 25 blocked scenes, I know that the tears were from all of my scenes...scenes that were connected by a river of nerve paths.

Using Karen as a starting point, my therapist carried me *up-stream* into my past by using the question, "Is there an earlier beginning?" It is one of the most powerful questions in therapy, because it is the question that takes you farther and farther into your past.

A USEFUL QUESTION

The question to take you "up-stream" into your past is:

"IS THERE AN EARLIER BEGINNING?"

Each time I told the story of Karen, my therapist would ask, "Is there an earlier beginning," and I would watch my viewing screen. Again and again she asked the question, and each time my viewing screen gave me a new picture. I saw myself at the age of 9...then 7...then 5 years old.

I was 5 when I met Karen, and I expected age 5 to be my earliest beginning. But she asked me again, "Is there an earlier beginning?" Suddenly I saw myself in the baby bed, and I found a new painful scene that had nothing to do with Karen. She asked me again and I found a scene in the hospital where I was born, and I found more pain. The tears continued to flow as I wondered, "How far back can I go?" She asked the question again, and I found painful scenes inside the womb.

Each time I found an earlier beginning, my therapist told me to "Run through the entire story from beginning to end." Starting with the womb, I would run through the events of my life, ending at age 12 when Karen left, and each time through I would find new details and new tears. She was sending me up the Mississippi River to the most distant creek, and back downstream all the way to the mouth ...over...and over again.

We call it the *river principle.* Here is the procedure in a nutshell:

- You find the *mouth of the river,* the scene connected to all the other scenes, by asking, "What was the worst day in your life," or "Tell me the 10 worst days of your life." There are many ways to ask it.

- Once you find an unblocked scene that makes your patient cry, you say, "Start at the beginning of the scene, and tell me what happened."

- After the patient tells the scene, you ask, "Is there an earlier beginning?" Wait until the patient finds an earlier beginning, then say," Starting with the earlier beginning, run through the entire story again and tell me what happened."

- Each time the patient tells the story, you ask for an earlier beginning. Repeat the same procedure again...and again...and again, until it stops working.

THE IMPORTANCE OF DETAILS

Specific details are important in finding pain. I'm always amazed how seemingly insignificant details can cause such an explosion of tears. When Karen told me she was leaving, I was standing on some fallen leaves. I exploded in tears as I told my therapist about the "leaves under my feet." When I talked about Amy's death, I did not cry about *death* or *love* or any obvious painful feelings. But the tears gushed from my eyes when I talked about a specific detail, "her little freckled nose sticking up out of the casket."

THERAPY PRINCIPLE NO. **15**

*Specific Details and Specific Words
From a Scene Can Cause a Patient
to Explode In Tears*

The reverse is also true: The patient can prevent tears by speaking in generalities and avoiding details.

Blocked Memories Are Not The Same As Forgotten Memories

In the early weeks of therapy, you may remember and cry about scenes from long ago. They will be painful, but that is not the same as being blocked.

The scenes that are truly blocked will come to you in pieces, like the pieces of a puzzle.

It's like looking at the scene through a small keyhole. You can see parts of the room beyond the keyhole, but you cannot see the whole room at once. If you look through the keyhole from different angles, you can see different details and then you can make a **guess** about what is going on in the room.

As you put the pieces of the story together, you may feel a little silly. You might say, "I don't know if this ever happened. I feel like I'm making it up." This is a natural feeling. In fact when the patient says, " I feel like I'm making it up," it's a healthy sign. It means that he can feel the difference between an old memory and a blocked memory and a fantasy. It's a sign of his intelligence. He wants to be sure that he's not fabricating a lie.

When he says, "I feel like I'm making this up," it's a pretty good sign that he has found a truly blocked scene. **The reason it seems so unbelievable to him is that he literally has never seen it before.** He was there physically when it happened, but a part of him blocked it before he really looked at it.

As you struggle to piece together your puzzle, you might not cry because you have already cried about it as a similar story (see pages 29-31).

Your similar story will not drain off all of the pain. There is more bawling ahead of you, but like the puzzle, you have to have all of the pieces before you feel the pain. Have you ever had a puzzle that you could not recognize the picture until the last piece was in place? That's the way blocked memories are. You may have ten pieces of the story without tears, and then when you find the eleventh piece, suddenly you realize what had happened...and then you will feel an explosion of tears.

I've gone to some length to give you a clear distinction between a *forgotten memory* and a *truly blocked memory* because I believe this distinction has eluded many professional therapists. A patient may tell a story of being molested or raped at the age of twelve or eight, and the therapist may believe that he has found the cause of the mental illness, but I doubt it. Most likely he has found the tip of the iceberg, an unblocked scene that was forgotten, not blocked. The patient has not thought about it for years, but *it is not a blocked scene.*

Neurosis is generally not caused by any one event. Most likely, as you do your therapy, you will find ten, twenty, or thirty scenes and when you add them together, the bottom line is, "My parents didn't love me. The only way I could get their attention was to give up being my real self" (see pages 34-38, What Traumatic Really Means).

Questions For Digging Out A <u>Truly</u> Blocked Memory

In digging out a blocked memory, you need a special set of questions. The following is a true story of a real blocked memory to illustrate these questions. The names have been changed to protect the privacy of the patient.

Nathan was 3 years old, and his sister Julie was 8. Nathan was playing in Julie's bedroom and messing up her papers. Mom and Dad were farming out in the field half mile away, so Julie was the boss. Julie got angry and grabbed Nathan by the arm and physically dragged him down the stairs, out the back door and locked him in a dark storage room in the barn. Nathan was afraid of the dark and he loved Julie, so the event was traumatic enough to become blocked.

It's a simply story. I told it to you in 30 seconds, but it took Nathan several months to dig it out.

The following is a dramatization of how we uncovered this scene. Our goal here is to make you familiar with the questions and what kind of response to expect. We've shortened this session to a few minutes for your convenience. In reality, this kind of digging could take several hours, and the patient might change the subject several times and talk a half hour about kids, problems at work and other unrelated subjects, before the scene is uncovered.

THERAPIST: What's the feeling?

NATHAN: I see (on my viewing screen) my boss ... hamburger... barn...my boss makes me mad.

THERAPIST: What's the feeling?

NATHAN: I see the barn. Flowers...

THERAPIST: What's the feeling?

NATHAN: I see the barn.

THERAPIST: Nathan, you've seen the barn on your viewing screen several times. Would you mind if I ask you about the barn?

NATHAN: Go ahead.

THERAPIST: What is it about the barn?

NATHAN: There were two storage rooms in the barn. One had a window, but the other didn't, and I was always afraid of the room that was so dark. (Nathan might talk ten minutes about various unrelated memories of playing in the barn.)

THERAPIST: What is it about the barn?

NATHAN: I keep seeing the dark storage room.

THERAPIST: What is it about the barn?

NATHAN: My Dad used to store seed and fertilizer in there. Sometimes a mouse would run across the floor and scare me.

THERAPIST: What is it about the barn?

NATHAN: I think I see something...not sure...I see a little boy laying on the bags of feed. He's laying with his knees tucked in his arms.

THERAPIST: What is it about the barn?

NATHAN: I don't know?

THERAPIST: What is it about the barn?

NATHAN: (Nathan doesn't answer for a few minutes)

THERAPIST: Are you falling asleep?
NATHAN: I feel dopey all of a sudden. Hard to keep my mind on the question.
THERAPIST: Would you like to take a nap?
NATHAN: Yes.

Nathan fell asleep quickly and slept a half hour. The dopey feeling is a clue that the questions are working. It suggests that we have found a blocked scene and the mind is not ready to let go of it. Generally a nap will actually help the therapy because the *rewiring* is done during sleep. The following is another session several days later:

THERAPIST: What is the feeling?
NATHAN: I see hands.
THERAPIST: What is the feeling?
NATHAN: Hands! They're pushing and shoving. Some kind of a struggle.
THERAPIST: What is it about hands?
NATHAN: I don't know. It's sort of fuzzy.
THERAPIST: What is it about hands?
NATHAN: I see the door latch...it might be the latch to the storage room in the barn.

It finally occurs to Nathan the possibility that the hands are pushing him into the storage room. At this point, both Nathan and the therapist are suspecting the presence of a blocked scene, but to be safe, the therapist asks permission:

THERAPIST: You might have a blocked scene here. Do you mind if I ask you some questions for blocked scenes?
NATHAN: Go ahead.
THERAPIST: What happened in the storage room?
NATHAN: I don't know.
THERAPIST: What happened in the storage room?
NATHAN: Maybe someone locked me in there.

THERAPIST: Who locked you in?

NATHAN: I don't know.

THERAPIST: Who locked you in?

NATHAN: I see flowers...pause...cloth...pause...maybe flowers on a dress...

THERAPIST: Who locked you in?

NATHAN: I don't know. I'm not sure anybody locked me in. *I feel like I'm making this whole thing up.*

THERAPIST: Who locked you in? Make a guess.

NATHAN: I don't think it was Dad. It would have to be Mom or Julie.

THERAPIST: Make a guess. Who do you think locked you in?

CAUTION: Guessing is useful as long as the **patient** does the guessing. It is serious and dangerous for the therapist to guess because he could be *planting* an untrue idea in the patient's mind.

NATHAN: It could have been Julie. She used to baby-sit me sometimes. *It feels like summer time and Julie would have been out of school.*

THERAPIST: Tell me the whole story. What happened in the barn?

NATHAN: I don't know the whole story. All I see is some hands, a flowered dress, a latch, and a little boy laying on a bag of feed.

THERAPIST: Tell me the whole story.

NATHAN: I just told you. I don't know any more.

THERAPIST: Watch your viewing screen. Is there an earlier beginning to this story?

NATHAN: I don't see anything.

THERAPIST: Is there an earlier beginning to this story?

NATHAN: I see a little boy playing with papers. He's throwing papers all over the place.

THERAPIST: What else do you see?

NATHAN: Nothing.

THERAPIST: Can you describe the room?

NATHAN: No.

THERAPIST:	Make a guess. What room is the little boy's in?
NATHAN:	I don't know!
THERAPIST:	Can you describe the room?
NATHAN:	It doesn't seem like the living room or the kitchen. It *feels* like it was an upstairs room. It might be my bedroom...pause...or Julie's bedroom.
THERAPIST:	Starting with the papers on the floor, move through the entire story and tell me what happened.
NATHAN:	I see a little boy playing with papers...I see a flowered dress...struggling hands...they're struggling with the latch...I see the little boy laying on a bag of feed.
THERAPIST:	What do you think happened? It's OK to guess.

Using the same procedure over and over again, Nathan eventually found the whole story. Did you get the procedure? When you dig out a blocked memory, these are the questions to use:

■ **"WHAT IS IT ABOUT THE BARN?** Whenever something pops-in to the viewing screen and stays there, or if it pops-in two or three times, it is the first clue to a blocked scene. So you ask "What is it about _____? (You fill in the blank, "barn", "hands" or whatever the pop-in is). We don't ask "What *happened* in the barn?" at least not yet, because that would be *planting*. At this early point, we're not sure anything happened.

■ **"WHAT HAPPENED IN THE STORAGE ROOM?"** This question is okay, and it is not planting, once the patient is pretty sure that something did happen.

■ **ASK FOR DETAILS.** "Who locked you in?" "Can you describe the room?" Typically the patient will say "I don't know" but it is amazing how many details he can find if you just keep asking. "How old were you ? Was it summer or winter? Morning or evening? What color was the room?" All of these details are in Nathan's mind, but they are out of focus or out of view. The patient may not see them, but he will *sense* them. He'll say, "It *feels* like it was an upstairs room." He'll find some details by logic. Nathan said, "It feels like summer time and Julie would have been out of school."

■   MAKE A GUESS. "What do you think happened?" The patient will have subtle feelings about what happened. When you give him permission to guess, his story will be created out of these subtle feelings. When he says them out loud, the story will become slightly clearer to him.

> **CAUTION:** It is a serious mistake for the therapist to guess because he could be *planting* an untrue idea in the patient's mind. But it is useful if the **patient** makes a guess.

The therapist must be careful not to plant suggestions. It interrupts the patient and gets him off track. In the worst case, it could lead to legal problems if the patient believes the therapist talked him into believing a false story. As long as the guesses come totally from the patient, there is little that can go wrong. And if the patient says, "I feel silly. I feel like I'm making it up," it is a healthy sign. It means that the patient can feel the difference between reality and a guess.

■   "IS THERE AN EARLIER BEGINNING?" Nathan's story ended in the storage room, but it started in Julie's bed room. We found the beginning of the story simply by asking for it.

■   "GO TO THE BEGINNING OF THE SCENE. MOVE THROUGH THE ENTIRE SCENE AND TELL ME WHAT HAPPENED." This is a formal way of saying, "Tell me the whole story from beginning to end," I'm sure it would work to say, "Run through it again." You might use this same question five, ten, or twenty times. Each time he goes through the story, he will find new details on his viewing screen.

If he finds the last piece of the puzzle that makes him recognize the painful feeling, he may explode in tears. But don't be surprised if he does not cry at all. It only means that this scene is not ready to discharge yet. Remember, all of the scenes are connected by the *river of pain*. The work you do today may result in a bawling session tomorrow that seems unrelated to the work you did today. Everything is connected and every discharge will move him closer to health. Trust his nervous system to decide which spoonful is ready to discharge safely.

It is critical to ask for an earlier beginning before you ask him to "Run through it again." You could assume the scene lasted only a day, while the real event might be a series of connected scenes that took place over a period of weeks, months or even years. Sometimes the scene will not discharge until it is recognized as it is connected to the other events. The only way to know for sure is to keep asking, "Is there an earlier beginning?"

How Do You Know It Really Happened?

One of the most common questions people ask me is " When I see surprising and unbelievable pictures on my viewing screen, how do I know if it's true? How do I know that my mind isn't just making up a fantasy?"

I always answer the same way. In the beginning, it might not matter if it's true. **The important thing is the crying.** Remembering by itself will not cure you. It's the crying that permanently drains off the pain.

Let's imagine the ridiculous. Suppose your picture screen gives you a picture of you on the planet Mars being chased by monsters, and as you are telling the story to your therapist you start to cry. Now assuming you have never been to Mars, the obvious question is, "Where are the tears coming from?" If it's not true, why are you crying?

Crying does not prove the story is true. Most likely, the Mars story is *similar to* a real story that is truely blocked. It may be a symbolic reliving (see pages 26-34 on the 3 kinds of reliving). The real blocked scene might be about some school boys chasing you, or your angry mother chasing you.

The real scene will remain blocked until you drain off some of the pain with the similar story. Remember, the scene was blocked in the first place because it was too traumatic. So why would you expect the scene to surface easily now? It was too much when it happened, and it is still too traumatic. That's why the mind lets you discharge the similar story before the real thing comes into view. As you progress farther into the therapy, eventually you'll know if it's true.

The following is a story I told you in Chapter 1. It is worth repeating because it graphically demonstrates one of the most important principles in therapy. One day I was listening to a cassette about Abraham Lincoln. When Lincoln's girl friend died, he disappeared for several days, and eventually his friends found him laying on the moist soil of his girl friend's grave. As I heard the story, I started to bawl. It was the kind of gushing bawl that signals that I had tapped into the enormous pile of childhood pain. The bawling went on for several sessions in a row. There was a lot of pain.

As with the story of monsters on Mars, I had to ask myself. "Why am I crying about Lincoln?" Was I there? Is it my imagination? Fantasy? Am I Lincoln reincarnated?

The answer began to surface weeks later. Working mostly with dreams, I began to piece together the real story, one picture at a time, as though I was putting together a puzzle. A little girl who lived in our neighborhood had died of pneumonia. I was 3, she was about 8. I loved her because she liked to play with me. My parents took me to the funeral. At the age of 3 I saw her little freckled face laying in the casket. I watched as they lowered the casket into the dark earth. It was too much for my little 3-year-old mind to handle, so I blocked it.

It is significant that the Lincoln story came easily to me, and that it came before my blocked scene. It is also significant that the Lincoln story came with gushing tears, while the real scene did not. I believe this is consistent in everyone's therapy: You will get the *similar story first,* you will bawl heavily and reduce your pile of pain, and only then will you begin to see your own real blocked memory. When the real scene comes, it may be fragmented into many pieces.

So it doesn't really matter if you see monsters from Mars on your viewing screen. If you're bawling, it's probably a similar story.

Your similar story can be something you create, it can be from a movie or a TV show or a novel or (as in my case) from history. It can be something that actually happened to you. For example, something that happened when you were 20 can be the similar story hiding something that happened when you were 5. What happened yesterday in your present life can be the similar story. Believe it or not, a story from your previous life can be the similar story.

Principle Number 5, page 31, is so very important to your understanding of therapy that it is worth repeating here.

THERAPY PRINCIPLE NO. **5**

Symbolic Reliving Is The Fastest Easiest Way To Discharge Old Pain.

Fragmented Reliving Comes Only After A Scene Is Discharged Symbolically.

4

How To Find Blocked Memories From Dreams

When I was 1¹/₂ years old, I was taken away from my mom. For six months I lived in a children's home. It was a white, two-story house with a big front porch. It had hardwood floors, a big hallway that lead to the kitchen in the back, and all the doors were painted light blue. The whole episode was a blocked memory.

The interesting thing about the children's home is how I was able to remember it. **It came to me in a dream.** And the first piece of the memory was a light blue door.

Dreaming is intimately connected with neurosis. In fact I'm convinced that dreaming is the mechanism of neurosis. Sigmund Freud was the first to make the connection between dreams and neurosis. He said "Dreams are the royal road to the subconscious." After digging 25 blocked memories out of my head, I can tell you that Freud was right.

THERAPY PRINCIPLE NO. **16**

Dreams Really Are the Royal Road to the Subconscious Because Dreaming is the Physical Mechanism of Neurosis

During the day, we receive millions of pieces of information, and they are stored in a part of the brain that I call the "temporary file." I'm not sure where it is but I suspect it is the hippocampus.

The temporary file is like the "in-and-out" box on a secretary's desk. It is not big enough nor is it intended for permanent storage. It is supposed to hold only one day's worth of information, no more, no less. Most of the information we receive in a typical day is trivia and only a small amount is important enough to be stored permanently.

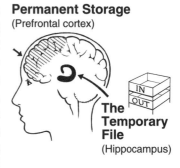

Permanent Storage
(Prefrontal cortex)

The Temporary File
(Hippocampus)

During sleep, your brain sorts through the temporary file, eliminates the trivia, and stores the important stuff in a permanent storage place, the prefrontal cortex. The new knowledge is connected to the previous important knowledge by new nerve connections. You experience this process as a dream.

Dreaming has many dimensions. Freud would say dreams are wish fulfillments. Hall and Perls might use dreams for self-understanding. A prophet would use dreams to foretell the future. All of these explanations are possible, and they don't contradict each other.[1] But the most important function of dreams is to eliminate useless data, and then *store and connect* important information so it can be instantly recalled.[2]

This *storage-and-connection* function insures our survival. But when a child is traumatized, it becomes distorted. It becomes the mechanism of neurosis. If a mother hates and mistreats her own child, what can the baby's little brain do with that information? **It literally does not compute! It is impossible!** It cannot be processed.

The only thing the little mind can do is to leave the information in the box, neither discard it, nor store it. If the information comes up during a dream, it must be disguised so the little mind won't recognize it. This is why neurotics have weird dreams.

Imagine an office secretary with a temporary in-and-out box on her desk. Under normal circumstances she is supposed to file everything and clear out the box every night. But one of the messages in the box is too awful for her to look at. The message says, "You're fired." ...so she leaves it in the box unfiled. The next day, the same message arrives again, and again she leaves the message in the box. Imagine that the same message arrives on the 3rd day, 4th day, 40th day, and the 400th day until her temporary box so full, it is spilling all over her desk.

Eventually the pile of messages is so big that it cannot be ignored any longer. But still she cannot allow herself to believe all those messages. She tries to disguise some of them. She files them under "My boss was drunk when he wrote these." But every day the same message keeps arriving. She busies herself with emptying the trash and sweeping the floor so she won't have to look at the overflowing box. This is the log jam in the office. Information is disguised, filed in the wrong place, or not filed at all.

Similarly, the little baby tries to avoid looking at the unbelievable truth that enters his temporary file every day. "My mom can't stand the sight of me." He tries to disguise the messages and file them under "Mom will love me if I get better grades in school," or "Mom has to work all the time." But the messages keep coming in day after day. Each night the temporary file is clogged with horrible messages. They cannot be discarded, and they cannot be filed.

Eventually the pile of messages gets so big that the child has to "split." The moment of the split is usually triggered by a traumatic event, but it can also be a seemingly unimportant event. A little girl falls from a swing and calls for her mother to come and help her. Suddenly she realizes, "Mom isn't coming because she doesn't care about me. She never has and she never will." And so the child splits. Her brain forms a new compartment to file the messages and then the compartment is sealed forever.

All neurotics have some sort of sleep problem, night-mares, insomnia, difficulty waking up. The connection between neurosis and sleep is absolutely fundamental. I've seen this connection demonstrated again and again. One of the most interesting examples is yawning. Frequently the patient will yawn during a specific question as though it were making him sleepy. And sometimes he'll yawn while telling a dream.

YAWNING and the "SLEEP-SWITCH"

The scientists seem to know very little about why we yawn, and this may be a good time to discuss it. We all know that yawning has something to do with sleep, but what? The popular idea is that yawning gives your brain an extra shot of oxygen, but this is unlikely. Recent scientific studies suggest that the yawn has more to do with controlling *pressure*, than with supplying oxygen.[3]

We have noticed that the patient frequently yawns during therapy, and with some questions, the patient will yawn heavily and continuously. Hubbard believed that a yawn is a discharge like crying, but I'm convinced this is not true.

Another popular idea is that yawning has something to do with boredom. But what is boredom? It is different in each person. At any seminar or class, one person may be excited, while another in the next chair is bored, and yawning.

The key to understanding the yawn is that it has something to do with *pressure*. In my opinion, the yawn is directly related to the "sleep-switch". The sleep-switch is not just a synapse (single nerve connection). I believe it is a relatively *big, physical switch*. It's so big that pressure control is a significant part of the system.

Let's pretend that your fingers are nerves. You can visualize the sleep-switch by gently placing your left fingertips against your right finger tips, and trying to make all five contacts simultaneously. Now imagine doing that if your hands had a billion fingers. To make things even more difficult, imagine doing it with a billion fingers,  and that some fingers must not touch because they represent blocked feelings that you are trying to keep under control.

If you can visualize this switch, then you can probably grasp the problem of the Super-Conscious as we approach sleep. If the contact is not perfect, a blocked memory would accidentally pop into consciousness with full force. The *yawn* is part of the delicate pressure control that helps this very big physical switch to make a gentle controlled contact, a soft landing, with some parts of the switch making clean contact while other parts are intentionally not in contact. This is the purpose of the yawn. And like all good theories, I believe it explains everything.

If I am right, I would expect neurotics to yawn much more than mentally healthy people because they need more delicate control when making the transition from awake to sleep.

Yawns are useful in therapy because they can tell us if a question is working. For instance, you may ask the question, "Why did you have to split?" Obviously if you have read the whole book up to now, the patient is not likely to answer that question. The question may shake the wires, loosen the log jam, and cause indirect discharge tomorrow or next week, but it is not likely to be answered today. **But if you see the patient yawn, that tells you that the question is having an affect. You are shaking the wires.**

The yawn is especially useful when you create a new question. After a month of therapy, the patient will have heard the core questions hundreds of times and may be slightly immune or at least accustomed to the questions. But a newly designed question will frequently stimulate yawns.

For example, let's pretend you have a patient who is afraid of cats. You might decide, on a hunch, to ask "Why are you afraid of cats?" If the patient feels tears, that could mean you have a good question, and perhaps you have stumbled across a spoonful ready to discharge. But what if the patient does not feel tears? Does that mean you should stop using the question?

There are two possibilities: 1) the new question has no effect at all, and 2) you are asking about a childhood scene that is not yet ready to discharge and this is where the yawn helps. **If the patient has no tears, but does yawn, that is a pretty good clue that the question is working,** and you should keep asking the question. I have seen a question asked 5 times cause a patient to yawn 5 times. I have seen yawns so big it almost breaks the patient's jaw.

Do you see what is happening? Why does the *question-that-can't-be-answered* cause a yawn? **It is because the Super-Conscious cannot answer the question until it does a little rewiring.** It must have sleep to do the rewiring, to give you an indirect spoonful and still keep balance. So by asking the question again and again you are forcing the patient to go to sleep, to close the sleep-switch, and the yawn is necessary to control the delicate switching process.

You may actually see your patient fall asleep in front of you as a result of your *question-that-can't-be-answered,* and that is what you want. You may find discharge fairly easy after a little nap. I have also seen the same thing happen with hypnotic commands. For instance, if you suspect a hypnotic command (see pages 103-109), and ask the patient to repeat the suspected phrase, you may find quick and easy discharge...or if the feeling is not ready, you may see the patient yawn heavily, or ultimately put himself to sleep by repeating the suspected command.

There is, of course, another possibility: The new question, or phrase, may really have no effect at all...no discharge and no yawns. In that case you will likely hear your patient say something like, "That question doesn't do anything. Let's change the question."

HEAVY SLEEP

Sometime during your therapy you may experience what Nancy and I call *heavy sleep*. This is a sleep so deep that you feel as though you are drugged or under and anesthetic, and you may find it very difficult to get out of bed. Almost all of the real work of therapy is done during sleep. If you wake up feeling like you've been working all night, you probably have.

Before you got involved in therapy, you may have needed only 8 hours of sleep because your old blocked memories and feelings were under control. We say that you were a "balanced neurotic," which means that the pain was successfully blocked by millions of wires disconnected and switches turned off. The wires and switches have been turned off since you were very little. It's the way you've always been. In a sense, you were comfortable. Your system was *balanced.*

The therapy will change all that. The questioning will stimulate the old pain and push it near the surface, but your nervous system does not want the pain to actually reach the surface. It was too painful when it happened, and it is still too painful. That's why you blocked it in the first place. So your brain chooses to compromise by blocking 99% of the pain and letting just a little bit of pain come through, just a spoonful of pain.

This whole process is a lot of work and it all happens during your sleep. A few million old wires may be reconnected for the first time in 20 years, and another million may be disconnected or re-routed. It's like rewiring a house with ten billion wires. **It's a lot of work, and you absolutely have to sleep until the work is done.**

When you experience this heavy sleep, all you can do is to give in to it, and allow yourself to sleep. I realize there is a lot of pressure on you to get up, go to work. People around you may make you feel guilty, but don't give in to their guilt-trip. You're not lazy. You're actually working very hard. You will not function well until the rewiring is done, so don't fight it. Sleep until your body tells you that your sleep is finished.

I am convinced that the rewiring is done during sleep not only because of the heavy sleep that Nancy and I have both experienced, but also because of something amazing that we have witnessed during Nancy's therapy. It's a remarkably consistent pattern: We'll start the session normally. I'll ask the usual questions. She'll answer them as best she can, with no feeling and no tears. Then she'll start to feel "dopey". (This is like feeling sleepy with the added feeling of being mildly drugged.) Then she'll fall asleep

While she takes a nap for 20 minutes to an hour, I take a break, read a book, or fix a snack. When she wakes up, I go back to my role as a therapist. I ask her the same questions I was asking before the nap, and within ten minutes, she'll be bawling.

While I cannot prove it with scientific instruments, It seems obvious what has happened. Before the nap, the questions were stimulating her blocked memories, but the brain would not let them reach the surface because of the danger of overload. The brain had to fall asleep so it could do a rewiring job, so it could give her a spoonful of pain instead of a truckload. Immediately after the nap, Nancy was able to discharge a spoonful...although the "spoonful" might be enough to make her bawl for a half hour and breathe heavily for another half hour after the bawling.

Sometimes, the feeling that finally discharges may not be the one we were asking for before the nap. It's as though the brain is telling us, "You're forcing me to drain off some pain, but the one you're asking for is too big, so I must give you a spoonful that is not too dangerous for you."

THERAPY PRINCIPLE NO. **17**

Your Brain Rewires Itself During Sleep

How To Find
Blocked Memories From Dreams

Nancy and I have found buckets of tears from our dreams. Some therapists will use "dream interpretation" to help a patient *understand* himself, but understanding will not cure symptoms. **Our goal is to find blocked memories and to cry.** Without the tears, dream interpretation is a pleasant, but useless, parlor game. The more you cry, the more your mind will heal itself, and when the pain is gone, the *understanding* will take care of itself.

FREE ASSOCIATION AND "FLOW"

The way to find old feelings in your dream is to break your dream down into pieces, then look at each piece and "free associate." In other words, you look at each piece and ask the question, "What does it remind you of?" One piece of the dream may remind you of something which reminds you of a second thing, and a third. You will be forming a "chain of associations."

Let's say for example that you see an old fountain pen in your dream, so you ask the question, "What does the fountain pen remind you of?" and you watch your viewing screen for the answer.

Let's say that the fountain pen reminds you of your grade school, so you ask the question, "What does your grade school remind you of?"

Let's say your grade school reminds you of your 3rd grade teacher, so you ask "What does your 3rd grade teacher remind you of?" And as you think about the teacher you might feel tears. Perhaps you'll remember that you loved your 3rd grade teacher, or that she looked like your mom, or she punished you severely. Eventually, with a little practice you'll find blocked memories by using the chain of associations.

You can also use the question, *"What is it about* the fountain pen?" *"What is it about* your grade school?" It has the same affect. Use whichever question is more comfortable for you.

Your chain of associations may have only one link, or it may have several. Just keep asking the question until you run out of answers.

A USEFUL QUESTION   *The way to find old feelings in a dream is to break the dream into pieces, then ask:*

"WHAT DOES EACH PIECE REMIND YOU OF?"

Free association is easy and natural for me, but some people have difficulty with it. Nancy had trouble with it in the beginning, but she eventually got better.

Learning to free associate takes practice. It's like being in a dark room and you have to develop your sense of touch to find your way around. It's a totally natural instinct for me. It's natural for you too, although you may not have used your instinct for a very long time. Once you develop this wonderful instinct, you'll be able to find the pain hidden in your dreams, without formal questions.

DREAMS ARE TRICKY

Sometimes you can free associate from your dream and not find any meaning, but the next day you'll suddenly know exactly what it means. So it pays to look at your dreams more than once. I have found new meaning and new tears from dreams over a year old.

Sometimes a dream will make no sense frontwards, but when you flip it around and look at the story backwards,[4] the meaning becomes clear. I honestly don't know why, but I've seen it more than once. Perhaps it is just a simple way to *disguise* the meaning. Freud helped me figure it out.

When I first started working with my dreams, I used to look at the major parts of the story and ignore the minor details. But Freud told us that you can find feeling from the most insignificant detail of a dream.[5] I did not believe him when I read it. (After all, everyone says that Freud is out of date.) I did not believe it until Sept. 10, 1989. Nancy and I were driving home from visiting our son in Kansas City. To make use of the driving time, I decided to tell Nancy a dream I had the previous night. I felt bright and cheerful that day and there was no reason to expect a discharge! I free associated from each part of the dream except I skipped over one minor detail because it seemed so insignificant. After running through the dream twice with no tears, I gave up and we changed the subject.

Twenty minutes later, on a hunch I decided to tell Nancy of the minor detail. It was a hole in concrete...that's all it was. It reminded me of Legos...then Tinker Toys...then Lincoln Logs. The childhood toys were suddenly vivid. I could smell the box and taste the Tinker Toys in my mouth. All of a sudden I was bawling, while going 60 miles and hour on Interstate 35.

Nancy quickly put on her seat belt and offered to drive. It was a powerful discharge, and it proved Freud's point that you can sometimes find feeling in the most insignificant details of the dream.

UNDERSTANDING YOUR DREAM SYMBOLS

When you look at your dream, you are looking at your own programming. A computer is programmed with numbers and letters and commands. Your mind is programmed by picture symbols. So it may be helpful to know a little about those symbols.

Freud believed that dream symbols had consistent meanings from patient to patient. For example, a cigar represents a penis and a bowl stands for a vagina...*in every patient.*

He would listen to his patient's dream then interpret the dream for the patient, as though the patient could not interpret his own dream.

Most modern students of dream analysis disagree with Freud on this issue, and so do I. In most cases, symbols mean different things to different people. **You are the only person who really knows what *your* symbols mean to you.**

When you look at your dream, trust your intuition. Only you can decide the meaning of a lion, a gun, a house, a car or a cigar. If you practice free association you'll develop a dream sense. You'll know what your dreams mean.

There are some subjects that seem to be common in many different patients: flying, falling, roads, cars, guns, spiders, just to name a few. But even though many people share a common symbol, there is little reason to assume they have the same meaning. So trust your instincts. You are the final word on your dreams, and if your therapist tries to interpret your dream for you, tell him what I said.

"STRUCTURAL" SYMBOLS IN DREAMS

I'd like to tell you about something exciting I have learned from my dreams.

I have received pictures in my dreams of how the brain works. I call them "structural dreams" because they are about the physical *structure* of the brain.

If the pictures are valid, it might explain why some (not all) dream symbols might really have a consistent meaning. After all, everybody's brain is constructed the same way, and if other people have structural dreams, there might be a few universal symbols.

I was tempted to leave this out of the book because it might be just my own personal symbols. I finally decided to leave it in because, if the pictures are valid, they might be useful to some future scientific studies.

I don't know anyone else who has experienced it, and I have not found it in any books by the famous dream scientists (Freud, Jung, Hall, Perls, etc.)

My first structural dream was of two silos side by side. The left silo was dark and empty, the right was light and full of people. To me (and not necessarily you) this means that when I split, I blocked out the left side and went to live in  the right side of the brain. I have also dreamed of two doors, two theaters, and always the left side is dark and the right side is light.

The idea of the "sleep-switch" (see page 84) could be discovered by logic, but I first saw it in a dream. I don't know where the switch is in the brain, but I can tell you something about its shape. Like all switches it has two parts that make contact. In a neurotic the lower part is concave like a bowl, and in the middle there is some fluid, like a little pond or lake. In my dreams I have seen this switch as a football stadium, a lake and a pond. It is interesting to note that in Jung's dream analysis, a lake often symbolizes the "interface between the conscious and the subconscious."[6] Thus a lake could be a symbol of a physical brain structure.

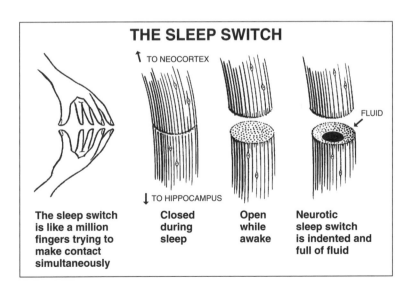

THE SLEEP SWITCH

↑ TO NEOCORTEX

↓ TO HIPPOCAMPUS

FLUID

The sleep switch is like a million fingers trying to make contact simultaneously

Closed during sleep

Open while awake

Neurotic sleep switch is indented and full of fluid

I suspect that in a mentally healthy person, the lower part of the switch is flat. Mine is indented to prevent a complete contact. The fluid is not suppose to be there. When my switch flattens out the way it is supposed to be, the fluid will dissipate.

I have had structural dreams about compartments. I have six compartments (see pages 171-173) in my head. I've learned about them in my normal therapy, but have also seen them in a dream as six ghosts.

One of the most common nightmares is about spiders and insects all over the bed, walls, and floor. I've had that dream too, and I suspect it is a structural dream about millions of blocked nerve connections trying to reconnect themselves. It's not a blocked memory about a spider attack when you were a child. It's structural! The millions of nerves really are trying to reconnect.

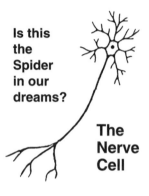

Is this the Spider in our dreams?

The Nerve Cell

You may or may not believe in the existence of a soul, but if there is a soul, it would explain a lot of things that happen in your brain. Whether you call it "self," "consciousness," "thetan" or "soul," let's imagine that "you" are a tiny bit of energy, rather than matter. *You* live in your body, but *you* can also exist outside of the body. In the daytime, *you* stay in one spot in the brain, like the captain of a ship must stay at the helm of his ship to do the steering. During the day, *you* are not particularly aware of what is happening in the rest of your brain...just as the captain of the ship is not aware of the cooking and scrubbing at the other end of his ship.

But at night, *you* are free to travel to billions of places in the brain...and when you get there, *you* are not the captain. *You* are more like one of the crew. Your viewpoint is no longer the captain's viewpoint.

Or another way to explain it: in the day, the *self* is like the king of a country, unaware of the activity of his subjects,

94

but at night, he leaves his castle and explores his kingdom, and as he explores each place he may be in the role of his subjects, instead of always being the king.

If you can imagine *you* as this particle of energy traveling down billions of nerve paths to explore your brain, then perhaps you can appreciate the symbolism of roads. I have had many dreams about roads and highways, sometimes traveling a thousand miles per hour, sometimes coming to an intersection and not knowing which way to turn, and sometimes going through dangerous neighborhoods. I believe roads represent nerve paths and the dangerous neighborhoods are dangerous parts of the brain where pain is stored.

Most of us have dreamed of flying. We usually assume it is symbolic. But what if it were not a symbol at all? Is it possible that this little particle of energy called *you* actually flies out once in a while?

In my most traumatic scenes, I usually see the event from a distance as though I were outside the body, looking at this little boy called "Tom." The more traumatic the scene, the farther the distance. Thousands of other patients have seen their traumatic scenes from the outside viewpoint. It could be a dream symbol, but it could be a physical reality. A dream of flying might be structural.

WHY WE REMEMBER SOME DREAMS
AND NOT OTHERS

If you have difficulty remembering dreams, you might want to keep a notebook and a pen by your bed so can write them down immediately.

Why are some dreams hard to remember, and others are crystal clear? The most common explanation is that we remember dreams if we wake up in the middle of them, but I think there is more to it than that.

I will often wake up during a dream, decide consciously to write it down, only to find that it has slipped out of my memory. At other times, I'll have a dream that is crystal clear, and easy to recall, and to tell the truth, I'm not so sure that I woke up during the dream.

In my experience, some dreams cannot be recalled no matter how hard you try, and some dreams are so clear that it's as though someone is sending you an intentional message. It's another reason I believe in the Super Conscious theory. It's almost as though He wants us to look at the dream.

When a dream is vague and fuzzy, and hard to recall, I just put it out of my mind and don't even try to use it. The fuzzy dream makes impossible work. I trust my Super-Conscious to tell me which dream to work on by giving me a clear dream.

DOING THERAPY WITH A NIGHTMARE[7]

A nightmare is a blocked scene coming up in the middle of the night. Theoretically, if you wake up with a nightmare and sink into the feeling instead of fighting it, you would have a primal, a complete, 3-dimensional, stereo, discharge of the scene.

Nancy and I have tried this early in therapy with no success. When the nightmare comes the patient is so shaken that he has no interest in sinking into it. It's hard to wake up the therapist (me), and when we tried to do normal therapy with the dream, we found the symbolism so thickly disguised that free association produced nothing.

Fortunately, as the therapy progresses and the pile of pain is reduced, the nightmares reduce in intensity, and the symbols are less disguised. The last time I had a nightmare, I was so calm that I just lay in bed and looked at it like a scientist.

I remember one night Nancy woke me up. She was having a mild nightmare. She was already crying when she woke up. We made no attempt to primal, but we did normal therapy as described in this book. We used the most basic question, "What is the feeling?" Very quickly, Nancy was bawling, and she bawled for 30 minutes followed by 25 minutes of heavy breathing. It was a very big discharge.

While I still consider it possible to primal from an intense nightmare, there may be no reason to take the risk.

Discharging a mild nightmare was a wild enough experience for me, and I'm sure for Nancy too.

A USEFUL QUESTION *If you try to do therapy in the middle of the night, use the question:*

"WHAT'S THE FEELING IN THE DREAM?"
or simply **"WHAT'S THE FEELING?"**

"PROGRESS REPORT" DREAMS

Some dreams seem to be sort of a "progress report" on the therapy, with clues about what to expect next. Patients in Psychoanalysis also have *progress dreams.* Nancy has only had a few, but I have had dozens. My *progress dreams* are useful and reassuring but I have spent months puzzling over the question, "Where does the *progress report* come from?"

The reports are mildly disguised, but once understood, they are very clever and clear communications. The clues about what is coming next seem to suggest strongly that the reports come from a source that is not only intelligent, but more knowledgeable about the therapy than I am. It is almost as though the report comes from another consciousness.

The only explanation I can come up with is that the Super Conscious is sending me an intentional message. The existence of this progress report is one of many reasons why I believe there is a Super Conscious, a part of me that is more intelligent, more knowledgeable than me and has a consciousness of its own.

To give you an idea of the predictive power of these progress reports, let me tell you a true story. In the early years of therapy, all of my reports were encouraging. They seemed to say "Keep going, everything is working" and they gave me clues of what was coming next. Suddenly I had a progress report that seemed to say, "You can't go any farther." Then I had 3 dreams that said, "If you keep doing therapy, you'll die for sure." I dreamed I was hit by a railroad train, a falling skyscraper, and an atom bomb.

I became discouraged. The therapy had worked so well, and so many symptoms had faded away. Why would it all come to such a sudden halt. A few months later I had a physical exam by the doctor. He discovered that I had a heart problem that could cause a stroke. I would have to take medicine the rest of my life to prevent the stroke.

Whoever sent me the progress report knew about my health problem before I did, and *before the doctor did.* The good news is that I have been taking my medicine regularly, and the doctor says as long as I stay on it, I'll live to be a hundred years old. And guess what. My therapy has resumed, although at a slower pace. Someone is definitely watching over me and I think it is my Super Conscious.

REPEATING DREAMS

If you keep notes on your dreams, you may notice that some dreams tend to repeat. I've had 19 different repeating dreams. They are very useful in helping you recognize your own symbols. I had several "cat" dreams before I realized that, for me, cats represent girls.

Whenever you have a repeat dream with a definite feeling, there is probably a blocked scene under the dream. It is repeating because the blocked scene is stuck in the temporary file and trying to come up. The feeling might be too powerful to discharge directly.

To find feeling in a repeating dream, use the core question, "What's the feeling?" You may not find the whole scene until late in therapy, but asking the question will shake the wires and force your brain to give you a spoonful of discharge within a few days.

A USEFUL QUESTION *When ever you have a repeat dream with a definite feeling, use the question:*

"WHAT'S THE FEELING IN THE DREAM?"
or simply "WHAT'S THE FEELING?"

As with nightmares, you can measure your therapy progress with your repeat dreams. I have a repeat dream about guns. In my early therapy, the dream went like this. A robber comes to my house, and I can't find my gun or my bullets. A few months later, when the same dream came, I would find the gun but not the bullets. Another few months passed, and I would find my gun and bullets, but I couldn't get the gun loaded. Next, I got the gun loaded, but couldn't aim. In the most recent dream, I have a gun, loaded, and I shot the bad guy. The dream is about my growing ability to confront people. I didn't cry about this dream. It was more like a progress report.

USING DREAMS TO "SHAKE THE WIRES"

Whenever you have a clear dream, always run through it during therapy and look for associations. If time allows, run through it several times. At the very least, run through it in your mind. You can do it while you're taking a shower or driving to work. Even if it does not lead directly to crying, you're making progress by "shaking the wires."

Running through your dream and asking the questions will put pressure on your nervous system and force discharge to the surface, if not immediately, then perhaps a few days later. When you look at a dream, you are looking into your temporary file, and that is exactly where the blocked memories are. If you are neurotic, every dream will have some connection to blocked pain. Even though you don't recognize it, believe me, it is there.

One way you can prove it to yourself is to watch for yawning and dopiness. When you free associate from your dream, you may not find any obvious feeling, but you may yawn continually, or feel dopey or sleepy, while you are trying to tell it. **You may think there is nothing in that dream, but your nervous system is being shaken by the questions.** The yawn and the dopiness means that the scene you are asking for is too much, and your nervous system will have to give you an indirect discharge later.

Quick Review:
How To Find Blocked Memories
From Dreams

1.   **Ignore dreams that are vague and fuzzy.** Work only with dreams that are clear and easy to recall.

2.   **Break the dream into pieces,** then look at each piece and ask the question, "What does _____ remind me of?" or "What is it about _____ ?" (You fill in the blanks.)

3.   **Don't ignore small details.** An insignificant detail may be the doorway to your hidden feeling.

4.   **Run through your dream the following day.** You may find a new meaning that you missed the first time.

5.   **Dreams are tricky.** Try running the dream backwards. Look for opposites.

6.   If a **nightmare** wakes you up in the middle of the night, you might be able to do therapy immediately. Use the question, "What's the feeling in the dream" or simply "What's the feeling?" If the nightmare is very intense, therapy might not work. But if it is mild, you should be able to find old pain.

7.   When looking at a **repeater dream** with a feeling, ask the question, "What's the feeling in the dream?" or simply "What's the feeling?"

8.   Even if you get no discharge directly from your dream, it pays to run through each dream because it **"shakes the wires."**

9.   Take **notes** on your dreams as soon as you wake up to be sure you can remember them during therapy.

FOOTNOTES CHAPTER 4

1. Ann Faraday, *Dream Power,* pp. 80-155.

2. Jonathon Winson, *Brain and Psyche,* read the whole book. Also, Ann Faraday, *Dream Power,* pp. 92-93.

3. "Yawning to Breathe Free," *Psychology Today,* Feb. 1987, pp. 9-10.

4. Sigmund Freud, *Interpretation of Dreams,* pp. 340-343.

5. Sigmund Freud, *Interpretation of Dreams,* pp. 167-195.

6. James A. Hall, *Jung: Interpreting Your Dream,* cassette.

7. Arthur Janov has had some success finding old feelings from nightmares, *Primal Scream,* pp. 260-263.

5

The First Week, Opening the Floodgate

After the patient gets the hang of doing therapy, a typical session is the ultimate in simplicity. The patient lays down on a davenport, reclining chair, or the floor, puts on a blindfold and starts talking. The patient will usually tell the therapist what question to use, because she already knows what's bothering her. She may say, "I want to tell you a dream I had last night," or "I want to talk about a problem at work," or simply, "Ask me what the feeling is." The therapist will ask her favorite question about every ten seconds and she does the rest.

Toward the end of my therapy the sessions were even simpler than that. I would work alone in the bedroom with music and find the old feeling by myself (See pages 19-26, Doing Therapy Alone). After I found the feeling and cried a few tears, I would go into the kitchen and ask Nancy to help me. We might sit at the kitchen table, with no blindfold, and as I told Nancy about the feeling, I'd explode almost with the first sentence. I might bawl for ten minutes and then I would feel much better. Nancy would go back to cooking lunch as if nothing had happened. She didn't even ask a question. She simply sat and listened.

Doing therapy is a little like driving a car. It's simple once you get the hang of it, and sometimes the hardest part is getting the darn thing started.

An experienced therapist can guide a patient to tears in the first session, but if you have never been a therapist before, don't be surprised if it takes several sessions to get started. It is important to try to get tears in the first session because it helps the patient overcome any skepticism she may have about the method. She will believe in the therapy and become anxious for the next session.

HYPNOTIC COMMANDS

Unfortunately, the most difficult session is the first one because the first feeling to surface may be blocked by a "hypnotic command" which is a little difficult to recognize. It is also a challenge for me to try to explain it to you. It's hard to explain because it is so simple. The *hypnotic command* will be screaming at you, but you will miss it because it is so obvious. The following is a true story that demonstrates the obviousness of a *hypnotic command:*

When Nancy first started The Therapy, we worked three sessions without a tear. She answered all the questions. She talked about her childhood, but there was something confusing in her speech. Her comments were general. She could not say anything specific. For example, she would say, "My father was always drunk," or "My parents fought all the time." When I tried to get her to talk about a specific day, or a specific fight, she could not do it. She would answer, "It was always like that."

For three days we got nowhere. Her answers had a common theme, but I didn't notice it. Can you spot it? It's as plain as the nose on your face. Whenever I asked her a question, her answers would contain words like, "always," "every time," "over and over."

Finally on the third day I began to suspect a *hypnotic command* and I asked her to repeat the word "always," and here is what she said, word-for-word:

"Always…always…always…always…always…ever …ever…ever…forever…forever…forever…never …never…never…" and then she started to weep, and then she cried.

She was crying as she remembered that her childhood had been always the same. No attention, no love, no hope. Nancy had spent her first two years of life caged in her baby bed, not allowed to get out and walk, not allowed to see anything, no conversation, no stimulation, just two years of near isolation. Her *never, ever* feeling was connected to a very big pile of pain.

At last we had found a leak in the dam, and this first memory gave us the confidence to keep working. Discharging the hypnotic command changed Nancy's speech pattern. She no longer answered every question with "always." She was able to look at specific days and moments. I hope you're getting the main point. The pain connected to the words "always" and "never" had given them a hypnotic effect as though some hypnotist had planted the words in her mind and commanded her to "never get specific."

While I was writing this book I struggled with whether to call it a *hypnotic command* or a *programmed command.* I finally decided to use them both. Both terms are descriptive. It's like a *hypnotist* had planted a command in her mind. It is also like a computer scientist *programming* a command into a computer.

> **DEFINITION**
>
> **A HYPNOTIC COMMAND** (Also called "programmed command") is a word or phrase that is connected to early pain, and that has a programming effect on the patient's speech, actions and viewing screen.

Where do hypnotic commands come from? Some are words that parents repeated day after day, for example, "Shut up," or "Hold still," or "Get lost," or "Don't cry!" Others are decisions the child made as early as 1 or 2 years old and later forgot, for example, "Don't trust parents," (Don't trust the therapist.)

Hypnotic commands were first discovered in the 1880's by Josef Brever and later by Jean-Martin Charcot. Both men were working on hysteria, a mental disease that is apparently caused by hypnotic commands.[1]

Hubbard believed that when a child is knocked unconscious, any words he hears from bystanders will become hypnotic commands. For example, a parent might say, "He's not moving." If Hubbard is right, imagine the effect if a man would hit his daughter while yelling, "You little slut!" He could be programming her to become one. Hubbard's theory is explained in more detail in chapter 10.

It is also possible to receive a hypnotic command while under anesthesia during an operation.[2]

The effect of these commands is that it is sometimes tricky to start The Therapy. When you ask the obvious question "What happened," the answer will be distorted by old programming. Words and decisions planted in the child's mind years ago will interfere with therapy, especially in the first few sessions. They literally have a programming affect as surely as if you had typed them in with your keyboard. And that is one reason why the hardest part of the therapy is getting started.

Therapists have known for a hundred years that neurosis is caused by childhood pain, yet they have not been able to dig out enough pain to cure the neurosis. One thing that has held them back is the *hypnotic* or *programmed command*. Once you get past that, the therapy will take on a life of its own.

THERAPY PRINCIPLE NO. **18**

Starting Therapy is Sometimes Difficult Because of Hypnotic Commands, (Also Called Programmed Commands.)

After the first few months, these commands become less important.

We found Nancy's hypnotic command by asking her to repeat the suspected phrase over and over, perhaps 10, or 20, or 30 times, while watching her picture screen. It is significant that Nancy started with the word "always," and ended with the word "never" which is the *opposite* of "always." **The brain frequently uses opposites as a defense.**

It is also significant that Nancy found the word "never," by herself with no training. She had not read this book nor any book on this subject. She found the word "never" and the feeling that was connected to it, *by following her intuition.*

THERAPY PRINCIPLE NO. **19**

The Way to Find Old Feelings From a Hypnotic Command (Programmed Command)is to Ask the Patient to Repeat the Phrase and Watch Her Picture Screen.

If you can appreciate the programming effect of Nancy's word "always," then perhaps you can also appreciate the devastating effect of some other common commands: "I can't see," "I can't move," "Don't trust anyone," "I can't believe it," just to list a few. The command, "I can't move" could program the body to feel stiff, and could prevent movement on the viewing screen. The command "I can't see" could give a person poor eye sight, and a blank viewing screen. "Don't trust" could program the patient to distrust the therapist.

Hubbard attempted to list all possible hypnotic commands. He cataloged them into groups which he called *holders, deniers, bouncers, groupers and misdirectors.*[3] For example, "I can't move" would be a *holder.* "Don't tell anyone" would be a *denyer,* and it could prevent a patient from telling anything personal to the therapist. "I can't go back" is a *bouncer,* and it could program the patient to not remember the past. Nancy's word "always" is an example of a *grouper,* which grouped all of Nancy's memories into a bunch so she would never have to look at a specific scene. "Start over again" is an example of a *misdirector* which could cause the patient to repeat everything.

I have given you only a small percent of Hubbard's list because it is impossible to list all of the possibilities, especially when you consider the infinite variety of people, the shades of meanings of words, and all the different languages and dialects. The possibilities are infinite. I prefer that you learn the basic principle, rather than memorizing lists.

Recognizing a hypnotic command is easier than you think because the command will be screaming at you, and once you make a reasonable guess, the patient's intuition will do the rest.

In Nancy's case, we had worked three days with no result, and yet the word "always" was popping into her speech practically every breath. If it had been a snake, it would have bitten us. She was practically screaming, "My first old feeling has something to do with the word "always."

The hypnotic command is bad news and good news at the same time. **It is a defense and a doorway.** Before we recognized Nancy's hypnotic command, it was a *defense,* preventing us from finding the pain. But as soon as we recognized it, it became the *doorway* into the pile of pain.

This principle will show up many times in therapy. A disguised dream is a defense and a doorway. Analysing is a defense and a doorway. A sexual fantasy is a defense and a doorway. It is one of the central principles of The Therapy.

THERAPY PRINCIPLE NO. **20**

Every Defense Is Also A Doorway.

For example, a hypnotic command
is a defense and a doorway.

I've said throughout the book that the patient does most of the work, but on this matter of hypnotic commands, the therapist has to be alert. If the patient reads the book, she may be able to spot her hypnotic commands, but it is a good idea if both therapist and patient are looking for it.

In my experience, hypnotic commands are critical early in therapy because they can prevent you from ever getting started. After several weeks they become less important. I suspect that every blocked memory has a programming effect and that discharging them will dissolve the bad programming. The early hypnotic commands, like Nancy's "always," are more interesting because the connection between the command and it's programming effect is obvious and visible. But the programming effect of the later blocked memories is so complex that it can be understood only by the patient.

The First Session And How To Instruct The Patient

Here is the speech I always give to the patient at the start of the first session. You may wish to reword it to fit your own personal style, or you can just read it as is:

"Put on the blindfold. Make yourself comfortable. Do you need a pillow?

I'd like you to form a picture of a tree in your mind. Do you see it? Good! The place in your mind where you see pictures is called your *viewing screen*. Sometimes I also call it the *picture screen*. During therapy you must constantly watch your viewing screen because when an old feeling comes to the surface, the first clue will usually be a picture on your viewing screen.

How good is the picture on your screen? Is it clear. Is it fuzzy or fragmented? Imagine the tree moving closer and closer to you. Now imagine it moving farther away. Imagine it with green leaves. Now imagine that it is autumn, and the leaves are yellow and gold, and now imagine that the leaves are falling."

If the patient has any kind of problem with her viewing screen it could be a clue that she has a *hypnotic command* stuck in her head. No movement might suggest something like "I can't move," or "Hold still." A blank screen might suggest "I can't see." The possibilities are infinite, **but if the patient has read the book, his intuition will help you find the command.**

If you or your patient find a phrase that might be a hypnotic command, ask her to repeat it and watch her picture screen. The first phrase you try may not be exactly right, so ask the patient to consider if there is another *similar phrase* that has some feeling. Ask her to repeat the *opposite* phrase. The patient's intuition will do the rest. When she stumbles across the right words, she'll know it because she'll feel something familiar.

Continue instructing the patient:

"You are going to cure yourself. You will do most of the work. The way you will be cured is by crying. Remember this simple rule: the more you cry, the more your mind will heal itself.

You must do the work because you are the only one who can see your viewing screen, and you are the only one who knows what you are feeling.

You must learn to recognize your own *brain feelings.* Some of them are pretty obvious. A *question* is a brain feeling. Other common brain feelings are *hunches, familiarity, curiosity.* You can feel the difference between a dream, and a real memory, because they each have a different feeling. You can find your blocked memories by trusting your brain feelings.

My job is to help you by asking qustions. In school and in business, when a question is asked, you are expected to answer it concisely and accurately. But in the therapy, you must learn a new way to answer questions. We call it "free association."

When I ask you a question, I want you to say everything that goes through your mind no matter how silly, childish, rude, disgusting or stupid. This is called "free association." If you can tell me every thought that goes through your mind, it will help you find your blocked memories.

Free association seems to loosen up blocked memories so small pieces suddenly pop into your viewing screen. We call it a "pop-in" when something new and surprising pops into your viewing screen.

A pop-in comes from the part of your brain that is blocked. It won't be the whole blocked memory...just one small piece. You can find the other pieces by free association and by trusting your *brain feelings.*"

Sometimes the memories you are looking for will be very subtle. When you find one, you may feel unsure. You will think you are making a big deal out of nothing. But follow your hunches and try to put that subtle feeling into words. When you find the right words, the tears will come.

Do you understand everything I've said?

Do you have any questions?

If you have no questions, let's begin."

Now ask the *starting questions* slowly, one at a time. The purpose of starting questions is to get the patient talking and to eliminate any problems that might distract her. You need to ask these starting questions only once, but be sure she is finished answering before you go on to the next question.

"How do you feel? Any strange body feelings?

Is there anything on your mind?

Anything you'd like to talk about?

Do you have a present-time problem?

Have you had a recent misunderstanding?

Do you have any negative feelings about the therapy?"

Some patients can free associate easily, and some can't. The ones who can do it easily will take charge of their own therapy quickly. If your patient has difficulty with free association, you'll have to help her along.

The patient who can't free associate might have a hypnotic command like "Shut-up," or "Be quiet." It is possible that she was ignored as a child and not allowed to talk. You can help her learn free association by using the starting question "Do you have a present time problem?"

She may talk about her job, or her boyfriend. Her talk may seem irrelevant to her childhood pain. You may think you are wasting your time, but have a little faith, and trust the patient's instincts. At the very least, the patient is learning that it is safe to talk to you, and that you won't laugh, interrupt, or tell her to shut up. Once the patient learns that lesson, you may see her slip into the past all by herself.

The patient may talk for twenty minutes about present time problems. It doesn't matter what she talks about. Just talking will stimulate old feelings. But after twenty minutes or a half hour it may be time to look for an old feeling.

Remember, there is only one feeling that is ready to come up. All you have to do is ask for it. You might try several different questions before you find the old feeling. At times you'll feel confused about which question to ask. But in the end, it's not critical which question you use, because the feeling is coming by itself no matter what you ask.

But still you have to make a decision which question to ask first, and here is how to decide it. The feeling is right there in front of you, but it is hiding. **There are only four places it can hide.** Think of it as though you are a hunter and there are four bushes in front of you. You know there is a rabbit behind one of the bushes but you don't know which one. So how do you decide which bush to shake? The answer is to shake all four, one at a time.

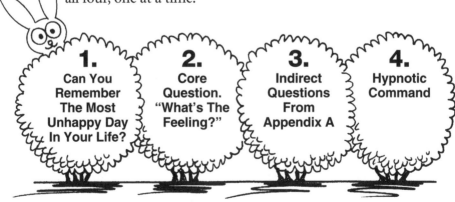

1.
Can You
Remember
The Most
Unhappy Day
In Your Life?

2.
Core
Question.
"What's The
Feeling?"

3.
Indirect
Questions
From
Appendix A

4.
Hypnotic
Command

Shake the **FIRST BUSH** by asking, **"Can you remember the most unhappy day of your life?"** With a little luck, your patient will be bawling within minutes. If she finds a scene that makes her cry, you have probably found the *mouth of the river* and you can use the procedure explained in Chapter 3. Briefly, you ask the patient to go to the beginning of the scene then describe what happened. You ask for an earlier beginning, and ask her to run through the whole scene again…and again…and again.

If you find the *mouth of the river,* you should count yourself lucky. This is the easiest way to find old feelings. Your patient will find buckets and buckets of tears by just looking for an earlier beginning and running through the scene. Unfortunately, every patient is a little different and some will not be able to find the *mouth of the river.*

Shake the **SECOND BUSH** by asking a *core question* like, **"What is the one feeling trying to come up by itself?"** or simply **"What's the feeling?"** Remind your patient to watch for pictures. Many times the *first picture she sees* will be a part of a blocked scene. It might be anything, a flower, a doll, or just a color. It won't be obviously traumatic. She may talk for a half hour and keep coming back to the very first picture. If she free associates from that picture she will probably find a scene that makes her cry. Keep asking, "What's the feeling?" Ask her for details. Ask her to tell the whole story. Once she finds a scene, try the river principle again by asking for an earlier beginning.

If she doesn't find tears, you may have to go to the third bush. Yawning is a sign that your direct question is shaking up her system but that she cannot answer the question *directly.* If she gets dopy or sleepy, it means pretty much the same thing. Your question is *shaking the wires,* but her tears will have to come up *indirectly.*

The **THIRD BUSH** is to ask the **indirect questions** in Appendix A. If your patient cannot cry from the first two methods, chances are that she will have to discharge *indirectly* before she can feel her real scenes. Crying in a movie is a simple example of indirect discharge. The movie is similar to the blocked scene. Crying in the movie will reduce the pile of pain even though the actual scene remains blocked.

The indirect question list is a *designed list.* It is a thorough checklist of every possible way the patient can discharge *indirectly.*

The **FOURTH BUSH** is to watch for a **hypnotic command.** You may see clues to the hypnotic command while you are shaking the other three bushes. The easiest clue will be if the patient has trouble with her viewing screen for instance, a blank screen, or no movement, or a color. But it can also be something in her speech habits, as with Nancy's "always."

If you shake all four bushes, chances are you will find some tears. I put them in sequence because I want you to try the easiest one first. The *river of pain* is the easiest way to find blocked memories. Many patients will explode almost immediately. Asking "What's the Feeling" is second easiest. The *indirect questions* is more work because there are a lot of questions to ask. If you go through the whole list, you might work for an hour or more just to get through the list. The *hypnotic command* is the last bush because it is the trickiest. But if your patient has a *hypnotic command,* you should be able to find it. It will be practically screaming at you. If your patient has read the book, she will help you spot it.

Which ever way you find the first old feeling, it will set the stage for many sessions to come. For example, if you find the *mouth of the river,* you can use that same procedure, asking for an earlier beginning, for the next several sessions. If the patient responds to "What's the feeling," you can use that same question in the next sessions. If the patient responds to the indirect questions, she will probably respond to them during the other sessions.

Hypnotic commands are an exception. There might be only one. Once the patient cries, her therapy skills will improve so she can more easily find feeling with the other

3 methods. So go back to the other bushes to find discharge. There may be another hypnotic command, but chances are that there is only one. But keep your eyes open just in case there are more.

Whatever question you use, ask it clearly and firmly as though you expect an answer. Keep asking the same question over and over. It is not unusual to ask the same question ten, twenty or thirty times. Keep asking the question until it is obvious that the patient is not reacting to it.

For example: you may ask:

"What is the old feeling?"…and the patient may talk
10 minutes.

"What is the old feeling?"…and she may talk a half hour.

"What is the old feeling?"…and she may talk 5 minutes.

Keep asking the question until the patient is tired of it. If you ask the question for an hour or more, and if the patient is not discharging (crying), and if the patient is not having any reaction (That's 3 ifs), then you may have a *stalled session* (see pages 127-128). You may wish to end the session and try again tomorrow. Have faith. Your work today was not in vain. During the night your patient's brain will do some rewiring so she can find old feelings more easily tomorrow.

WHEN THE PATIENT STARTS TO CRY

If the patient stops talking, be careful. Be as quiet as possible, and be alert. She might be close to a feeling. She might be hiding her tears. Anything you say can be an interruption. Look at her lips and nostrils for signs that she is starting to cry.

Use the *probing questions* in Appendix A. They are designed to give the patient a little nudge without interrupting. When you say something, say it in a whisper, "What's the feeling?" One of the most beautiful probing questions is "What are the tears for?"

If her lips and nostrils are not moving, there are other possibilities. She might be experiencing *lethargy* which is a form of discharge. She might feel stiff, paralysed, unable to lift her arms. She will have difficulty talking. She is discharging as surely as if she were bawling. You can help her through it by asking "What's the feeling." Listen patiently as she tries to talk. It should last about twenty minutes or half hour.

Silence can also mean that she is feeling *dopy or sleepy*. This means that the questions are shaking up her system. Her computer can't give you an answer without some rewiring. Your questions are forcing her to fall asleep. You should ask her, "Do you want to take a nap?" Let her sleep and try therapy after the nap. You may find discharge almost immediately after she wakes up.

KINDS OF DISCHARGE

There is some controversy about what is a valid discharge. In some therapies, patients are encouraged to get angry, to confront each other, and to beat on pillows, as if that would make them more healthy. Hubbard believed that laughing and yawning were forms of discharge.

Let's be clear about the meaning of the word "discharge." The blocked scenes are stored in the form of chemicals with electrical potential, like the chemicals in a battery. A discharge is valid if it physically drains away the stored-up chemicals.

I believe it is self-evident that bawling and screaming about a blocked scene will discharge and reduce the size of the pile. I am also sure that lethargy is a valid discharge.

Yawning is most definitely not a discharge. It is part of a pressure control for closing the sleep watch.

Anger and laughter are questionable. No doubt they are healthy emotions and may stimulate some chemical flow that make the patient feel better. They may even improve the health of the body. But I don't believe they reduce the pile of stored chemicals in the brain.

Janov believed that anger is a defense that covers the pain.[4] It is sometimes instructive to watch a patient get angry, yell obscenities, and a few seconds later she is bawling. **It's the BAWLING that reduces the pile of pain.**

Is fear a discharge? Probably not. In one of Nancy's most recent sessions, she told of a scene when her Dad was drunk and angry. He knocked over the Christmas tree and smashed a chair. Nancy said, "I forgot how scared I used to be," **and then she cried.** She felt *fear* when it happened but she discharged it with *tears* 30 years later.

I hope you don't think it is necessary to cry in every session. Once you get started, and the therapy is going full speed, you may have one session of bawling followed by a session of discovery, insights, and connections. Then another bawling session, and so on. Actually, the session of discovery and connection is pretty good evidence that there has been a valid discharge and that some rewiring has taken place.

ENDING THE SESSION

Before you end the session, be sure to shake the third bush, the *indirect questions.* The patient who tells you that no feeling is coming up may suddenly start bawling about something very indirect, like a dream, a movie, or something in the news.

If you get discharge from an indirect question, it may occur to you that you have been wasting your time by asking the core questions for an hour, but it was not a waste. The core question created the pressure on the brain. It shook up the system. The core question forces the mind to answer the question, which it cannot do without exploding. The brain solves the problem by giving your patient an indirect discharge. The pile of pain is reduced slightly, and your patient becomes slightly healthier.

After tears, the nervous system has to rebalance because it will never again be the same. The dam has a leak. The log jam has lost its first log, and every single log has shifted position slightly. The rebalancing may mess up the patient's sleep for a while. He may need more sleep, or be unable to sleep. He may have nightmares. This simply means that the mind is having some difficulty rebalancing. It may take 2 or 3 days. Sleep is critical to the therapy because that is when the rewiring is done.

Gradually your sessions will become simpler and simpler. You'll reach a time where you can do the whole session with one or two questions. You may have to use this *first session procedure* for a few days, a week, or a month. Trust your instincts to decide when to stop doing the whole routine.

At times, you'll experience stalled sessions, and you may want to return to the *first session procedure* to get the ball rolling again.

FOOTNOTES CHAPTER 5

1. Jonathan Winson, *Brain and Psyche,* pp. 7-77

2. Arthur Janov, *Primal Man,* p. 263

3. L. Ron Hubbard, *Dianetics,* pp. 403-409

4. Arthur Janov, *Primal Scream,* pp. 322-350

6

Tips on Being
A Good Therapist

The best preparation for being a therapist is to experience being a patient. You'll experience blocked memories popping into your viewing screen. You'll learn what it feels like to burst into tears while telling the details of a scene. You'll experience the earlier beginning, programmed commands, doorways, and brain feelings.

If your therapist is new at his job, you'll see how his mistakes can interrupt you just when you are close to feeling. If he is too talkative, if he tries to analyze or label you, if he gives you sympathy, or if he judges or disagrees with what you say, you'll see how all of those mistakes can interfere with your progress.

LISTEN WITHOUT JUDGING

Traditionally the psychiatrist's job is to sit quietly and *listen without judging*. Sounds pretty simple! This was one of Freud's greatest contributions. He discovered that if the therapist will be quiet and listen, the patient will get better just by talking. We call it the "talking cure." It is so simple and yet so rare. Consider for a moment who among your friends can listen even one full minute without interrupting.

If you can master this simple formula of *listening without judging,* you will create an environment in which the patient can cure himself. Talking to you will focus his thoughts much more than when he is alone. Your very presence will stimulate his old feelings. The faster and more freely he talks, the more he will go into a kind of a trance in which old feelings will surface more easily. Just being there with him will make him feel safer when he starts to cry. You accomplish all of this by sitting in silence and listening without judging.

If you disapprove or disagree with anything he says, he will quickly learn that it is not safe to talk to you. He will begin to pick and choose carefully what he tells you. This is a disaster because when he hides his honest thoughts from you, he is simultaneously stopping the *flow* of old memories.

Painful feelings will pop-in most easily when the patient is talking fast and freely without judging his own words. If you accept everything he says, no matter how silly, childish, rude, disgusting or stupid, he will feel safe with you and his *flow* will increase.

A normal psychiatrist listens without judging, but in The Therapy you will go beyond what the psychiatrist does. You will give some instructions, ask questions and sometimes discuss which question to use. But the basic psychiatrist attitude of silence is a great starting point. Silence is the foundation. You add a touch of gentle conversation. When in doubt, it is always safer to be quiet. When you talk, it is better to be too brief than to be too talkative.

READ THE BOOK

You must read the entire book, and make sure that your patient reads the whole book. Refer to it often while doing therapy. We have a tape version for slow readers.

The most difficult sessions will be the first two or three because *hypnotic commands* are such tricky little devils. You would be smart to read Chapter 5 about the first session several times, and to have the book opened to that chapter while attempting the first session.

Ten Guidelines Of A Good Therapist

The following guidelines should guide you on the road to being a good therapist. If you vary from these guidelines, you will slow the therapy and make extra work for yourself.

1. **ASK EACH QUESTION OVER AND OVER AGAIN.**
   You may ask the same question 10 times, 20 times, 30 times. You might even use the same question for several sessions. The patient will tell you if the question is having no effect, and then you can move on to a different question.

2. **BE AS QUIET AS POSSIBLE.**
   Even a squeaky chair can be a distraction. Each time you ask a question be totally quiet while the patient is answering it. If the patient doesn't say anything, count to 10 silently before you ask the question again. Silence becomes more important as the patient gets closer to feelings.

3. **NEVER SYMPATHIZE.**
   If the patient is crying, squirming, or yelling, be quiet and listen. You may be tempted to comfort him, but realize that you are comforting him by just being there. If you say anything at that moment, you will interrupt him and cause him to loose the feeling. Think of it as a trance, and your interruption will bring him out of the trance.

   Later in therapy, there may be times when a touch or a hug is appropriate. It may actually help the patient cry more. Trust your instincts. You'll know when the time is right. This has nothing to do with sex. It is a fatherly or motherly hug...a hug for the soul.

4. **NEVER JUDGE, EVALUATE, OR DISAGREE.**
   It is perfectly okay for the patient to be wrong, stupid, silly, immature, unreasonable, childish, selfish, hateful. All of these feelings will eventually correct themselves after the old pain is removed by crying.

5. **BE WARM, FRIENDLY AND COURTEOUS.**
   Be a friend. The patient will tell you nothing if he does not trust you. One famous psychiatrist once said, "I've

never had much success with patients that I don't like."
But rest assured that the more the patient discharges his
pain, the more you will grow to like him.

6. **INTERRUPT VERY CAREFULLY.**
If the patient becomes silent for a long time, he might be
in the middle of a fragile thought that you can't see. So
ask him in a whisper, "Where are you now?" or "Are you
in the middle of something?" If he falls asleep, let him
sleep. Your questions may have forced him to sleep to do
some rewiring. Go read a book until he wakes up.

7. **DON'T THEORIZE, ANALYZE, OR LABEL.**
It does not help the patient to say, "You have a mother
complex," or "You need to improve your self-esteem."
Keep your target clear. The more he cries, the more he
gets cured. Only removing the old pain will help. Even if
your analysis is valid, saying it out loud will interrupt his
concentration, and it tells the patient that you are not
really listening with your heart.

8. **DON'T TRY TO GUESS WHAT HAPPENED IN A SCENE.**
The patient can guess, but the therapist must never guess.
Even with good intentions, your guesses will just interrupt
and confuse the patient. Worst of all, the patient might
believe your guess instead of looking inside himself and
piecing his own puzzle together.

9. **PICK THE RIGHT TIME OF DAY.**
Don't attempt therapy if either the patient or therapist is
sleepy. Try to find a time of day when both are fully awake.

10. **DON'T TAKE IT PERSONALLY.**
If the patient says you are ugly or stupid, you know that is
not true. It is his old pain that is saying those things. So
be quiet, bite your tongue, and help him to find his pain.

The scan question, "Do you have negative feelings
about the therapist?" may actually invite the patient to
attack you. If you are tempted to defend yourself, here
is a way to do it without interrupting his "trance." You
can say, "Yes, that is your feeling." You are agreeing with
him, and reminding him that while his feeling may be
valid, he might be feeling it toward the wrong person.

7

The Long Journey,
Overcoming Obstacles

Depending on how many blocked memories you have, your therapy may last several months or many years. It could be a very long journey, and you will undoubtedly encounter some road blocks along the way. If you don't know how to handle them, you might get discouraged.

You will have an advantage that we didn't have. You have this book. When we ran into barriers there was no one to tell us to keep going. We came close to quitting more than once.

The purpose of this chapter is to prepare you for the long journey, to describe some of the stumbling blocks, and tell you how to handle them.

To start your journey on the right foot, set a goal for yourself to become 100% cured, totally mentally healthy. Like all goals, you may never get there, but if you get only halfway to mental health, the quality of your life will improve 1000%.

Setting the goal of a total cure will take you into uncharted territory. Most other therapy methods barely scratch the surface. They completely underestimate the enormous quantity of pain stored in the nervous system. Very little is known about reaching a total cure. You are in a sense a pioneer.

Your therapy will be similar to mine, but not identical. This chapter will give you the most common barriers, but you will undoubtedly run into a few that are unique for you. You can solve your own problems by using the principles in this book, and I hope you will write and tell us what you did.

Don't be afraid to take the long road. I'll be with you every step of the way. Trust your own instincts and trust the basic principles in this book. Together, we will get the job done.

The Importance of Notes

One of the most valuable tools to help you on your long journey is notes. When you look back at several weeks of therapy from your memory, it may seem like you are going in circles, talking about the same feeling.

The solution is to look at the larger picture, and that can only be done by looking at written notes. Write a brief summary of each session, listing the date, what questions were asked, what feelings and scenes came up and how much crying. I usually note how many minutes of crying, and how intense (weeping, soft-bawling, loud-bawling or screaming).

On the opposite page I've copied one page of my session notes to show you how I do it, but of course you should keep notes any way that is convenient for you. There is no right way to do it.

If you keep a record of each session, you'll be able to look back after 6 months and see plenty of progress that you could not have seen without the notes. We quickly forget how we used to be. I used to have headaches 2 and 3 times a week. It has been so many years since I've had a headache that I sometimes wonder if I ever really had them. Only my notes can tell me how I used to be.

I recommend that before you start therapy, you write a list of your symptoms. Put it in a special place, perhaps write it in this book so that some day you can look back and see how many symptoms have improved.

Notes can be written by either the patient or the therapist, but it is probably better if the patient writes them. The therapist is observing everything second hand. The patient is the only one who sees the pictures and feels the feelings.

On the following pages, we'll discuss the most likely barriers and recommend a solution for each one.

SAMPLE OF SESSION NOTES

SESSION SUMMARY
NANCY SATURDAY MARCH 18, 1988

QUESTIONS →

PREVIOUS EVENING:
NANCY TALKED 2 HOURS ABOUT DOUG!
SOME IMPATIENCE WITH TOM
— ANGER AT DOUG.

2:15 AM
NANCY WOKE UP IN MIDDLE OF THE NIGHT ✗✗
CRIED FOR 20 MINUTES IN THE BATHROOM ✗
ABOUT PEOPLE WHO "STAB HER IN THE BACK ✗
— SOFT BAWL 20 MIN.

TOM:
DO YOU HAVE A PRESENT TIME PROBLEM?

SHE TALKS ABOUT PEOPLE AT WORK.
"I'VE GOT 5 PEOPLE MAD AT ME
AND I DID NOTHING!"
"I'M DEPRESSED." "NO INTERESTS"
"I'M TIRED OF IT ALL [POP IN:] DAD IN HAY/MOW
[POP IN:] I SEE THE BARN STEPS
— SESSION STARTS 8:30
FAST FLOW TIL 9:12

NANCY
WHAT IS IT ABOUT THE BARN?

N: WHAT HAPPENED IN THE BARN
IIII IIII IIII IIII

— NO REACTION
JUST SILENCE
YAWN YAWN
YAWN YAWN YAWN
— KNOT IN HER STOMACH
— PRESSURE IN FACE
CHEST FEELING

"I FEEL TIRED BUT
NOT SLEEPY, ITS MORE
LIKE A TRANCE"
YAWN YAWN

NANCY:
WHY CAN'T YOU REMEMBER

POP-IN SCENE → NANCY IS SICK, HIGH FEVER, SLEEPING IN HER MOM'S BED
— FULL BAWL 20 MIN

AS SHE CRIES, SHE ROCKS BACK AND FORTH

NANCY SAYS: I SEE NO PICTURES BUT I KEEP THINKING ONE WORD: ✗ ✗
✗ MOMMY! ✗✗
✗✗
✗ WHERE IS MY ✗✗
✗ MOMMY ✗✗
✗ ✗ ✗✗ ✗ ✗
10:20 - 10:50
FOLLOWED BY 25 MIN HEAVY BREATHING TOO TIRED TO SIT UP

SAMPLE OF SESSION NOTES: I always put date and year at the top. In left column, I write what questions we used and who chose the question, and how many times did I ask it. On the right edge, I write times and what kind of emotion: yawn, tears, bawling, screaming. In the middle, I write the most important words the patient says, especially the words that cause her to cry.

Programmed Commands

The first barrier you will probably run into will be *programmed commands*. I also call them *hypnotic commands*. If you don't find tears in the first several sessions, you might become discouraged. Believe me, I understand. In my own therapy, I found tears within the first hour, but when we started Nancy's therapy, she went 3 sessions without a tear.

Nancy had a programmed command that was driving me crazy. We already talked about it earlier but it is important enough to mention again. Programmed commands are tricky little devils.

As a general principle, exact, specific thoughts lead to tears, while general, vague thoughts prevent tears. Nancy would talk about her past in very general language: "Every day was the same." "It was always like that." She could not seem to focus on a specific moment or event.

After 3 sessions, I began to suspect that "every" and "always" could be the programmed command. I asked her to repeat the word "always," and here's what she said:

> "Always… always…always…always…always…
> ever…ever…ever…ever…forever…forever…
> forever…never…never…never…never"

As she felt the meaning of those words, she began to cry. The word that was interfering with therapy was also the doorway to her first pain. Everyday had been the same and that in itself was painful. Nothing to look forward to…no love…no attention…no answer…no hope.

In my therapy my first programmed command was "Hold still!" It had the affect of clogging up my picture screen so I could not move to the next picture.

The solution is to repeat the command out loud ten, twenty, thirty times and watch your picture screen. If you get a picture, then you should free associate starting from that picture.

Take a look at the list on page 107 to get an idea of what possible commands you might run into. The possibilities are infinite, so you'll have to trust your intuition to recognize the programmed command.

The solution to the PROGRAMMED COMMAND
is to repeat the command 10, 20, 30 times
while watching your picture screen.

Stalled Sessions

Sometimes the therapy doesn't seem to work no matter what you do. We call it a "stalled session" if you work several hours and nothing happens.

We do not consider it a stalled session when you have a "connection" (new understandings, discoveries, insights, etc.) even though you may not cry. We have found that when the therapy was going full speed, we would usually have one session with lots of bawling, followed by a session with many connections, then a third session full of bawling followed by a fourth session of connections, and so on. A truly stalled session has no tears and no connections.

Stalled sessions are frustrating, but they can't be helped. Sometimes we would keep digging an extra hour and finally get to a discharge, and then we'd say, "It really pays to keep digging." Other times the extra hour would do nothing and then we'd say, "The extra hour was a waste of time!"

At times the patient starts the session with a lot of nervousness, and he believes, "The way I feel, I know I'm going to discharge a lot today," and then nothing happens. Other times the patient starts out calm and happy, and ends up bawling within 10 minutes. **It's sometimes just the opposite of what you'd expect.**

This "opposite effect" is more evidence of the existence of the Super Conscious, who is more interested in balancing

127

the needs of the entire body than in curing the neurosis. If you are tense and have a headache, you might think that you are really close to finding an old scene, and you're right. You are so close to the pain, that it is dangerous, so the Super Conscious, instead of letting you explode, will do the opposite. It prevents the discharge completely.

During your sleep, the Super Conscious rebalances your nervous system, and then during the next session, you may start bawling within minutes. The Super Conscious has given you a controlled spoonful of pain, and kept the whole body in balance. I have seen Nancy do this many times. We'll work for an hour with no discharge, then she'll doze off. After her nap, she'll find feeling and tears within minutes.

Here is my advice on stalled sessions. Long sessions are expensive, and there is no harm in quitting too soon. Whatever old feeling is trying to come through will still be there tomorrow.

When you have a stalled session, you may feel that you wasted your time, but nothing could be further from the truth. The therapy keeps working after the session ends. The process of questioning and looking at your viewing screen will "shake the wires." You are creating a pressure that will cause a discharge tomorrow or the day after.

To be doubly sure that you have shaken the system before you quit, run through the list of *scan questions* (Appendix A). The *scan questions* are designed to put pressure on old feelings in every possible hiding place. It is a guaranteed wire-shaker. **The most powerful wire-shaker on the list is to look at your dreams.** The other *scan questions* will work at individual times, but looking at dreams will always put pressure on your old feelings. Every dream has some connection to your old feelings.

The solution to the STALLED SESSION
is to "SHAKE THE WIRES"
by asking the scan questions, and especially
by running through your dreams.

Plateaus

A Plateau is three or more sessions in a row without discharge. When we first ran into plateaus, we didn't have anyone to tell us to keep working. We were very discouraged. But after every plateau, just when we started thinking the therapy didn't work, and were ready to quit, we'd find more old feelings and a lot of bawling.

Janov noticed plateaus in his therapy, and he considered it a "resting period" for the body. Since our method is more gentle than Primal Therapy, the "resting period" explanation makes less sense.

In my own therapy, when I experience a plateau, it has frequently turned out that the next old feeling was a big one. I have found that my worst scenes are very hard to dig out. I believe that a plateau is a time when the Super-Conscious is struggling with how to chop a traumatic scene into small comfortable spoonfuls. It takes some fancy rewiring to discharge a big scene without loosing control. A headache is a pretty sure sign that something big is trying to come up.

When you are in a plateau, my advice is keep going, keep working, don't quit. Do shorter sessions to minimize the wasted time. A half hour session every two days will keep the pain stirred up and keep the Super Conscious busy trying to break big scenes into small pieces. Be sure to use the scan questions and especially work on your dreams to be sure you are shaking the wires every session.

Normally, isolation is not essential for therapy, but if you are anxious to end the plateau, you might try a whole day of isolation. Read pages 215-219 about our experiences with isolation.

> *The solution to a PLATEAU is the same*
> *as the solution to a single stalled session.*
> *Keep "SHAKING THE WIRES"*
> *by asking scan questions and especially*
> *by running through your dreams.*
> *You also might try a day of isolation.*

Patient Can't
Free Associate

Many people have difficulty with free association. When you ask them a question, they will answer with one word and then go silent.

So far in this book I've given you two definitions of free association. First, we defined it as "Say everything that goes through your mind." Then when we talked about dreams we told you to break the dream into pieces and ask "What does each piece remind you of?"

But the two definitions are really the same thing. If you say everything that goes through your mind, you are saying one thing, which reminds you of a second thing which reminds you of a third, and so on.

Nancy is a pretty good example of why a person might have difficulty with free association. All through her childhood she was taught not to talk. When she tried to talk she was either told to "Shut up" or she was completely ignored, and these are the kinds of things that become programmed commands.

Try to imagine all of the possible programmed commands that might interfere with easily flowing thoughts: "Forget it!" "Don't tell anyone!" "Shut up!" "Stop your talking!" "I can't remember!" A programmed command can be actual words from a parent such as "Shut up!" or it can be a firm decision by the little child, "I don't want to talk," or "I want to forget."

When Nancy had difficulty with free association, the first thing we did was to look for programmed commands. Her *Dinner Table Scene* was perhaps her biggest discharge. It was a scene where her father would not let her talk. He interrupted every time she tried, and she finally gave up trying. Her free association got better after that scene.

At the beginning of every session, I would ask Nancy if she had a *present time problem,* and she would immediately start to talk about problems with people at her job. It was her favorite subject and she would talk very fast. She thought it was a waste of time, but it wasn't. There is some value to just talking fast. We call it "flow." She was learning to say everything that went through her mind. Her words were "flowing."

Talking works like a funnel, or like a lens. All of your knowledge and feelings become funneled and focused and come out of your mouth in an instant. This process of talking fast and freely seems to loosen up blocked feelings. It lubricates the brain. If the patient is talking fast, we say she is having "good flow!"

Nancy would usually talk about her job for 20 minutes, and eventually she'd wind down and be ready for therapy. She always thought the 20 minutes was wasted, and yet gradually her free association has improved. I'm convinced that her *good flow* about her job has improved her ability to *flow* on all other subjects.

There is always one subject that your patient will talk about. You can find her subject by running through the starting questions and the scan questions. Once you find it, encourage her to talk about it as much as she wants. It may seem like a waste of time, but it will improve her ability to free associate, and it actually stirs up the old feelings.

At times I would help Nancy with her free association by prodding her with questions. If your patient is good at free association, one question may cause her to talk for 20 minutes. In Nancy's case it was sometimes necessary to ask a question 5 or 10 times while she watched her picture screen. I would prod her by asking, "Is there anything on your picture screen?" or "Does that remind you of anything?" It seemed slow and tedious. I wasn't sure we were getting anywhere. Looking back, I can see that her free association improved rather quickly.

When the patient has difficulty free associating,

1) Look for programmed commands.
2) Encourage the patient to "flow" on any subject that makes her talkative.
3) Prod the patient's thoughts by asking starting questions and scan questions.

Negative Feelings About the Therapist

One way your brain controls pain is by "transferring" feelings on to the wrong people, places or things. That's why we get mad at hammers, scream obscenities at other cars in traffic, and are afraid of the monster in the closet. All of these are examples of transferring feeling outside of ourselves so we can handle the childhood pain.

It is hard to recognize your own transferred feelings. They seem so real. It feels like your wife is purposely trying to irritate you. The driver in that other car purposely pulled out in front of you. The hammer purposely missed the nail and hit your thumb. Your feeling is real but you are aiming it at the wrong target, and there is little you can do about it, because **transferring is an automatic reaction.** Even if you are able to recognize your own transfer, you cannot change it until you experience the childhood pain that is hidden under it.

As a neurotic, you may feel irritation or some other feeling toward your therapist. Chances are 99% that you are experiencing old feelings about Mom (or Dad, Sister, etc.) transferred onto the therapist. Of course, there is a 1% chance that your therapist really is an "insensitive, opinionated, two-faced jerk."

Transferring feelings onto the therapist is common in all therapies. Psychoanalysis uses the transfer intentionally as a therapy tool. The patient gradually transfers old feelings about Mom and Dad onto the psychoanalyst, and then re-experiences the child-parent relationship with the doctor.

In The Therapy, transferring feelings to the therapist can be confusing and may interrupt progress. **But every defense is a doorway.** If you handle it right, the transfer can be a doorway to blocked feelings.

When I was in psychoanalysis, I told my doctor that she was ugly and fat. I was transferring old feelings onto her. Her reaction was to listen calmly as though nothing had happened. That's what a psychoanalyst is supposed to do. She accepted my outburst so that I could learn that it is safe to say anything to her. She did her job perfectly.

A professional analyst is trained to accept insult without getting mad. He knows that the patient is transferring feelings, and so he does not take it personally. But the amateur therapist might not have that much self-control. If you insult your therapist, he might defend himself, get angry, or get his feelings hurt. He can easily accept your tears, or screaming and cussing as long as it is directed at someone else. But he might have a hard time accepting criticism directed straight at him.

The problem gets even worse if you are married to the therapist. Can you imagine how the conversation might go in a husband-wife therapy session:

> **PATIENT:** You're not listening to me.

> **THERAPIST:** Yes, I am.

> **PATIENT:** You never listen to me. You have never really paid any attention to me.

> **THERAPIST:** Well, I might listen if you'd ever say something worth listening to.

Very quickly the patient learns that he (or she) cannot be totally open or honest, and this makes therapy impossible. The only way therapy can work is if the therapist is willing to accept every word, no matter how childish, vulgar or insulting, that comes out of the patient's mouth.

The last question on the scan list is, "Do you have a negative feeling about the therapist." It is a powerful, yet dangerous, question. Dangerous because it invites the patient to attack the therapist, and he must be strong enough to take it. Powerful because it can uncover some big feelings.

I remember asking the question to Nancy. For several months she would chuckle at the question, as though it were a silly question. Then one day when I asked it, she became silent as though she was deep in thought, but she did not answer it. For three sessions in a row, when I asked the question, she became quiet, as though she was working up the courage to say something. Finally, on the fourth session she decided to answer it, and she exploded in tears.

She talked about a time when we had broken up early in our marriage, and how much it had hurt her. She bawled heavily for a half hour, followed by heavy breathing for 20 minutes. Heavy breathing is a good sign of valid discharge. It was one of her biggest discharges ever. We found it by asking, "Do you have a negative feeling about the therapist?"

I was able to listen without disagreeing, because I was pretty sure she was transferring, and yet I was very uncomfortable. She was criticizing me, and telling her side. I had to bite my tongue to keep from telling my side. It was important to not interrupt and to let her feel safe about being honest. This is one advantage of the blindfold. She could not see that I was squirming in my chair.

There is another way to handle negative feelings about the therapist. There were times when I felt negative feelings toward her, but I chose not to say them to her because I was pretty sure that she would tend to defend herself. I suspect that many amateur therapists would react this way, and it need not disrupt the therapy. **The important thing is to recognize and cry about your negative feelings toward the therapist. Whether or not to confront the therapist about it is a separate issue.**

My solution was to do the therapy alone using self-therapy (see pages 19-26). Another solution would be to temporarily find another therapist for this one issue.

In some counseling methods, husbands and wives are encouraged to "fight it out." I don't object to a good fight, but let's put first things first. First, drain off the old pain and become mentally stronger. There will be time later for a good healthy argument. Nancy and I almost never fight, but when we do, it is a thousand times more constructive than our fights were before the therapy.

Whether you choose to confront the therapist, or handle the issue in self-therapy, or with a temporary therapist, start with the question, "Do you have negative feelings about the therapist?" As always, ask the question over and over, watch your picture screen, and say everything that goes through your mind. If you get tears while talking about the therapist, that's great. It's like crying in a movie. It is a *similar story* discharge. You are really discharging about the scene that is hidden underneath.

If you want to dig out the real old feeling, wait until the feelings about the therapist are drained away, and then ask, "Was there an earlier time when something similar happened?"

For example, suppose you feel that the therapist never *believes* you. After you cry about the therapist not believing you, ask the question, "Was there an earlier time when someone didn't *believe* you?" and watch your picture screen.

You might not have to ask about the earlier time. I remember years ago, early in our marriage, before we ever thought about therapy, Nancy and I would sometimes get into an argument. Nancy would talk a half hour about what I had done, and then she would gradually shift the conversation from me to her Dad. She'd end up saying, "My Dad did the same thing," and then she'd talk an hour about him. The point is that she shifted into the past with no knowledge of therapy methods, and without my coaching her. I suspect that it is natural to slip into the past, if someone will only listen long enough.

It is one of the reasons that The Therapy is so simple. The patient has natural instincts that take her in the right direction. It is natural to slip into the past, and to sort out your own thoughts, if only you can find someone who can listen without judging.

A USEFUL QUESTION

The way to handle TRANSFERRED FEELINGS is to ask the question,

"DO YOU HAVE NEGATIVE FEELINGS ABOUT THE THERAPIST?"

If your therapist cannot handle criticism in silence, you can use the same question in self-therapy (pages 19-26) or temporarily find another therapist for this one issue.

Death Feelings

You might assume that you have never been near death and yet if you had been near death as a child, the memory would most likely be blocked, and you would be unaware of it.

There have been many books written about the near-death experience. Thousands of people say that they have flown out of their bodies during a car accident or a heart operation. It is possible that they were not only near-death, but actually dead for several minutes.

If you were near death as a child, you might experience an unusual style of discharge other than just crying. In my therapy, the normal pattern of remembering and crying went on for several years, then all of a sudden, something in me changed. I lost all of my enthusiasm and I became obsessed with death. I was dull, dry, and lacking emotion, and I went on in that condition for six months.

During that time, I collected songs that reminded me of death, and I played them during my therapy sessions. I actually enjoyed the idea of death. I would spend my free time in a grave yard. I would read the names on the grave stones and cry for the person who was buried there.

One of the scenes that came to me during those months was about Amy, the little girl in my neighborhood who had died of pneumonia. I remembered seeing her little freckled nose in the casket, and watching as they lowered the casket into the ground.

For six months, I cried about death from every possible viewpoint: the senseless death, the courageous death of soldiers, the leader's decision to send someone else to his death, my death, and other people's deaths. My death feelings seemed to be endless, and again I started to doubt the effectiveness of the therapy.

Looking back, it was a short six months. But at the time, it appeared that the therapy was making me dull and negative, just as my professional therapist friend had told me it would. And now I want to tell the happy ending, so you will know that it is just a passing stage.

After about six months, I started to come out of it. I remember driving along in my car, listening to my death music tape, and suddenly the music no longer reminded me of death, but rather it reminded me of "waking up" and "coming out of a coma." It was the kind of joyful feeling you might feel if your child or some one you love had been sick for several days, and then suddenly sat up in bed and said, "I'm hungry."

In that wonderful moment, I suddenly understood that I had been reliving my own death, and now at last it was over. It had taken six months and buckets of tears to get through it. I had been experiencing my death and the death of the little girl all mixed together, and it was a very big pile of pain.

Crying is the normal way you will discharge the stored up pain energy, but it is not the only way. I believe that I was discharging for six months by experiencing the dullness. Nancy has discharged in the form of lethargy (see pages 115-116). Some therapists believe that laughter is a discharge. I don't think it is, but I won't rule it out as a possibility.

In the months that followed, my energy became more than I had ever dreamed possible. **For the first time in my life I experienced brief periods of perfect mental health, quicker reactions, brighter personality, and the pure pleasure of being alive.** At first, the experience would last for a whole day. Later, I experienced several days in a row, and then two weeks at a time. I was becoming more mentally healthy than I had ever been in my whole life.

I don't know if you will experience death feelings, and even if you do, it may be different from my experience. Everybody discharges a little differently. The point of this chapter is that at some point you may experience a long slow discharge that takes several months, and it might not be about death. During that time, you might wonder if the therapy is still working.

The existence of this long slow discharge should tell you how much pain is stored inside of a neurotic. An event that may have lasted only a few minutes had to be spread out over six months before I could handle it.

If you experience death feelings, or some other long discharge, just keep on going. It may seem endless, but I'm living proof that if you keep doing the sessions, sooner or later there will be an end, and you will emerge brighter and more alive than ever before.

> *The solution to "DEATH FEELINGS"*
> *is to sink into it, embrace it, cry about it,*
> *and keep doing The Therapy.*

The Exploding Patient

During your therapy, you may find yourself, or your patient yelling and screaming violently, and it may appear that the session is dangerously out of control. Please believe this: there is inside of you a mechanism that controls how much pain you can take. It's a lot like the governor on a motor that makes it impossible to run the motor too fast.

I've seen it work in my therapy, in Nancy's and in Beth's. Just when you are sure the patient is ready to explode and splatter all over the walls, suddenly she will calm down.

This mechanism, whatever or whoever it is, is very intelligent. It not only controls the amount of discharge, but it also controls the sequence. Some scenes will come up early in therapy because they are relatively easy to handle, and the worst traumas will be saved till the end of therapy when you are most prepared to handle them. The governor is even aware of your health problems, and will slow down your therapy rather than risk a heart attack.

Every patient will have a different style of discharge. I tend to bawl and yell for five minutes and calm down immediately. Nancy will sometimes bawl for 20 minutes, and then she needs an hour to recover. Her recovery time has changed a lot. In her early therapy, after a bawling session, she would be sad and withdrawn for days. Gradually her recovery time has changed from days, to hours, to minutes.

The most violent session I've ever experienced happened after a day of isolation (see page 218). Nancy may have thought I was out of control. I was actually very comfortable although I was a little scared of what was coming. My voice got louder and louder and I began to scream. My chest expanded as though it was being pumped up like a balloon. I yelled 20 minutes straight, loud enough to scare my neighbors, and yet I was never in real pain. It was a controlled spoonful.

Nancy and I are fortunate in that neither of us have ever used drugs or alcohol. I believe this has made us perfect test subjects for this therapy. My daughter Beth, on the other hand, has used marijuana for about eight years. I tell you of her drug problem because drugs might affect your style of discharge.

When Beth did therapy, she would become terrified that some one was under the bed. I'm sure her husband was very concerned. I have a hunch that her drugs were a part of the problem. Every drug affects the nervous system differently. Heroin deadens childhood pain and makes reliving impossible. LSD and marijuana stimulate blocked traumas and bring them closer to the surface, which creates fear...fear that the old feelings might slip through. Hallucinations are a last ditch defense to prevent the reliving.[1]

All of us when we were young experienced a fear of the dark, fear that there was a monster under the bed or in the closet. Fear of the dark is really fear of an old feeling that is near the surface. In the dark it is more difficult to keep old feelings under control. Neurotics have to do something all day long in order to keep from feeling old pain, read, watch TV, smoke, chew gum, work, start an argument. In the night, you cannot do these things so feelings come closer to the surface. As a defense, your mind transfers the feeling outside of you to the monster in the closet, so you won't have to know that it is really inside of you.

When Beth experienced "someone under the bed," it was a good sign and a bad sign. It was a sign that the therapy had brought her close to her old feeling. It was also a sign that the real old feeling would not come up. It was too much feeling, too close to exploding, and so the *governor* prevented the discharge by creating the hallucination. Beth and her husband may have experienced a lot of fear for nothing. It is possible that Beth's violent fear was a discharge, but I personally don't think it was. With a few exceptions (see pages 116-117) 99% of your discharge will be tears. Fear and anger are normally defenses that prevent the tears.

If you experience fear and anger during a primal, a **total reliving,** then of course it would be a discharge, but in that case you would know without doubt that you were discharging, because the memory would be coming up in 3-D stereo with all of the smells and sights and feelings of the total blocked scene. You would not need me to tell you that you were discharging. You would know! **However, most of the discharge using The Therapy will be from symbolic reliving or fragmented reliving, and it will come up with tears most of the time.**

Beth's fear of the dark might not have been a total waste. She may have found tears the day after the fear session. Unfortunately, I was not there to observe. Beth and her husband live about 150 miles from us.

How do you handle the exploding patient? First, ask him if he is on any medications or street drugs. Be sure to read the section about brain chemistry (pages 193-201).

Next, be sure your patient does not have a mineral or vitamin deficiency. It is possible that the governor will not work without the essential nutrients. It is safest just to be on a complete supplement program (see pages 199-201).

Encourage your patient to get a physical check-up from a doctor before you start the therapy. There could be physical problems beyond the scope of this book.

If your body is healthy, and if there are no drugs in your system, you can safely sink into your feelings and let them overtake you knowing that your governor will never let you go too far.

The solution to the EXPLODING PATIENT is to,
  (1) Get a physical check-up from a doctor.
  (2) Get drugs out of your system.
  (3) Start a program of complete vitamin and mineral supplements (pages 199-201).
  (4) Trust your built-in governor.

Theorizing and Analyzing

Many therapists will tell you that you should avoid theorizing. In Primal Therapy, Janov tells us that theorizing is a way to avoid the pain.

My experience is slightly different. I believe that the *therapist* should absolutely avoid theorizing and analyzing because he will interrupt the patient's thoughts. But I have never seen any harm done by letting the *patient* analyze. Even though the analyzing may defend him from totally reliving his pain, it may also be an indirect doorway that leads him to a controlled spoonful of pain. Remember, every defense is a doorway.

In a restaurant, or at a party, the analyzing person might talk aimlessly for hours, but in therapy and wearing a blindfold his analyzing will more likely lead him in a productive direction. The decision to not theorize is unrealistic. If the patient's brain is clogged and compartmentalized, with parts of the brain not working, the patient has no choice but to use what's left. **Theorizing might be his only open door.**

In my own therapy, logic was all I had to work with. I recall many sessions when I explored my logical path for 45 minutes, while Nancy was saying, "Stop theorizing! Get to the feeling!" Thank God I followed my instincts, I explored my logic, and ultimately found lots of pain. Theorizing had actually lead me to tears. It's another reason why I believe strongly in letting the patient follow his instincts.

I have seen the same thing happen when Nancy was the patient. She would talk about stuff that I thought was trivial or irrelevant, and just when I was thinking, "What a waste of time," suddenly she would start to cry. She did it all by herself, by following her own hunches.

> *The solution to the THEORIZING patient is to be sure she is wearing a blindfold and watching her picture screen, and then let her theorize, and trust her instincts. The Therapist should never theorize.*

Sleeping Late

Some symptoms go away in the first week. Others go away in a few months. Sleep problems are unique in that they may come and go and come again until the last scene is discharged. I've said in other parts of the book that I've grown to almost perfect mental health. But it would be more accurate to say "perfect mental health *as long as I finish my sleep.*" If I don't sleep until I'm done, I will be a little dull for the whole day, but still 1000% better than I was before therapy.

In my experience, if I discharge a big scene, I will feel great for many days afterwards and I will sleep like a baby. Then a few weeks later, as another scene is trying to come up, I will have sleep problems again.

As I write this book, I have discharged 24 scenes and I know I have one left. I believe it is the most traumatic of all my scenes, and that is why it has been saved to the last. The one last scene is hurting my sleep for the same reason that the other 24 scenes hurt my sleep. I still have a scene stuck in my temporary file. But still, if I *finish my sleep,* I'll feel great all day. I tell you this so that you will know that your sleep problems might reoccur until the end.

Be sure to read the section about brain chemistry and vitamins, pages 193-201. If you have blocked memories, your brain will work harder at night time than it does during the day. And you can solve your sleep problems, and speed your therapy by giving yourself the nutrients your brain needs *before you go to bed.*

Avoid sleeping pills, especially barbiturates because they prevent dreams. Avoid eating sugar snacks before sleep because it will release insulin which destroys growth hormone. Eat a banana or milk for the amino acid *tryptophan.* Chicken is a good snack because it stimulates growth hormone. Take 2 grams of vitamin C, and a good dose of a B-complex formula that contains B1, B3, B5, B6, and B12. A little extra B3 (niacin) will also make you drowsey. It has the same effect as a barbiturate without any of the dangers. Try to always sleep until you are done. If you must wake up before you are finished, try to take a nap later in the day.[2]

How Do You Know Where The End Is

We end this section where we began it, with the importance of notes. The most difficult problem for you as a therapist is that since you cannot know how many hours are left, you will start doubting the therapy. You may wonder, is there one more hour? ...10 more? ...1000 more?

At times the patient will appear to be getting worse. Discharging an old feeling will increase his mental health, but then as the next old feeling comes close to the surface, the patient will become tired and dull again. It's a lot like remodeling a house. It gets worse before it gets better.

You'll have doubts during the first session when you're up against the programmed command. Later in therapy you'll experience stalled sessions and plateaus. If the patient has death feelings, they may seem to go on forever. And perhaps the biggest test of your faith will be when you have a disagreement with the patient.

You'll start to wonder, "Maybe the professional therapists are right. Maybe there is no end. Maybe The Therapy is just a fraud created by Mr. Stone just to sell books to naive people. Maybe it really is just a chemical imbalance. Maybe we should just take an anti-depressant pill."

These thoughts are normal. I had them continually during my therapy. **The solution to your doubts is to keep written notes.** The only way you can be sure that you are making progress is to remind yourself of how you were just a few months ago, by looking at your notes.

Have faith that there is a higher power guiding your therapy along. Have a little faith in me, and in your own instincts. Go back and read the book to reassure yourself that you are not the first one to cross these barriers. And finally, it might be helpful to buy a cassette version of the book so you can hear these words over and over again in my voice, with honest feeling that only comes with real experience.

Is It Really A Cure?

Before therapy, I had a rash on my face, now it's gone. I used to have headaches and nightmares, now I don't. I was depressed, now I'm cheerful. I used to be irritated by people and things, but today nothing irritates me.

Before therapy, I would procrastinate. Today I start projects immediately. Before therapy I could not understand mechanical things. Last summer I rebuilt a transmission.

Before therapy I had not read two books all the way through in my whole life. Since therapy I have read over 200 books on subjects ranging from history to economics, religion, banking, mythology, sports, war, self-defense, salesmanship, sex, public speaking and politics.

I used to have a miserable marriage. I would get insane crushes on other girls. Now I have a wonderful marriage and I no longer have insane crushes. I still notice girls, but it does not interfere with my life.

Before therapy I did not enjoy the beauty of nature, and autumn leaves made me feel depressed because they reminded me of blocked scenes. Last September I took a two day trip to Wisconsin for the sole purpose of looking at leaves.

I wish I could tell you that I am 100% cured, but I know that I am not. I'm still afraid of heights, which is a clue that there is more pain inside of me. I have found at least one traumatic scene that has not discharged yet, and perhaps it never will.

As I write these words, I am 52 years old and I have a minor heart ailment which seems to be interfering with therapy. If I had started therapy when I was 20 and if I had kept my body healthy, I'm sure I could have reached total mental health, but I wasted my youth not knowing I was neurotic and I lost another 10 years searching for a method that really works.

I don't know if I am 90% cured or 50%. All I know is that the quality of my life is 1000% better than it used to be. I can't imagine going back to my life before therapy. If I am ever to be punished for a crime or indiscretion, the worst punishment I could imagine would be to send me back to my old life. It was like being in hell. I was sinking in quicksand and no one to pull me out. I was in a fog and could not see three feet in front of me. I was miserable, I was sad, I was lonely, I was lost. I thank God for the great works of Freud, Janov, Hubbard, and all the other people who helped me find a way out of the darkness.

Even though my heart ailment may prevent my total cure, there are three reasons why I am convinced that other people, using this method, can eventually discharge their entire pile of pain and reach mental health. For most people who read this book, the question of a total cure may not be important. Even if you get half way there, your life will improve 1000%.

For the serious scientific researcher looking for a total cure, I urge you to take the following information seriously. I have been given a gift, a special ability to study and observe the brain from an inside viewpoint. I have made discoveries that could not be made any other way. Here are the three reasons I'm convinced The Therapy can lead to a total cure:

1. DISAPPEARING SYMPTOMS

The first reason is that I have witnessed the disappearance of many symptoms. On pages 18-19 I have listed 20 major symptoms that have disappeared, but it is not a total list. There are *hundreds* of other symptoms such as walking stiffly, and saying things twice, and talking about myself constantly, that are too trivial and too numerous to put on the list.

It seems obvious to me that if 10 hours of therapy will cure a few symptoms, and if 50 hours will cure several more, logic would suggest that more hours would eventually cure all of the symptoms.

2. HUBBARD'S ACCIDENT

The second reason is that I believe that Hubbard accidentally brought some of his patients to a *total reliving* by using methods very similar to ours. In his technical bulletin he talks about his attempt to cure the "psychotic break" but he never explains what he means by the phrase, "psychotic break."[3]

I suspect that his therapy method accidentally threw his patient into a primal, which might have helped the patient, except that Hubbard did not know what it was. He was frightened by the sight of a patient experiencing old feelings with full intensity, and he thought the patient was dangerously out of control, and so he tried to stop it. He did not know what a primal was because Janov's book had not yet been written.

In the movies we often see this typical scene: A woman starts yelling and screaming hysterically and immediately everyone around her tries to calm her down. Someone says "Call a doctor." They give her a pill or a shot to quiet her.

If they had let her yell until she was done, it would have moved her closer to mental health. But in movies, as in life, we always want to quiet someone who is upset. The pills and the shot are not for the lady who is screaming, but for the other people who can't stand to watch, *because her scream is stimulating their blocked pain.*

Hubbard's accidental psychotic breaks suggest that this kind of therapy will eventually lead to a total reliving. Our method is a combination of discoveries from Hubbard, Janov, Jung, Winson and Freud. Hubbard's first therapy book was interesting, but in my opinion he got off track when he tried to cure the patient in 25 to 100 hours. He became impatient and started looking for short cuts.

3. MESSAGES FROM THE SUPER-CONSCIOUS

When I first got involved in self-therapy experiments, I would frequently find myself gagging. I knew from Janov's writings that his patients frequently experienced gagging at the moment before they primal (pages 219-221). So when I felt the gagging feeling, instead of drinking water to stop it, I lay down on my back, closed my eyes and tried to primal. As the gagging feeling came over me, I took some deep breaths, and the gagging became a loud yell, practically a roar. It's lucky we lived in the country, or we would have frightened the neighbors. It was all very noisy, and yet I could not break through to a complete primal discharge. (Janov tells us that gagging is a defense that prevents the primal.)

Many months later during a session, I had my first and only complete reliving, but it was very brief. I was working on a scene about my mom leaving home with my two brothers, and leaving me behind. I was clinging desperately to her neck. The only way she could get me to let go was to shove me into the house and close the door. My Dad hooked the door from the inside so I couldn't get out.

For a split second, I could smell the summer air, I could hear the door latch. I saw my Mommy's face as she said "good-bye" to me through the locked screen door. **This was not a fragmented memory. It was the real thing. I was there!** I was 3$1/2$ years old for a split second, and I had gotten there by using the methods described in this book, and an amateur therapist.

But I wondered why it had been so brief. The gagging had signaled that I was near primaling, and the split second reliving proved that I could get there. It was obvious that our do-it-yourself method was definitely pushing scenes and feelings to the surface, and yet I could not stay there very long.

I wondered what was wrong? Why could I not primal? Was there something missing from our method?

Going back to the most basic principle in this book, we decided to ask the obvious question, and watch the picture screen. Again and again Nancy asked me,

"Why can't you primal?"

"Why can't you primal?"

"Why can't you primal?"

Within a few seconds the answer came to me as a *symbolic picture* on my viewing screen, and I immediately knew what it meant. It would be tedious and boring for you to try to understand my picture symbols so I have decided to skip the symbolism and simply tell you the message. (For the serious research scientists, the symbolic answer to the question is shown in Appendix B, page 255.)

This was the message on my picture screen: "Your old pain is all connected like a long turd that wedges its way out of your anus, so that once it starts to come out, you won't be able to stop it. It will be safer if we chop your pain into small manageable pieces and let them out one at a time."

The symbolism was so clever, so concise, and so efficient, that I began to wonder where the message had come from. Some writers had talked about the subconscious mind as though it was a big dumb filing cabinet full of stored tapes. But the message on my view screen was so clever that I began to suspect the presence of another consciousness that was not only intelligent, but who knew more about the therapy than I did with all of my books. It was the first time that I became aware of the existence of my Super Conscious.

A few months later I had a progress report dream, which I now refer to as my "Yellow House Dream" (see Appendix B). Again the symbolism was so clever that it obviously came from a source that understood therapy better that I did. My progress report dreams actually *predict* what scenes are coming next in therapy. I have found scenes that were predicted a year earlier by a progress report dream. This is not voo-do or clairvoyance. The Super-Conscious very simply has access to parts of the brain that are blocked for me.

The message of the *Yellow House Dream* was this: Because your childhood scenes are so painful and terrifying, the only way you can handle it is to do it in two stages:

In **STAGE 1,** you'll experience each scene lightly and indirectly. You'll feel enough of the pain to reduce the intensity, and you'll become familiar with all that happened to you.

In **STAGE 2** you will experience each scene completely. It will be less terrifying because you will know in advance what is coming next and because the intensity of the feeling will be reduced. Stage 1 will be like a rehearsal and a road map for Stage 2.

A month later I had another progress dream which I call the "Yellow Truck Dream" (See Appendix B). The meaning was, "Your traumatic scenes happened to you in chronological order. When you finally discharge them, they will come to you in the opposite order, just as a semi-truck is loaded and unloaded in opposite sequence."

Now I want to summarize the third reason I'm sure this is a total cure. My logic goes like this:

- My Super Conscious has successfully predicted what scenes will come up in therapy.

- My Super Conscious seems to know more about the therapy than I do with all of my books.

- I consider my Super Conscious to be an accurate source of information.

- The Super Conscious seems to be saying, "Yes, you can discharge the entire pile of pain, but for your own safety, we'll have to break the pile into small portions and give them to you in two stages. The first stage will prepare you for the second stage.

- The final discharge will come out in reverse chronological order.

- Conclusion: My Super Conscious is saying, "Yes, it can be done."

Even though my progress dreams are unique to me, I'm convinced that their meaning is universal. There is tons of experience to suggest that everyone who does this or similar therapy (psychoanalysis, Dianetics, etc.) will initially discharge scenes first as a *symbolic* reliving and as *fragmented* reliving, (Stage 1). The problem is that up until now, the methods have been so slow that no one has ever gone to Stage 2. I believe that anyone who takes The Therapy far enough will eventually experience *total reliving* (Stage 2) of scenes in reverse chronological order.

You may rightly ask why I have not yet reached the total reliving of stage 2. As I've said in other parts of the book, my therapy progress came to a sudden screeching halt when I developed a mild heart problem.

Also, as I've said many times, once you get half-cured, you get so busy with life that you don't have time to do the therapy. Even so, and even without formal sessions, my therapy has restarted at a much slower pace, and I expect to reach stage 2 eventually.

I recognize that these are internal experiences that cannot yet be documented or measured, and of course, you have to trust my power of observation. And yet I am not the first to experience the Super Conscious. Other writers including Hubbard and Jung, have had similar experiences. They just use different language. Hubbard talks about the "file clerk" who intelligently finds the answer to every question that is asked. Jung called it the "archtypal self" and he said it is the "real center of the personality."

In a completely different field, many chiropractors diagnose illnesses by using kinesiology which is simply a physical way to communicate with the Super Conscious.

If you will proceed with your own therapy, I'm sure that eventually you will become aware of your own Super Conscious.

CONCLUSION

I'm convinced this method can lead to a total cure because of 1) the obvious disappearance of my symptoms, 2) Hubbard accidentally threw his patients into a total reliving by similar method, and 3) the Super Conscious seems to be saying that the method can lead to a total discharge of all the pain.

I wish we had a million dollar budget and a thousand case histories, but we don't. If you have success with this method, please write and tell us. If you and others like you will write to us, I plan to summarize letters and make the information available, perhaps as a second book.

Eventually millions of people will read this book, and among them a few scientists will undertake to prove its contents. Some day they may find the physical location of the sleep switch and the temporary file. Or perhaps they have already found them but did not know what they were for.

I am content to leave proof to future generations. My job is to report how Nancy and I have changed our lives, and to explain our method in a way that other people can do The Therapy too. From the viewpoint of a scientist who believes only in things that can be measured, these writings might fall short of his expectations, but I would be untrue to myself if I would change a single word.

FOOTNOTES CHAPTER 7

1. Arthur Janov, *Primal Scream,* pp. 351-367.
2. Durk Pearson and Sandy Shaw, *Life Extension,* pp. 125-136, pp. 167-195.
3. L. Ron Hubbard, *Technical Bulletin,* 1973, Volume VIII, pp. 239-241.

8

Growing to Maturity

If you could wave a magic wand and instantly cure your neurosis, you would still have a long journey ahead of you. Your traumatic childhood did much more than just damage your mind. **It also created a void inside of you.** Curing your neurosis is like erasing the pages of a bad novel, and what you end up with is a lot of empty pages. Your therapy will not be complete until you rewrite those empty pages.

You were taught that you were stupid, and now you have to discover how smart you are. You were told to shut up, and now you have to learn how to shout. You became self-centered because your needs were never met. Now you must learn to fill your own needs, and then focus on other people.

In short, it's time for you to grow-up and become an adult. It's time to learn how to talk, to take responsibility, become a giver instead of a taker. It's the way you were supposed to be, if your parents had allowed you to be yourself. The adult is there inside of you, and The Therapy will help you to find it.

In the early part of therapy, you will cry about what happened when you were little, perhaps violence, the death of a parent, or just being ignored. But in the later stages, you will find yourself bawling about *maturity* subjects. You'll cry about the mess you've made of your life, what you have lost, and what you could have been. At times you'll cry for people other than yourself.

These *maturity* issues may come up by themselves, without asking questions. They will come up in dreams, or during free association, or during conversations with your spouse. They will often be accompanied by exploding tears. Frankly, I can't explain why you must cry about these kinds of subjects. They're not necessarily connected to blocked scenes. But there is definitely some pain attached to each issue. It's as though your whole brain has been in a coma. It is stiff, or dead, or dried-up from under-use, and now it hurts to bring it back to life.

THERAPY PRINCIPLE NO. **21**

The Therapy Method Continues To Work Even When You Are No Longer Looking For Blocked Memories

---

The following are specific maturity issues you are likely to run into and examples from Nancy's and my therapy:

YOUR LOST YOUTH

The first time I cried about a maturity issue was in May of 1990. It was not a therapy session. Nancy and I were just talking and suddenly I realized that I had lost 40 years of my life. I exploded in tears as I added up my losses: I had missed my childhood, my teen years, my college years, my honeymoon, and I had missed the wonderful years when my children were little. I had been there physically, but I didn't get to enjoy them. I have almost no joyful memories.

My tears were not about my childhood traumas. These tears were about the present, a feeling of waste, self-pity, the unfairness, and the permanence of my loss. My body shook in Nancy's arms as I knew once and for all that those wonderful days were gone forever, and I would never, ever have them back. Since that day I have been comfortable with my lost youth and the thought of growing old doesn't scare me.

LONGING FOR YOUR OTHER HALF

The movie *Ice Castles* is about a teenage girl who becomes a champion ice skater. It's a typical athletic story about hard work and struggle leading to one perfect performance in the last scene. It's a mediocre movie but the music and the skating is superb.

I saw the movie before I started therapy, and it did not make me cry. But during therapy, I saw the movie again, and at the end of the movie I exploded in tears. I stayed home from work the next day and watched the ending 23 times, bawling my eyes out for 3 hours straight.

What was I crying about? This movie was not about death or lost love. It was about *achievement!* And it was about a girl, while I am obviously a guy.

When I saw *Ice Castles* before therapy, my feeling was that the girl was cute and had nice legs (pretty deep, right?). But when I saw it again during therapy, my feeling was, "That is how I was supposed to be, *smooth, graceful, and perfect!*"

Nancy and Beth experienced similar bawling sessions on the same subject. Beth found a musical video called *U-2 Rattle and Hum.* It had the same effect on her as *Ice Castles* had on me. She cried about their *success, their skill,* and the feeling that she could have been like them. But U-2 is an all male group, while Beth is obviously a girl.

The fact that I was reacting to a girl, and Beth was reacting to men is noteworthy. There is a little male and a little female in all of us. The left side of the brain is much more verbal (more female). The right side is more mechanical (more male).[1]

In order for any of us to reach our peak performance, we need both sides of the brain working together without barriers or compartments. We need an unblocked electrical flow to every part of the brain. But when we split, we tend to live more in one side of the brain, and we lose the talents from the other side because it is blocked.

And so we have neurotic men who can rebuild an engine, but they can hardly speak in full sentences, and we have neurotic women who can talk for hours and pronounce every word perfectly, but can't plug in a toaster. The mechanic, if he had access to his feminine half, would be a mechanic who could express his thoughts. He would not be more feminine...just more complete. A woman who is connected to her masculine half would be feminine and motherly, but if she needed to, she could do anything a man can do.

My feeling in the *Ice Castles* movie was the *longing to be complete again.* I wanted my feminine half back in working order. Believe me, I am not gay, but I do long for the smoothness and grace that I was born with. My daughter Beth was longing for the male qualities missing from her personality.

Nancy also had a similar experience. She watched the ending of an old classic love movie *Wuthering Heights* over and over. She cried so much that she was physically exhausted and could hardly stand up. Her tears were not so much about love but rather about *being complete,* and *joining with her other half.* In the movie, Kathy said "I don't just love Heathcliff. *I am Heathcliff!*" The two halves are really one whole.

Many times I've seen my other half in my dreams. She is represented as a very tiny, sometimes sickly girl, meaning that my other half is barely alive. Nancy's other half seems to be a female. In her dreams, she is frequently accompanied by a girl who is always with her. It may be that Nancy has more access to her masculine side.

This longing for your other half is not my discovery. Carl Jung called the other half "anima." I have never understood why scientists create technical language to describe simple ideas. I prefer to call it "your other half."

As always, the important thing is the tears. **It was pain that forced you to split from your other half, and you will feel some tears as your brain tries to reconnect.** It's the crying that cures your brain. When I was crying about *Ice Castles,* and Beth cried about *U-2* and Nancy cried about *Wuthering Heights,* I believe it was the beginning of a reconnection process.

Carl Jung has suggested, and I tend to agree, that the feeling of longing for your other half is somehow connected to the feeling that you call "falling in love."[2]

WHAT IS LOVE?

Have you ever been in love? Have you ever had the thought, "I can't live without her (or him)?" Have you ever felt desperate about your need for that other person?

Love is a wonderful feeling, but when you are neurotic, love feelings get mixed up with your childhood feelings and with your longing for your own *other half.*

If Carl Jung were alive today, he would say that falling in love is really "unconsciously projecting your anima onto someone of the opposite sex." Translation: When you feel the longing for your other half, and you cannot find it inside your head, you look for it in someone else, and then you fall in love with that person.[3]

It isn't necessarily sick. In fact, it is so common that it may be the natural way to fall in love. It might be the glue that holds a marriage together, and yet, if the feeling is too strong, too desperate, it can destroy the marriage with possessiveness and jealousy.

I'm not saying that falling in love is sick, but the degree of *desperation* is definitely sick. A mentally healthy person does not feel *desperately* in love. He feels passionate, and affectionate, but it does not cloud his judgement. He can get over the loss of a loved one in a few months, while the neurotic will feel the pain for many years.

When I "fell in love" with Karen, I was 5 years old. I was devastated when she went away forever. I never really got over it until I did this therapy at the age of 41. That's a total of 36 years. That's how long a neurotic can carry around the pain of desperate love.

For me, Karen's leaving was the *mouth of the river* (see pages 65-67). We used the question, "Is there an earlier beginning?" and very quickly I was bawling about things that had happened when I was less than a year old. I found scene after scene about my first 3 years of life. I relived a day when my Mom left me just before my fourth birthday. She was only gone a few weeks, but I didn't know she would come back, and so I blocked the memory.

After many months of crying, my pain about Karen

finally went away, and the word *love* took on a different meaning. Today it is no longer a painful word.

Several years later in the therapy, I became aware of my *other half,* and I noticed that the feeling that I had called *love* was similar to my longing for my other half.

What is love? I'm afraid that I cannot tell you what real love is. My own ability to love may be damaged beyond repair. But I can tell you that if you feel a *desperate* longing, your love feelings are probably connected to blocked pain from early childhood.

WHY ARE YOU SO NEGATIVE?

I used to think that people who smile a lot were phony and insincere. I have read success books that advocate positive thinking, but I've had a hard time learning it. I used to have so much negative inside me that whenever I tried to act positive, I would feel dishonest.

One day Nancy and I were visiting a psychic friend and I asked the psychic for some advice on my career. She advised me to not take my career so seriously, and to think of it as a hobby instead of a job. In that moment I realized what a negative person I was. I tended to see the negative side of everything, and I miss the positive side.

As Nancy and I drove home I started asking myself an obvious question, "Why am I so negative," and then I started to bawl so hard that I had to pull the car off of the road. I bawled about all the negativity that had been stuck in my head, and now it was time to let it go. Since that day I have become more and more positive, and it is no longer just an act.

You will never learn to be genuinely positive when your mind is full of childhood pain. You will accomplish more by sinking into the negative, and letting yourself cry. But after you have bawled uncountable hours and reduced your pile of pain, the day will come when you can honestly see the positive side of things.

BEING AWARE OF THE WORLD AROUND YOU

When I was a child, I loved to play with Lincoln Logs. The toys of my childhood were real. They were like real life in miniature. But some time during the '70s the world around me underwent a change. Lincoln Logs were replaced with Legos. Children's play was no longer to learn about life, but rather play for the sake of play...or play so you won't interrupt Mommy. It's as though our whole society went from real to unreal during the '70s.

The change in our society is not just my imagination. The great economics expert Peter Drucker has said, "Sometime in the mid-70s America moved into the age of chaos." The years 1950 through 1975 were the most prosperous years in the history of the world, but it all came to a crashing halt around the year 1975. Our country went into a dangerous recession, and we took desperate measures to get the country moving again. Our government resorted to more and more money creation. Our business leaders lost touch with people. They stopped selling what people *needed,* and started selling them whatever people *wanted.* The whole country started to live for pleasure, and nothing more.

When these changes were taking place, I was too neurotic to notice. I lived inside myself. I did not read the newspaper or listen to the radio news, and I didn't have the slightest understanding of how the world works, and so I was unaware of the subtle changes in the economy the 1970s.

Gradually, after several years of therapy, I became more aware of the complex world around me. One day Nancy and I were driving home from visiting our son in Kansas City, and I decided to tell her a dream. Within minutes I was bawling. The dream was not about a childhood scene, but rather about my *sense of history.*

The dream was about Legos (brightly colored toy building blocks). For some reason, I have never liked Legos, and I didn't know why until that day. The reason was because, in my mind, Legos symbolized the change in our society around the year 1975. Before Legos, children played to learn about life. After Legos, children were taught to play just for the sake of pleasure.

I've always hated Legos because deep down inside, I did notice the change! **I was crying because, in that moment, I knew that a hidden part of my brain had recorded it all.** The conscious *Me* may have been in a fog, but there was an other part of me, a subconscious part, or a Super-Conscious part that was paying attention, and it was saving the information for the day when I would come out of the fog. I did notice the change, retroactively, almost 20 years after the event.

My tears were about the reconnecting process, the rewiring of my brain. But part of my tears were tears of joy because I realized how fantastic my brain, and everybody's brain, really is. **Even when my brain was sick, it was recording everything.**

Ever since that day, I have been more alert to the world around me. Before therapy, I did not notice events unfolding right before my eyes, and previous history was a distant blur. But since therapy, the events of thousands of years ago are vivid in my mind. The Civil War, the discoveries of Isaac Newton, and the ancient Roman Empire are real to me, and that is how every mature person should be. Everything in your life, your language, your clothes, your food, has evolved over thousands of years. How could you ever understand your world without knowing your own history.

WHAT IS A MAN? WHAT IS A WOMAN?

In a healthy childhood, you would admire your parents. They would be your heroes, and you would want to be like them. It is a *natural* and *effortless* way to learn.

But if your parents were abusive or weak, you won't have anything to imitate. You won't know what it means to be a "real man" or a "real woman." You will need to find a role model before you can ever grow up.

This might be a bigger issue for men than for women. Nancy and Beth don't seem to have many heroes, but I have dozens, and without them, I could never discover my own values and goals. It's as though the "real man" is genetically coded inside of me but I can't find it by myself. My heroes have helped me to recognize different facets of the man who is hidden inside of me.

Don't be surprised if you find yourself crying as you discover your heroes. The tears seem to be a part of the regrowth or reconnection process. At first you may admire your hero in a vague, undefined way. But as with all of therapy, tears and feeling will come when you get *specific.* As you tell your therapist about your hero, you'll eventually find just *exactly the right word* for what you admire, and then you'll know deep in your soul **that is how you were supposed to be.**

I remember crying about one of my heroes, Michael Douglas, the movie star, when I realized that he never puts on an act to please others. My tears came at the specific thought, "He doesn't give a shit what people think." He is himself all the time, and that's the way I want to be.

I have many other heros who have helped me to discover myself. Each one has a different talent for me to imitate. Harry Browne the economist, Barbara Streisand, Benjamin Franklin, Harry Truman, Ronald Reagan, just to name a few.

Obviously my heroes will be different from yours. You are a unique and special person with your own destiny, but I want to share one of my best heroes with you because he might help you too. His name is James E. Tolleson. He is the most amazing person I've ever known, and I believe he is as close to perfect mental health as I've ever seen, and that's what you're looking for in a hero: what would a mentally healthy person do?

Mr. Tolleson is a self-made millionaire. That in itself is not unique. There are thousands of self-made millionaires. What makes Mr. Tolleson unique is that he has *recorded his whole personality* on cassettes and videos. All of his thoughts, his motives, what he would do in every life situation is recorded in his own voice, with feeling, with humor, with sternness and sometimes anger, and with great caring for the human race. He recorded it all so that other people could imitate him.

His mental attitude is on such a high plane that no matter how much I learn and grow, he is always a step ahead of me. I listen to his tapes over and over and always learn something new.

161

If it were not for Mr. Tolleson, I would have never written this historic book. He taught me that my worst problem is also my biggest opportunity, because millions of people have the same problem. He taught me to be positive, to think big and to never quit. And while I was writing this book, it seemed like everyone in the world, including three so-called "professionals" told me I was wrong. Mr. Tolleson was the only voice in my whole life who ever convinced me to *trust my instincts*. This book contains no less than 30 new discoveries on curing mental illness, and the only way I know they are true is by *my instinct*.

Of course there are hundreds of other books and tape programs to help you fill your blank pages. You can find your heroes among your family, or where you work, or in the movies, but if you can't find a hero of your own, you might consider listening to the Tolleson tapes (see back page).

FACING REALITY

On the last page of this book, we have listed some cassettes on subjects other than neurosis. I'd like to tell you how they came into existence.

During the first 40 years of my life, I was living in the fog of neurosis. I was like a man wearing blinders. My perceptions of the world were narrow and fragmented. I was unaware of how society functioned. I had very confused ideas about people, business, government, history, sex, and money.

You may not be as poorly informed as I was, but I can guarantee that every neurotic has to some degree a distorted view of the world.

One of the most invisible symptoms of neurosis is the tendency to follow the crowd almost in a hypnotic trance. If you are neurotic, you are susceptible to everyone who speaks in an authoritative voice. Your mind is full of ideas planted in your head by friends, teachers, doctors, lawyers, TV commercials, movies, thousands of businesses, government agencies and non-profit groups. They all speak with authority, but very few of them have your best interest at heart.

Your tendency to follow the crowd and to believe people who speak with authority can be suicidal. People who speak with authority do not always know what they are talking about. An incompetent doctor looks and acts just like a competent doctor.

I sometimes think about the Holocaust in World War II and I imagine a German soldier telling a line-up of Jewish people "You are going into this building to take a shower." Perhaps a few of them would question the soldier's orders, but way too many assumed the soldier was telling the truth. It's a tragic example of the neurotic tendency to follow the crowd and to believe anyone with an authoritative voice.

When I started to come out of my neurosis, I quickly realized that my perceptions had been distorted, and I needed to do some catch-up studying. My instincts told me that whatever I do with the rest of my life, I need a clear picture of *reality* as a foundation for my thinking. And so I started to read everything I could get my hands on. I was forty years behind, and I needed to catch up.

I looked for the best, wisest, most knowledgeable people in every field. Inspired by Mr. Tolleson, I looked for experts who were doers instead of observers, people who got results, people who had common sense and a simple way of explaining their ideas, instead of trying to impress me with big words.

Once I chose my experts, I read their books, and summarized them on cassettes. My original intent was to play the tapes over and over to program my own brain. Later I made copies for my kids, to teach them things I should have told them when they were growing up. Since then many of my friends, including 5 millionaires, have listened to these summaries, and they tell me the tapes are very good.

The tapes represent reality as I see it. There are many realities. Ultimately you will have to do your own reading and thinking to fill in your own blank pages. But if you are a slow reader, as I was, and if you want to give yourself a quick, basic, overview of the world from history to business to sex and religion, consider listening to the *Reality Tapes.* (see page 279)

USING THERAPY
TO FACE NEW CHALLENGES

As your mind continues to grow, you'll take on challenges that you would not have dreamed of when you were neurotic. Before therapy I was completely without a sense of humor. After therapy, I joined a public speaking club and won first place in a humor contest. I rebuilt a transmission, and volunteered for a political group.

Nancy went back to school and earned a second degree, won first place at a marketing conference, and was promoted to manager at her job. All of these changes would have been out of the question before therapy.

Whenever I face a new challenge, I still use The Therapy as a way to handle my fears. Most recently I've had the challenge of raising money for a business project. I talked to fifty people and endured fifty rejections before I found the first investor. Before therapy I would have crumbled after 3 rejections. But with my newly found mental health I was able to learn from each rejection and keep moving forward.

At times like this the positive thinking crowd might say, "Think Positive!" but I did just the opposite. I used The Therapy. I made a list of all the reasons that I knew I would fail, and I sunk into the feeling. I said it out loud, "I don't want to do this! I can't do it! I can't do it!" I pouted, I whimpered, I hung my head and cried...and an hour later, the negative was gone out of me. I've used the same technique more than once during this challenge. Since then I have found seven investors and raised enough money to start the project.

Throughout this chapter I've tried to convey the message that you are going to cry whenever your brain attempts to reconstruct the adult that you were supposed to be. The therapy is a tool you can use for the rest of your life. The method is the same: ask an obvious question, watch your picture screen, free associate, and look for feelings. But in the maturity stage you'll be creating your own unique questions: "Why are you so negative?" "Why can't you confront people?" "Why can't you sell?" "Why can't you tell the truth?" "Why can't you be yourself?"

It's the opposite of positive thinking, and I think it's more permanent! Positive thinking attempts to hide the pain. Therapy removes the pain forever. Ultimately you will be able to use positive thinking, and it won't be an act. If you allow yourself to feel the pain and get it out of you, eventually your positivism will be real.

FOOTNOTES CHAPTER 8

1. Peter Russell, The Brain Book, p. 54

2. James A. Hall, *Jung: Interpreting Your Dream*, cassette

3. Same.

9

Scary Things In Your Mind

Fears, Phobias, and Panic Attacks

There is a difference between a fear and a phobia. Fear is reasonable. A phobia is unreasonable.

Fear is healthy and useful to your survival. When you were little you probably burned yourself on a stove, and yet you do not have a phobia about stoves. Most likely you cook your meals on a stove every day. If I would push your hand close to the burner, you would feel a mild fear, and if I pull your hand back from the burner, your fear would calm down. This is normal, healthy fear.

A phobia is different than a fear. It is illogical, and unreasonable. It seems to serve no obvious purpose. The most common phobias are fear of the dark, fear of heights, fear of spiders or snakes, fear of small places, and there are many others.

A phobia is very much like a nightmare. It is essentially an old blocked feeling trying to come up. You can prove this to yourself if you consider for a moment what a nightmare feels like and what your phobia feels like. The feeling is the same. It's a feeling of *panic*.

Even though a phobia is apparently unreasonable, it is in fact a healthy self-defense mechanism. It does two jobs: It disguises the old feeling coming up, and it gives you a way to control it. A phobia is essentially a natural method for controlling your old feelings. For example, if you are afraid of the dark, you can control it by turning on a light. A healthy phobia will always focus on something specific like spiders, snakes, and small places, so you can control your old feelings by avoiding spiders, snakes and small places.

167

A panic attack is the same as a phobia with one difference: you can't control the old feeling by leaving on a light, avoiding spiders, snakes, and small places. Your inability to control your old feelings could be a physical problem: adrenal exhaustion from years of neurotic stress; a food allergy possibly to milk; hypoglycemia (low blood sugar); damage to your nervous system by drugs; vitamin and mineral deficiency caused by years of stress, especially deficiency in vitamins B1, B2, B3, B5, B6, B12, chromium, calcium, magnesium, and the amino acid L-tryptophan.[1]

When you start The Therapy, it is possible that the questioning will stimulate your nightmares, phobias and panic attacks. You might be terrified because there is a monster in the closet or under the bed.

You might take all of this terror as a sign that The Therapy is really working and that your are close to a *total reliving*. It's true, you are close. It is theoretically possible that your feelings could come up full force,...but in actual practice you are not likely to achieve a *total reliving* this way.

When you have a nightmare, phobia or a panic attack, you are feeling the power of more than one scene. The traumas of your childhood are wired together like a string of light bulbs. When you do The Therapy the right way, you will discharge one scene at a time, while the others remain blocked. But when you have a nightmare, phobia or panic attack, you are feeling too much, and your nervous system will have to stop the discharge by putting up more and more defenses.

Your nervous system will use every trick possible to keep the feeling hidden. It will *externalize* the feeling (the monster is in the closet rather than inside of you.) It will give you hallucinations to disguise the real blocked scene. It will use *opposites* (the monster is male while the attacker in the real scene was female).

If the mental defenses fail, your body will give you physical defenses, *shallow breathing, swallowing, yawning, giggling* and *gagging*. You may think you are ready for a total reliving, but there is another part of you that very much wants to prevent it.

You may think that your nightmare or phobia can give you a clue to what happened in the blocked scene. You may think "I'm afraid of spiders because I was once bitten by a spider," or "I'm afraid of heights because I fell out of a tree," or "I'm afraid of the closet because I was raped by a man who hid in the closet." But most often the phobia has no obvious connection to the scene. Janov tells of one of his patients who was traumatized by her father and became afraid of spiders. Another woman was raped and became afraid of heights.[2]

If your goal is to cure yourself by a *total reliving*, it is doubtful that you can do it at home, but not impossible. With few exceptions, 99% of your discharge will be in the form of tears from *symbolic reliving* or *fragmented reliving*.

If you are feeling nightmares, phobias and panic attacks, you are not discharging. Instead of discharging, your body is putting up a very tough last ditch defense.

If you really want to use your panic attack as an entry into a *total reliving*, the safest way to do that is to go through Primal Therapy. The Primal Institute does not recommend self-primalling and neither do I. However, it is possible that you might primal accidentally when you do The Therapy. If that happens, I have a few suggestions:

1. Put yourself on a complete vitamin and mineral program as described on pages 193-201,

2. Read the Primal Scream, by Arthur Janov,

3. Read my experiments on pages 215-221.

4. Get a complete physical checkup to be sure you have no physical health problems.

If you are like me, you may eventually decide that you cannot achieve a *total reliving* by yourself. And yet the violent fear you experience with your phobias and panic attacks may not be completely in vain. You may be forcing your nervous system to give you a *symbolic* or *fragmented* discharge a few days later. And at the very least, you will become aware of the enormous pile of pain that you have been carrying inside of you for your whole life.

Multiple Personalities, Compartments And Hearing Voices

The multiple or split personality makes a great movie theme. *Dr. Jekyll and Mr. Hyde* was the story of a kind, loving doctor who turned into an evil, selfish, bully at night. *Three Faces of Eve* was a true story of a woman with 3 personalities. And *Sibyl* was a true story of the ultimate split personality...a woman with 21 distinct personalities, each one capable of taking over the entire body, and each one unaware of the others. This is an excellent movie. Sally Fields does a fantastic job of portraying the different "persons," and I'm sure it will bring a tear to your eye. Go rent it tomorrow!

Movie makers tend to focus on the exciting and entertaining subjects, and sometimes they don't tell the whole story. I personally believe that a split personality is so common that it occurs in virtually all neurotics, *to some degree.* After all, why do you suppose that Janov constantly uses the word "split" every third sentence in his book.

I've had several friends (and you have too) who seem to be a "Jekyll & Hyde"...dominating and confident one minute, then suddenly panicked and shy...or warm and generous, then suddenly selfish and cruel. Split personalities are relatively common, but extreme cases, like Eve and Sibyl, are rare, and they obviously result from excessive and continuous brutality.

To help you understand how a multiple personality is possible, I'd like to introduce you to the idea of "compartments" in the brain briefly mentioned on page 94. *Compartmenting* is a very logical safety device to protect the brain from an overload of pain. When a little child is so badly mistreated that the pain is unbearable, that child could actually die. But rather than die, the nervous system automatically builds a *compartment* around the pain to keep it from spreading to the whole brain. I assume the compartment is a wall of synapses (electric switches) turned to the *off* position. A section of the brain becomes unusable, and the child goes about life with perhaps 10% less brain capacity.

When you look outside of therapy, compartmenting is a very common safety device. In submarines and ships, every room has a watertight door, so that when one room is damaged, it can be sealed to keep the flood water in that one room. The rest of the ship is dry and functioning. Our modern school buildings have steel doors on every room and especially stairwells, for fire safety, to keep fire from spreading from one room to the next.

Similarly, the brain, when it is overloaded with pain, will automatically compartmentalize and sacrifice a small part of the brain, so the rest of the brain can keep functioning.

It is possible that one of your compartments may be able to create words, and you may have the experience of hearing voices. This can be very unnerving, if you don't understand what is happening. You may think you are really crazy. After all, hearing voices is the ultimate insanity, right?…wrong! More likely, it is simply a matter of chance. I have had at least 6 compartments in my head, and I don't hear voices, because those sections of my brain have no control over words. I assume that if you have a compartment in a word-area of your brain, you may hear voices. You're not sicker than me. You just have a different compartment than I do.

The words you hear can be like a tape recording, as though from an unthinking computer, or a parrot…no life or intelligence; or the words can be life-like, as though coming from a living, intelligent person. Both are possible, and it may be useful to make the distinction before using the knowledge in therapy.

Compartments form in chronological order. In the Sibyl story, one "person" would be 12, another 10, and still another 9. In my own compartments, one person is pre-birth, another is age 3, another is 5, and so on. It seems obvious to me how this happens. First, early trauma accumulates until it is unbearable, then a compartment is formed and the personality is made out of the feelings and images of life at that early age. Perhaps a year or two later, mistreatment again accumulates to the unbearable level, and another compartment is formed, with the feelings and images of the later age, and so on, third, fourth, fifth compartments are formed, in sequence, and chronological order.

I had 6 compartments in my head, and it seems that much of my left prefrontal cortex was blank. I suspect that the compartments were located in that part of my brain. I don't really care precisely where they were, and it is not necessary to know their locations.

It might be entertaining to hear the names of my *persons:* Triangle Monster (pre-birth), the Black Monster (age birth to 6 months), Devil Boy (age about 3), Horse (age about 5), Salt-Shaker Girl (age 8), and Johnny, a 2-year old who is very neat and tidy and well groomed. As an adult, I'm a bit of a slob. I lost the neat and tidy part of me when I was 2.

Don't panic if you have persons of the opposite sex in your brain. It does not mean you are gay. It is perfectly normal. Every great man has some feminine qualities like sensitivity and warmth, and every great woman has male qualities like strength and vision.

Nancy has not yet discovered any compartments, but she has a repeating dream about a pile of 15 or 20 boxes which might suggest her compartments. It's something we need to work on a little more.

How do you use this compartment knowledge in therapy? First, don't be overly concerned about it. Just do therapy your normal way as described in chapter 2. **Remember that your goal is to cry.** Your compartments may be formed by millions of nerve connections turned to the *off* position and as you cry out your pain, they will gradually reconnect and be turned *on* again. The more you cry, the more your mind will heal itself, and your compartments will dissolve by themselves.

If you are hearing voices, and you'd like to use that in The Therapy, I'd start by deciding whether your voice is a lifeless mechanical recording, or is it a living personality who creates it's own original thoughts.

If your voices are mechanical, then I'd suggest treating them as *pop-ins*. In other words, create your own question around the words. If, for example, you are hearing the words "Hurry, get a taxi!", then your therapist should ask something like this: "What is it about the taxi?" Another technique is to treat it as a *hypnotic command* and repeat the phrase "Hurry, get a taxi" over and over, and watch for pictures. Repeating of the question or repeating the phrase will have the same effect.

If your *voices* seem more alive and intelligent, I'd consider talking to it as you would to a friend. Perhaps he can help with the therapy. Ask him the therapy questions. I once asked Johnny "Don't you want to relive those painful scenes and get them off our backs, so we can be perfectly healthy?" The answer came back, "Are you kidding? I don't want to go through that again." I felt a chill up my spine, as I realized that Johnny was actually alive inside of me. He knew better than I did what the pain was like. For me the pain is a theory. For Johnny, it was real.

I'd be careful about obeying orders from your *voice*. Even if it is alive, and intelligent, it is working with only a small portion of your brain. It may be all logic, or all emotion, or all anger, rather than a balanced person.

The most important lesson about split personalities and compartments, is to not be afraid of them. They are normal in all neurotics. **They are more of a safety device, than a sign of insanity.** Napoleon Hill actually used this *compartments* in a positive way. He intentionally created 21 compartments in his mind. He called them his "guides" and gave each one a job to do. One was in charge of health, another was in charge of money, and so on. His friends thought he was nutty, but he lived to be very old, and very wealthy. Today his book *Think and Grow Rich* still sells 1,000 copies a day.[3]

Schizophrenia

The conventional wisdom today is that schizophrenia is caused by a chemical imbalance in the brain. Somehow that seems just a bit illogical to me. The human body is a miraculous machine. It is capable of repairing, enlarging, and rerouting damaged parts. The human body is a self-regulating organism that manufactures over 50,000 complex chemicals and regulates their quantities. If there were a shortage of any chemical, the body would just make more of it. A chemical imbalance might make sense if the organ that makes the chemical is dead, or if the diet is so deficient in vitamins, minerals and amino acids that the body does not have the raw materials to make the chemicals.

I have no doubt that the schizophrenic does in fact have a chemical imbalance, but I question whether the chemical imbalance is the cause. It is more likely the result. The blocked traumas cause the chemical imbalance. I suspect that the extra work of maintaining the blockage consumes vital nutrients like zinc, calcium, phenylaline, choline, vitamin C and all of the B-vitamins and a dozen others. **The body is unable to make enough chemicals because of a lack of raw materials.** The physical differences in the schizophrenic brain, the smaller hippocampus and larger ventricles, may be a result of vitamin and mineral deficiencies.

Some scientists have pointed out that schizophrenia runs in families, and so they conclude that it is genetic. If you think about that for 15 seconds, your common sense would tell you this is nothing more than a guess. The only way to prove a genetic link would be to raise 3 generations of humans in a laboratory, in a controlled environment, prevent all traumas, control their diet and a million other variables. The experiment would last 60 years.

Psychotic patients and their parents are quick to believe the chemical-imbalance-and-genetics explanation because the drugs offer a fast reduction of symptoms, at least temporarily. And the genetic cause is kinder and easier to accept than the possibility of mistreatment in early childhood.

Blocked traumas can occur very early in life, for example abortion attempts in the womb, or trauma during the first year. This could explain why sometimes twins both become schizophrenic even though they are adopted and grow up in separate homes.

There are many sets of identical twins where one is schizophrenic and the other is not. While a genetic link or a genetic tendency is certainly possible, I believe there is a simpler explanation. Mentally ill people make lousy parents. They ignore, ridicule and abuse their children. Of course if you ask them for the sake of a scientific study, they will say, "We love our children, and we would never hurt them."

Even the kindest, most well-intentioned neurotic parent will damage his own children because he is incapable of giving them enough attention. A mentally healthy child is energetic and demanding. The neurotic parent has very little energy to give. I believe that the reason schizophrenia runs in families is because mentally ill parents traumatize their kids who grow up and traumatize their kids, and so on.

I am troubled by the drug solution to mental problems. There can be many side effects, vomiting, lack of coordination, memory loss, constipation, sexual disfunction. In the worst cases some drugs can cause tardive dyskinsia (muscle jerking) or drug-induced Parkinson's disease.

The brain often develops a tolerance for the chemical so it stops working. Sometimes there is a rebound effect in which the drug intended to stimulate a specific neurotransmitter can actually deplete the supply of that same chemical leading to deep depression, the very symptom it was supposed to cure.

If, as I suspect, the blocked memories are causing the chemical inbalance, then treating the illness with drugs would be self-defeating. It is interesting that drugs intended to improve memory sometimes have "side effects" that might not be side effects at all, but rather a natural result of stimulating blocked memories. Many of the memory drugs will cause insomnia, irritability, and higher blood pressure. Choline which should normally help depression will in fact increase depression of a manic-depressive patient.

One common way to treat schizophrenia is to use a chemical that blocks dopamine receptors. Obviously this is not a case of a brain failing to make its own chemicals.

I hope you can see the paradox. The patient's nervous system may have intelligently decided to make less of some neurotransmitters and more of others as a way of controlling the blocked trauma and balancing the whole body. The doctor may adjust one chemical while the patient's nervous system is trying to balance 50 neurotransmitters, and 50,000 enzymes, hormones and other chemicals. It's hard for me to imagine that even our most clever scientist could ever balance all of those chemicals as skillfully as the patient's own nervous system.

I believe that the only difference between a schizophrenic and a neurotic is that the schizophrenic has a bigger pile of pain, and that he has depleted his vitamins and minerals in attempt to maintain the blockage. Even LSD-induced schizophrenia is a result of blocked memories. LSD weakens the brain's ability to maintain the blockage. The old memories come up and have to be disguised as hallucinations.

The fact that the schizophrenic suffers from hallucinations tells us two things. First, he has so much old pain that he can no longer keep it blocked, probably because his illness has consumed all of his nutrients. Second, it tells us that the human brain has a *governor,* a wonderful self protection mechanism. The hallucinations are a last ditch effort to protect the patient from remembering the trauma.

Blocking the old pain is not sick, it is healthy. A normal neurotic can carry around an enormous quantity of blocked pain and keep it under control. He can hold a job, raise a family, and not even be aware of his neurosis.

I am very hopeful that the schizophrenic can be cured if you drain off the pile of old pain. I believe they can be cured because of my own experience in digging out my own extremely violent traumas, and also because Janov and Hubbard both suggest that psychotics can be cured.[4]

The most difficult problem in treating a schizophrenic or any psychotic is that they cannot focus their attention enough to cooperate with the therapy. A second problem is that by the time they read this book, they most likely have been on prescribed drugs for many years.

If you are schizophrenic, or paranoid, or manic-depressive, and if you wish to start digging out blocked memories, here is what I suggest:

1. For the time being, stay on the drugs prescribed by your therapist. You'll need them to keep your mind clear while you get started.

2. Immediately start taking minerals, vitamins and amino acids as described in Chapter 10 to insure that your body has the raw materials to build your own chemicals. Ask your therapist if the drug he prescribed can have any dangerous interaction with your vitamins and minerals.

3. Read the book. Get it all in your head. You must understand the therapy better than your therapist.

4. Ask your therapist to read the book. Don't be surprised if he does not believe it. Many people resist new information. You may have to find another therapist.

5. Using a professional therapist, do the therapy as described in this book, and stay on your prescribed drugs.

6. After you have reduced your pile of pain by extensive bawling, ask your therapist to gradually reduce the dosage of drugs, but keep up the vitamins, minerals and amino acids so your body can make your own chemicals. I would not reduce your prescribed drugs until you have been on vitamins and minerals for at least 4 months.

7. Write and tell us about your therapy so others can learn from your experience.

These suggestions are theoretical. I have not yet tried the therapy on a schizophrenic. If you try The Therapy, you will be pioneering in new territory. I wish you luck. Even if everyone tells you that you are sick, I'm telling you that you are also a genius with unlimited potential. Trust yourself. Trust your instincts. And if your therapist will read this book, you can trust him too.

Do We Leave Our Bodies?

When you find scenes that are truly blocked, you may be surprised to see yourself from an *outside view*. As you look at the picture on your viewing screen, instead of saying, "I was laying on the bed," you might say, "The little boy was laying on the bed" as though you are a separate person observing what happened.

If the scene has a lot of pain, you may view the "little boy" from a very long distance. I remember one scene where the sadness was so overwhelming that I saw the little boy (me) from what seemed like 100 feet in the air.

This outside view is not unique to me. I have seen it in Nancy's therapy, and in Beth's. Hubbard noticed this outside view with all of his patients. It is so universal that even the movie makers use it as a technique to show great pain. At the moment of the greatest sorrow, they'll pull the camera high in the air and show the actor from a great distance.

There are two possible explanations for this out-of-body viewpoint: First, it could be merely a fabrication, a kind of symbolism that is built into our human nature. The second possibility is that we really do fly out of our bodies.

The whole issue is impossible to study by the normal scientific method, and yet we hear many stories suggesting that people do, in fact, fly out during a trauma. The book *Life After Life* by Raymond Moody is full of stories by people who claim to have left their bodies during a car accident or operation. I recall an interview with a famous movie star who had been raped. She said that she witnessed the rape from an outside view.[5]

The experience of flying out during trauma is more common than you might think. If you would ask 10 of your friends, chances are one of them has experienced the out-of-body state. One of my dearest friends claims to do it as often as once a month. My first reaction was skeptical, and yet she has shown me some very impressive evidence.

Fortunately, you and I don't have to decide whether it is a reality or symbolism. This book is not about psychic experiences. It is about curing neurosis by removing old blocked memories. I simply want you to know that when a blocked scene comes into your viewing screen, you might see yourself from an outside view. The farther your view is from your body, the greater the pain in the scene.

More important than that, I want you to know that whatever you see inside your mind really could be true. Movies and television have given us a confused idea about mental illness. They use the words "nuts" or "crazy" or "insane" as though neurotic people are incapable of any accurate thought. **The truth is that mentally ill people are very intelligent.** The less intelligent people died during their traumas. But people like you and I stayed alive by cleverly rewiring our brains so we could continue to function in spite of the trauma.

You may have problems in life, but there is no reason to question what you experience inside you own head. You can *feel* the difference between a dream, a fantasy, and a reality. You can *feel* the difference between a reconstructed memory and a real memory. If you think you have flown out of your body, and if your sister and mother think you are "crazy," there is no reason to assume that they know more than you do. On this subject, they are just guessing based on second-hand information. Only you have a front row seat.

Fantasies and Fetishes

When my daughter Beth was a teenager, she told me a secret. Sometimes when she was alone, she would pretend to be a tough super-hero named Joe, and she would live all kinds of adventures. She was so embarrassed to tell me, you would think she was confessing to a murder.

If you have a fantasy, sexual or otherwise, believe me, you are not the only one. More than 50% of the population has some sort of fantasy.

It is not unusual for women to fantasize about being prostitutes, or strippers, or being spanked, or having sex with many men, or with an anonymous stranger, or with other women or even animals. The most common male fantasy is about dominating women, but some also fantasize about being dominated, or sex with other men, or wearing women's clothes, masterbating in public and many more. Fantasy is not evil or bad. Rather it is a creative way that your mind handles blocked pain, and it can be a source of comfort.

I have had fantasies about dominating women. When you consider that my mother was physically violent, you can easily see that **my fantasies grew out of my childhood traumas. And the same is true of you.**

Your fantasy is a doorway into your hidden past. Tell your therapist about your fantasy, then try to create questions about it. Your fantasy may seem obviously sexual, but the trauma hidden under it could be about fear, hatred or need for parental love. A good question is "Other than sex, what is the feeling in your fantasy. As usual, ask the question over and over and watch for pop-ins.

FOOTNOTES CHAPTER 9

1. Joel Wallach, *Let's Play Doctor,* pp. 85-86.
2. For the research scientist: I suspect that the content of a phobia follows the same principle as a structural dream (see pages 92-95). Instead of the spider symbolizing what happened in the scene, it might symbolize what happened physically inside the brain. The spider might symbolize nerve endings (see page 94). The fear of heights might have something to do with flying out of the body during the trauma, rather than falling out of a tree.
3. Napoleon Hill, *Think and Grow Rich,* cassette version.
4. Janov's *Primal Scream,* chapter 20, and Hubbard's *Dianetics,* page 59.
5. L. Ron Hubbard, *Dianetics 55,* read the whole book.

10

Scientific Basis

Scientific Basis For The Subconscious

The word "subconscious" is as old as Sigmund Freud. I'm sure you've used the word in conversation, and yet I wonder if it is real to you. Do you really believe that there is a part of your mind that is hidden from you? I'd like to tell you the story of how the subconscious was first discovered and why we know it is real.

Scientists first became aware of the subconscious because of a mental illness called *hysteria*. We use the word "hysterical" today to describe someone who is crying or laughing uncontrollably, but that was not the original meaning. Hysteria in the 1800s and early 1900s was a mental disorder in which a patient could have *physical symptoms without any physical cause.*[1] For example, a person could be blind even though his eyes were perfect. For some reason, hysteria is rare today, but 100 years ago, it was very common.

In the year 1836 a 12-year-old Swiss girl suffered paralysis after a fall. She was taken to a doctor named Despine, who determined that her paralysis had no physical cause. He suspected hysteria and decided to try hypnotism. Her paralysis went away, as long as she was hypnotized.

Hysteria was almost totally a female disease. Only about 5% of cases were men. It was more common among poor country girls and prostitutes than it was among wealthy families. Hysteria was frequently accompanied by multiple personalities. Our main concern is with the *physical symptoms without any physical cause* because that was the first evidence for the existence of the subconscious.

One of the most famous cases of hysteria was the case of "Anna-O" around the year 1885. She had many bizarre symptoms, slurred speech, bad vision, severe cough, both legs and one arm paralyzed. Her doctor, Josef Breuer, was able to relieve her symptoms, at least temporarily, by hypnotism.

The 12-year-old Swiss girl and Anna-O were the most famous cases, but there were thousands of others. It was so common that it became the subject of much scientific research.

Around the time that Josef Breuer was treating Anna-O, a neurologist named Jean-Martin Charcot was famous for his work in treating hysteria. In one experiment, Charcot created hysterical symptoms in patients by hypnotizing them and giving them commands like "You cannot move your arm," or "You cannot speak." The result was symptoms exactly like hysteria. This experiment strongly suggested that hysteria may be caused by an *accidental hypnotic command* stuck inside the patient's brain.

Hypnosis is closely related to, and may be the same as, "authority" or "self direction" or "will power." For brevity I shall use the word "Will." A mentally healthy person cannot be hypnotized because he has his own *Will*. A neurotic can be hypnotized because his *Will* is somehow missing, hidden, or asleep, and this makes him susceptible to the authority of other people. A hypnotist would say he uses the "power of suggestion," but I prefer to say that the neurotic hears the suggestion as a command because his own *Will*, his own sense of authority, is missing, hidden or asleep. This is why neurotics are uncomfortable around persuasive sales people, because they know that they might buy something they don't need. They know they can't resist his authority.

As a result of Charcot's experiments, scientists became convinced of the existence of the subconscious mind. Their logic went like this:

- Anna's paralysis has no physical cause.
- Anna's paralysis can be cured, or created by mere commands (hypnosis).
- Conclusion: Someplace in Anna's mind there are commands that Anna is not aware of and that she cannot change…we call that "place" the "subconscious."

When Josef Breuer was treating Anna-O, he developed a method of asking her, under hypnosis, to go back into her past and tell in chronological order all the times her symptom had appeared. When she eventually told about the earliest time, her symptom would disappear. This might be where Hubbard got some of his ideas for his Dianetic method, but there is a slight difference. Hubbard tried to go back to the earliest *trauma*. while Breuer took his patient back to the *first time the symptom appeared,* which could be days or years after the hidden trauma.

Hubbard believed that when a child is traumatized he is in a hypnotic state because he is partially unconscious.[2] His own *Will* has been disconnected. In this hypnotic state, words spoken by people near the child (parents, doctor, etc.) might become *hypnotic commands stuck in the child's mind.* It is easy to imagine a child falling and bumping his head, and then a parent might say, "He's not moving!" which could become a hypnotic command that causes paralysis. Or imagine a cruel parent who beats his child while shouting "You're an idiot," might literally be causing the child to become an idiot.

Doctors who do operations have also noticed that hypnotic commands can be planted in a patient accidentally while he is under anesthesia. In one case, the doctor said, during the operation, "Oh my, it's malignant." It turned out later that the tumor was not malignant, but the lady patient could not recover from the operation until she discovered, under hypnosis, the hidden command, "It's malignant."[3]

This could possibly explain hysteria, but it would not explain all neurotic symptoms. I know that hypnotic commands do exist in the subconscious because I have experienced them. But they are not, as Hubbard thought, the main cause of the illness. Rather they are one kind of symptom among many symptoms. The real cause of neurosis is the trauma of not being loved, not allowed to be yourself (see pages 34-37).

Sigmund Freud was a friend of Breuer and eventually used Breuer's method to treat hysterical patients. In 1892 Freud and Breuer co-authored a book on treating hysteria in which they suggest that the cause of hysteria started in early childhood. They also thought the cause had something to do with psychic pain from sexual seduction by an adult.

You might think that hypnotism should be an ideal treatment for mental illness, but both Freud and Breuer found the results to be inconsistent and temporary and many patients could not be hypnotized.

Hypnotism is important not because it is a cure but rather because it helped us discover that there is a hidden part of the mind. Hypnotism is used today by many therapists. If the patient cries and feels the pain, hypnotism can be helpful. And yet many hypnotherapists do just the opposite. They tell the patient to go back and look at the traumatic event as a detached observer with no feeling. They are trying to protect the patient from the pain instead of making him feel it. If hypnosis helps you to remember without tears, the pain is still locked inside of you.

Frankly, I wonder if hypnosis can find a *truly blocked memory* (See Three Kinds of Reliving, pages 26-34). A hypnotist might help a patient to remember being raped at the age of 13, and both the patient and the hypnotist might assume they have found the trauma that caused the illness, while there may be ten, twenty or forty other traumas that remain blocked around the middle years, ages of 3 to 8 years old. These memories may be so blocked that hypnotism does not touch them.

I don't mean to say that hypnotism is bad. Hypnotism does a lot of good, and there are many situations where it is a useful therapy tool. But if you want to find all of your blocked memories and cry about them The Therapy will get you there faster.

Scientific Basis For The Temporary File

The one quality that makes the human superior to other animals is his ability to *learn,* and to make long term *plans.* Dogs, cats and rabbits can solve a problem involving a half-hour of time, but only the human will study a problem for several years and then form a plan that will be executed many years into the future.

The prefrontal cortex is the part of the brain that is used for studying, theorizing, analyzing and long term planning. You might naturally expect that humans would have the largest prefrontal cortex of all the animals.

As amazing as humans are, there is another animal that has an even larger (as a percentage of the brain) prefrontal cortex. The animal is called the echidna, an Australian ant eater about the size of a rat.[4] With such a large prefrontal cortex, we might assume it is a very intelligent little animal, but it isn't.

Why does the echidna have such a large prefrontal cortex? The answer is because he does not have a *temporary file*, he does not have *off-line processing*, and he does not *dream*. We know he does not dream by measuring his eye movements during sleep.[5]

Let's back up and give you a brief history of brain evolution, and then you'll understand the significance of the echidna. As you know, life on earth started in the sea, first as one-celled animals, later crustaceans and fish. The first animals to leave the ocean were reptiles, lizards, snakes, etc.

Up to this point in evolution, animals did not need to learn. Everything they needed to know was encoded into their instincts and reflex actions. Shrimp, fish, lizards and snakes do not learn in the sense that we learn.

When mammals started to evolve about 180 million years ago, Mother Nature had to develop a more efficient brain, one that could learn. Nature's first attempt was to give the brain a larger prefrontal cortex to record and process new learning experiences.

Apparently the bigger prefrontal cortex did not work very well, because all of those early mammals died out except two, the echidna and the platypus.

Nature's second solution was to create the *temporary file* and *off-line processing* (much like computer off-line processing) which higher mammals experience as *dreaming*. This method allows the brain to store and process thousands of times more information in much less space.

The echidna has a bigger prefrontal cortex than man because it has to store everything it learns, no matter how trivial or useless. If mammals had continued to evolve along these lines, eventually the head would be as big as a house.

The higher mammals, including humans, have a much more efficient system. Everything that happens during the day is stored in a *temporary place* until night time. Then during sleep, the information is *re-processed.* First, the trivia is eliminated. Ninety-nine percent of the day's events are not important to survival, so they are discarded. The important information is stored for future use and it is *doubled-up.* In other words, it is added to other similar experiences by *symbolizing.*

Symbolizing has the effect of condensing a large volume of information into a small package. One tree is very much like another tree. All trees are pretty much the same. If the echidna studies ten different trees, he would have to store that knowledge in ten different places in the brain. But we humans can record ten experiences with ten different trees in one place by using the symbolizing principle: all trees are similar.

When the trivia is eliminated and the important ideas are condensed by symbolizing, the information is sent to the prefrontal cortex for more permanent storage. This process of sorting and symbolizing information is done during the night, and you experience it as a *dream.*

The existence of the temporary file is crucial to the understanding of the mind, because it is the mechanism of neurosis, and it may be what Freud called the "subconscious," or at least a big part of it. It is possible that the hypnotic commands are stuck in the temporary file. I don't know the physical location of the temporary file, but there is some evidence that it is the hippocampus or something connected to it:

1. We know that the echidna does not dream, so it is logical to assume that he does not have a temporary file. It would further be logical to say that whatever part of the brain is oversized in the human and undersized in the echidna would be a likely candidate for the temporary file. What part would that be? You guessed it, the hippocampus.

2. We know that removing the hippocampus in the human brain will destroy short term memory, while leaving long term memory beyond three years in tact.[6]

3. We know that the hippocampus is interconnected with the prefrontal cortex in a way that suggests *off-line processing*. Dr. Jonathan Winson of Rockerfeller University has identified an electrical processing loop in animals with brains similar to man. When the animal receives information, there is an electrical current, called *theta rhythm*, that travels first to the prefrontal cortex, then to the hippocampus, and back to the prefrontal cortex again.[7]

   My guess is that new information goes first to the prefrontal cortex to be used immediately in present time. Then it goes to the hippocampus to take on an emotional quality and to give the person a *feeling* of relative importance. For example, a rattle snake is dangerous! Apple pie is nice! A fly is unimportant! Next the event with it's emotion is stored in the hippocampus for later off-line processing to be done at night. And finally, during the dream, it is sent back to the prefrontal cortex for permanent storage.

4. In the study of schizophrenia, scientists have noticed abnormalities in the hippocampus.[8] Under a microscope they have seen unusual structures or shapes. In a neurotic, chemicals that transmit information across synapses get physically dammed up and unable to fulfill their normal cycle. It is possible that in the schizophrenic, so much fluid is dammed up that it is actually visible. The scientists might be seeing a physical picture of the *river of pain*.

All of these pieces of information when viewed together suggest the strong possibility that the hippocampus or something connected to it is the physical location of Freud's subconscious, and what I call the temporary file.

Toward A Complete Theory

Any complete theory of the mind must explain blocked memories, hysteria, hypnotism, sleep problems, nightmares, multiple personality, neurosis, psychosis and chemical imbalance. So let's put it all together:

1. **Blocked memory.** When a child is traumatized, the event goes through the prefrontal cortex, but it gets stuck in the temporary file before it can take on it's emotional quality. The child may have *seen* the event, but he has never really *experienced* it. He has not *felt* it. The event remains stuck in the temporary file. It is never processed or symbolized for long term storage.

2. **Hysteria and hypnotism.** Simultaneously with the trauma, the child is to some degree unconscious. His own *Will* is temporarily suspended, hidden, disconnected or put to sleep. This is apparently a safety mechanism to protect the brain from overload. Whether the child is hit on the head or witnesses the death of a parent, there is some unconsciousness.

I don't know what or where the Will is. It could be a part of the brain, or just a unit of energy, or it could be what religious people call the "soul." It could be a process instead of a thing...the process of all brain parts working together, or the process of focusing thoughts.

Once the Will is disconnected, asleep, dead or lost, the child can be hypnotized by a professional, or accidentally by people near the child during the trauma. If the hypnotist says "Jump," it is as though the child's own Will has decided to jump. If a parent or brother standing near the child says "He's not moving," that phrase could accidentally become a hypnotic command stuck in the brain. This accidental hypnotism could possibly explain hysterical symptoms, and it could explain what we call hypnotic commands, but it would not explain all symptoms.

3. **Sleep problems.** If the child is traumatized continually day after day, his temporary file would become overloaded. It is small and can hold only a little bit of information.

Whenever it gets full, the child will feel sleepy. Attempts to process the traumatic information during sleep could cause the child to wake up to avoid a total reliving. If the pain is accidentally felt during sleep, the child would have a nightmare.

As more and more traumas get stuck in the temporary file, it becomes more tricky to close the gap on the sleep switch. Big yawns are necessary for pressure control to make the fragile connection without accidentally reconnecting the traumatic scenes.

4. **Compartments in the brain.** In an effort to empty the overloaded temporary file, entire weeks, months or years of a child's life could be "dumped" without processing from the temporary file into an isolated part of the prefrontal cortex. It would be as if the secretary in your office would just dump her unfilable papers into a shoe box and shove them into a file case without sorting or processing.

If the brain would actually dump painful events out of the temporary file into the prefrontal cortex without processing, then that part would have to be sealed off, forming mental compartments, just as you might seal a burning room to save the house, or seal a leaking compartment to save a sinking ship. It is conceivable that this dumping could be experienced as a nightmare.

5. **Multiple personality.** If the child continues to be traumatized, the temporary file will again become full, and again will have to be dumped into another sealed compartment. As traumas continue, the child may form a third, fourth, and fifth compartment. Each compartment will be loaded with experiences from a specific time period. For example, the first compartment might be age 3, the second age 6, the third age 8, etc.

If the compartments come to life and take over the body, the person would have a split personality. If the first compartment comes to life, you would meet a 3-year-old. The second compartment is a 6-year-old, and so on. In most multiple personalities, each personality is a different age.

The fact that these compartments can and do come to life suggests the *possibility* that the Will is a unit of energy that can travel from one compartment to another.

If the compartments do not come to life, the person may experience his compartments as ghosts or monsters during his dreams. I have had six compartments in my head, and yes, they were all different ages. I assume they are gone because I have not seen them in a very long time.

The compartmented parts of the brain are blocked and useless, thus reducing the person's potential talents and thinking speed. In my brain, the right side is very alive and active, but the entire left side was compartmentalized and unavailable for normal thinking. However, as my mental health has grown, I believe that my left side is gradually coming to life.

6. **Neurosis and psychosis.** If a child is traumatized only a few times, he would grow up "neurotic." He would be nervous and shy, have headaches and nightmares, but he could hold a job and have a normal life. But if the child has 30 or 40 traumas, he could grow up "psychotic" because his symptoms would be so serious that he could not function.

7. **Chemical imbalance.** The psychotic brain has to work possibly ten times as hard as a healthy brain and it consumes perhaps ten times as much energy and raw materials. Thus he creates a deficiency of chemicals because he doesn't have enough raw materials to make them.

The above "Complete Theory" of mental illness is not based on experiments with rats or mice or 800 volunteer human subjects. I did not have a $1,000,000 research grant from a government agency. Rather it is based on what I have observed inside my head during my own illness and my own cure. It is also based on my admittedly limited reading of experiments which seem to verify what I have observed.

I hesitate to say, and yet it would be dishonest not to tell you, that much of my observations came to me in dreams. It is as though someone is trying to give me a clear description of brain functioning, so I can pass it on to you. That someone could be a hidden part of me, perhaps my Super Conscious, or even a higher power. I really don't know the source. I realize this may not sound very "scientific." But I look at it this way. There are many things which are true that cannot yet be measured or proven. My job is to tell you how I cured my own neurosis, and to document what I did as accurately as I can. I leave that to some future scientist to prove or disprove it.

What Causes Headaches?

20,000,000 Americans suffer from headaches. Some migraine sufferers take up to 30 aspirins a day to control the pain, and often have to go home from their jobs because they can not work.

If you ask an average doctor what causes headaches, he'll likely tell you something like this: "We don't know what causes headaches. Sometimes they can be triggered be a food allergy."

If you go to the top specialist at one of America's six major headache clinics, he might say, "Headaches occur when neurons in the back of the brain stem become unstable, causing an imbalance of **serotonin,** thus causing depression of nerve cell function in the cortex and causing the blood vessels in the scalp to expand."[9] This sounds very scientific, and it's probably true, but it does not solve your problem. We still don't know what causes the "neurons in the back of the brain stem to become unstable?"

There are 3 kinds of headaches: migraine, tension and cluster. *Migraine* headaches and *tension* headaches are caused by blocked childhood pain. These headaches occur when an old memory is trying to come up, and you are trying to shove it back down. This painful struggle is your headache. Very little is known about *cluster* headaches, but they might also be caused by blocked pain. My own headaches disappeared after a few months of therapy. Janov's patients have also had their migraine headaches cured.[10]

I can remember therapy sessions when my face would hurt around my eyes. It was the beginning of what I used to call a headache. But as I started to cry, the feeling in my face would turn into bawling, and then I knew that my "ache" was just me physically blocking my tears. Draining off the pain by crying has permanently cured my headaches. It seems self-evident that blocked pain was the cause.

Obviously, all headaches are not neurotic. There can be some physical problems such as meningitis, flu, eye strain, just to name a few. About 3% of headaches are from physical problems, and you should contact your doctor to eliminate that possibility. But if your doctor gives you a thorough check-up and ends up saying, "We don't know what causes headaches. It might be a food allergy," then you can be pretty sure you are in the 97% who has a neurotic headache. There may indeed be a food allergy, but that is not the cause. In most cases the blocked memory causes the headache and the allergy.

Should you attempt the therapy while your head is hurting so badly? In most cases, I would say not yet! Read the next section about brain chemistry. It should help you get your headaches under control before you start therapy.

If you cannot control your headaches by nutrition, and if you must try therapy during a headache, you might find immediate tears by sinking into the headache. **Sometimes a symptom is the doorway into old pain.** Stop fighting it! Feel it! Say it out loud, "My head hurts! Somebody help me! I can't stand it any more!" Ask your therapist to use the question "Why does your head hurt?"

But your safer choice is to start a program of vitamins, minerals, and amino acids, as discussed in the next section. We want your old feelings to come up in small controlled spoonfuls. We don't want to explode your head in the process. Blocking old traumas is a natural defense mechanism and it should be reasonably comfortable. If your nervous system has all of the nutrients it needs, you should be able to maintain your blocked memories without headaches, though you may feel nervous and irritable.

Understand Your Brain Chemistry

In theory, if you are in perfect health, you could do the therapy without reading this section. But in reality, if you have emotional problems, you probably also have some brain chemistry problems. You can solve them by knowing a little about brain chemistry and proper nutrition. If your body has all of the vitamins, minerals and amino acids it needs to make your brain chemicals, then your therapy will go much smoother. With a little luck, eating the right nutrients might reduce some of your symptoms before you start therapy.

Over the past 30 years scientists have made remarkable progress in understanding brain chemistry. They have developed miracle drugs that can control the symptoms of neurosis, depression, schizophrenia and manic-depression.

The effectiveness of these drugs has lead some scientists to conclude that many mental problems are caused by a chemical imbalance in the brain. But I have to ask, "What causes the chemical imbalance?"

I have no doubt that a chemical imbalance can cause neurotic symptoms, but I suspect that most of the time it is the other way around: the extra work of maintaining blocked memories consumes vitamins and minerals so the brain cannot make it's own chemicals, thus causing the imbalance.[11] A neurotic burns up twice as much energy as a mentally healthy person. That's why neurotics are always tired. It is a lot of work to maintain the blockage and to process information when your brain is clogged up.

In my own case, the cause of my neurosis seems simple and obvious: before therapy I had symptoms (headaches, depression, etc.) and after therapy my symptoms disappeared. I have never been on any kind of drug, alcohol, or vitamin except coffee and an occasional vitamin C during a cold. So in my case the obvious cause was blocked childhood trauma. But that might not be true of you. You would be foolish not to at least consider other possibilities.

I believe that your headaches are a combination of blocked memories and vitamin and mineral deficiencies. The extra burden of keeping the memories blocked has consumed vital nutrients that you need to build your own brain chemicals. Without the raw materials, you can't make the chemicals and you can't keep the memories hidden, and so your head hurts.

It would cost a billion dollars in research to prove whether the neurosis causes the deficiencies or the deficiencies cause the neurosis. Either way you need to make sure that your body has all the nutrients it needs. If you are low on vitamin C, B5, B6, B12, zinc or any of 90 other essential nutrients, it can slow down your therapy unnecessarily. Your body knows when it has a health problem, and it will not allow you to discharge if you are in bad health.

If you have an imbalance of chemicals in your brain, there are two ways to fix it. First, we could give you the missing chemical. Second, we could give you the nutrients you need to manufacture your own chemicals. You probably have already guessed that I favor the second choice.

The wonderful thing about vitamins and minerals is that with a few exceptions[12] you can take enormous quantities of them and let your body decide how much to use. (Be sure to read footnote no. 12, page 224, for the exceptions.) For example, you can take one gram, ten grams or up to 100 grams of vitamin C per day with no ill effect other than possible diarrea. Compare that to my heart medicine. My daily dosage is 50 mg. If I take twice that much, it would be dangerous. Vitamins and minerals are simply food. They allow your own nervous system to decide what to use, and throw the rest away.

The chemicals that transmit information in our brain are called "neurotransmitters." About 50 neurotransmitters have been discovered so far. All of them can be rebuilt and replenished with a knowledge of vitamins, minerals and amino acids.

For example, one of the most important neurotransmitters for the neurotic is *norepinephrine.* A shortage of this chemical will cause a feeling of depression. Replenishing it will restore energy and motivation. A patient who has used amphetamines and related drugs, (including some drugs used to treat hyperactive children) may have depleted his store of norepinephrine leading to depression, depressed immune system, and shortage of growth hormone. The non-prescription solution is to eat the amino acid *phenylaline* in doses ranging from 100 to 1000 mg. per day. In the presence of *vitamin C* and *vitamin B6,* the brain will convert the amino acid into the needed neurotransmitter. Phenylalanine is twice as effective for relieving depression as the most common anti-depression drug. It is a natural substance found in meat, eggs and cheese. You can buy it at the health food store.[13]

Another neurotransmitter *acetylcholine* is important for improving memory, and it's absense can cause depression. It could be useful in therapy. You can increase your acetylcholine supply by taking a B-complex vitamin called *choline* at 3 grams per day. Also *vitamin B5* is necessary for the conversion. You can get choline by eating fish. The old wives' tale that fish is good for the brain is actually true.[14]

Another memory chemical is *vasopressin,* a natural pituitary hormone, (brand name Diapid® made by Sandoz). As a nasal spray it has been able to restore memory to amnesia victims within hours. Even though it requires a prescription, it is a natural substance. When your body makes acetylcholine (previous paragraph) it will also release vasopressin. Marijuana and alcohol inhibit release of vasopressin.[15]

Serotonin is a neurotransmitter that helps us sleep. A shortage of serotonin has been linked with migraine headache.[16] I believe it is needed to maintain blocked memories.[17] You can increase your serotonin by taking an amino acid *tryptophan,* found in bananas and milk. Vitamin C and B6 are needed for conversion.[18]

Dopamine is another neurotransmitter linked to mental problems. One way to treat schizophrenia is by *blocking* dopamine receptors. This suggests to me that a shortage of brain chemicals is not the problem. Apparently the schizophrenic brain is perfectly capable of making dopamine. Also damage to dopamine receptors will lead to Parkinson's Disease. *L-dopa,* the amino acid used to make dopamine is a prescription drug. But perhaps more important than L-dopa is the fact that dopamine receptors are easily damaged by oxidation. You can preserve your dopamine system and possibly prevent Parkinson's Disease by taking plenty of the anti-oxidants, *vitamins A, E, C, B1, B5, B6, zinc, and selenium.*[19]

Dopamine stimulates the production of *growth hormone*, which is necessary during sleep. You can also stimulate more growth hormone by eating *arginine* and *ornithine*, two amino acids found in large concentrations in chicken meat.

All of the neurotransmitters discussed above have been shown to increase the life span in mice 20% to 50%. They improve energy, sexual activity and endurance.[20]

RNA or ribonucleic acid is considered to be the memory molecule. It can be purchased as a natural substance in the healthfood store, or you can get it by eating fish. But the best way is to take *vitamin B12*, about 1000 micrograms (1 milligram) per day, to stimulate RNA growth.[21] Be sure to take all the B vitamins together to maintain balance.

Cellular waste products in brain cells, called *libofuscin*, can be removed more quickly by using the B complex vitamin *choline*, plus the anti-oxidants *vitamins A, E, C, B1, B5, B6, zinc* and *selenium.*[22]

You might ask your doctor to prescribe tryptophan because of its role in controlling headaches. It is frustrating that the amino acids *tryptophan* and *L-dopa* require a prescription. Amino acids are simply the building blocks of proteins. If you eat milk, cheese, eggs, especially chicken and fish, you will have the amino acids, as long as you simultaneously eat plenty of vitamins to make the conversion.[23] If you are concerned about cholesterol, you might like to know that cholesterol does not come from eggs and meat. Rather it results from too much sugar and not enough vitamin C and vitamin B3 (niacin).[24]

In some research studies, we have found that specific vitamins improve mental disorders without necessarily knowing precisely how they work. **The vitamins do more than one job, and the chemical deficiency may have more**

than one cause. For example, there can be a neurotransmitter shortage because the brain is not making it, or because the raw materials are not being transferred across the blood brain barrier, or across the cell walls, or because the food is not being digested. The possibilities are almost infinite. It's another reason why I prefer to give your body all of the nutrients and let your nervous system solve the problem.

In 1939, Cleckley, Sydenstricker and Geeslin successfully treated 19 patients with severe psychotic symptoms by large doses of *vitamin B3* (niacin, niacinamide, nicotinic acid). The dosage was up to 1.5 grams per day, about 100 times the RDA. Since 1952 Doctors Hoffer and Osmond have advocated B3 for treating schizophrenia.[25]

A 1965 study by Edwin, Holten, Norum, Schrumpf and Shaug found that a significant number of mental patients in Norway suffered from a deficiency of vitamin B12.[26]

Ron Hubbard tells us that without vitamin B1 during therapy, you will have more nightmares. He suggests a dosage of 10 mg. per day.[27]

There is mounting evidence that any emotional stress, including therapy, can drain your body of zinc. The symptoms of zinc deficiency are listed as depression, fatigue, insomnia, irritability, and paranoia.[28]

Potassium is necessary to move the waste matter out through your cells. A deficiency in potassium can cause fatigue.

Nobel Prize winner, Dr. Linus Pauling has shown us that vitamin C is needed for brain functioning. Nerve cells contain 100 times as much vitamin C as the rest of the body. In one study a dose of 180 mg. per day (a very small dose) in school children increased IQ scores almost 4 points. Separate double blind studies by Dr. Ruth F. Harrel and by Dr. Henry Turkel have shown that vitamins and mineral supplements can raise IQ scores of retarded children by as much as 25 points if administered early in childhood.[29]

The minerals bioton, choline, calcium, copper, folic acid, iodine, iron, magnesium, niacin, phosphorus, potassium, sodium, zinc, lithium, and vitamins C, D, B1, B2, B3, B5, B6 and B12 have all been linked to depression and mental illness.

Minerals are as important as vitamins because minerals are the raw materials of all those brain chemicals. Vitamins are catalysts that cause chemical reactions. Without minerals as the raw materials, the vitamins cannot do their job.

It is popular to believe that we get plenty of vitamins and minerals in our food, but it is unfortunately not true. Our bodies have evolved over a million years on a diet that was about half meat and half wild fruits, roots and vegetables. The meat was from wild animals low in fat. The plants were full of vitamins and minerals because the soil was full of nutrients. Our caveman ancestors were actually taller than the Romans and the Greeks.

It is only in the past 5000 years that we have moved out of the wilderness. We cook our food to kill germs but we also destroy many vitamins. We farm the same soil year after year and deplete it's minerals. We preserve our food with sugar which does untold damage to our body.

Probably the two most destructive problems in our modern diet are the excess of sugar and the shortage of vitamin C. Today we eat 50 times as much refined sugar as our ancestors did just 100 years ago. Diabetes used to be a rare disease. Today it is the number 3 killer. Heart disease is the number 1 killer and it is also sugar related. Contrary to popular belief the cholesterol in your blood is not a result of eating cholesterol. Your body makes its own cholesterol, and table sugar increases the amount you make.

The Recommended Daily Allowance of vitamin C is only 60 mg., but our caveman ancestors were accustomed to forty times that much. Like it or not, your body needs about 3 grams or 3000 milligrams of vitamin C every day.[30] When you're sick you need much more. Vitamin C is the most well documented and completely understood of all the vitamins. It does many jobs and without it you will be sicker more often and longer than necessary. Vitamin C does the following:

- Helps make collagen, a protein in tendons, gums, blood vessels.
- Fights virus and bacteria, including colds, flu, hepatitis, herpes, mononucleosis.

- Prevents cancer and extends life of people who already have cancer.
- Reduces side effects of chemotherapy.
- Reduces cholesterol in blood.
- Improves IQ scores of genetically retarded children.
- Controls allergies by controlling histamine release.
- Improves arthritis if used with vitamin B3 and B6.
- Needed to make adrenaline.
- Reduces need for insulin in diabetics.
- Destroys cancer causing nitrates in blood.
- Prevents cataracts in eyes.
- Increases healing time after operations by 2 days.
- Essential for manufacture of neurotransmitters.
- Seems to help AIDS victims (no formal study yet).
- Slows aging by removing free radicals.
- Removes lead poisoning from blood.
- Vitamin C reduces damage done by smoking.[31]

I tell you about Vitamin C as an example of how one vitamin can do many jobs, and why it is better to eat the right nutrients and let your body make the decisions.

If you are planning to do the therapy, why not take a few precautions. Get a complete physical check-up from a doctor to be sure you have no physical problems. Then consider starting a program of daily supplements.

Be careful about asking your doctor's advice on vitamins and minerals. Many doctors are not up-to-date on the subject. They seem to get their education from the drug companies who are not interested in vitamins because they can't be patented. The FDA also seems to be 20 years behind the times on vitamin research. Doctors are excellent for diagnosis after you get sick, but many doctors have a lot to learn about prevention. If you want to learn about vitamins, I suggest you read *Life Extension*, by physicist Durk Pearson and biochemist Sandy Shaw. Also read *How to Live Longer and Feel Better*, by chemist and Nobel Prize winner Linus Pauling. I am neither a doctor nor a chemist. Most of what I know is based on Pearson, Shaw and Pauling.

All of the major vitamin companies and health food stores are offering one-dose supplements that attempt to supply a full range of vitamins and minerals. It is a wonderful trend. But you need to do a little reading to help you recognize the right combination of nutrients. The vitamin companies are not aware of the special needs of a person doing therapy.

Dr. Joel Wallach, who was nominated for a Nobel Prize in 1981, tells us that your body needs 7 major minerals, 53 trace minerals, 16 vitamins, 12 amino acids and 3 fatty acids every day.[32] If you purchase that many supplements individually, you'd spend a fortune. His company offers a product that has all of those nutrients in a single dose. It's much cheaper in the long run, and I personally recommend it.

One of the cassettes offered on the last page of the book is by Dr. Wallach. I urge you to listen to the tape even if you do not buy his products because it is the best explanation I have ever heard about why your body needs trace minerals. I use his supplements every day, and so does my family.

I did not take supplements during my therapy, and looking back, I wish I had. I suspect my heart problem could have been prevented by trace minerals, and once it started, my therapy progress came to a screeching halt.

If you don't use Dr. Wallach's product, consider taking the amino acid *phenylaline.* Eat bananas and milk to get *tryptophan.* Eat protein, especially fish, for other amino acids. Take the minerals *selenium, zinc, potassium, calcium,* the *vitamins A, E, C, choline,* and all of the *B vitamins.* Shop around and see if you can find them all in one pill.

Vitamins are acids and can irritate or damage your stomach. To prevent this, 1) start with a small dose and build up gradually, 2) use powder or liquid instead of pills, 3) take them immediately after eating so pills don't lay on your bare stomach lining.

Spread the doses throughout the day. Take some at breakfast, lunch, supper and bedtime. **Your brain will work harder at night than it does in the daytime, so be sure to save some vitamins for bedtime.**

The single most important vitamin is vitamin C. You should take a minimum of 3 grams per day. That's 3000 mg.

per day. If you are schizophrenic take 10 grams or more per day. If you still have neurotic symptoms after taking vitamins and minerals for several months, then you can be pretty sure that old blocked pain is the cause.

Don't expect the vitamins and minerals to make you feel great. They might have the opposite effect. If they help old feelings come up more easily, you can temporarily feel sad or irritable until you cry about the feeling.

If you wish to create your own nutrient program, it may be difficult to decide the right dosage. As I write this page (January 1995), we are contracting with a pharmaceutical company to make a vitamin-mineral-amino acid supplement which will include all of the nutrients we have talked about in this section in the right proportions to support someone doing The Therapy. Hopefully, it will be available by the time you read these words.

If you get a physical check-up and take vitamins, minerals, and amino acids, you will be covering all of the bases, and when your body has all the nutrients it needs, your therapy will go more smoothly.

The 20 Great Discoveries

Whenever I am being interviewed on a talk radio show, the host inevitably asks me, "How is it possible that you could find a cure for mental illness, while all the doctors and scientists of the world have not been able to?"

The answer is that I didn't come up with it all by myself. The method is built on discoveries by other researchers plus a few of my own. All I did was put them together, and get rid of the technical voodoo language.

Frankly, I wouldn't be surprised if there are many therapists out there who understand the principles in this book. Most of the ideas were discovered before 1956. It is highly unlikely that I am the only one who has put it all together.

If indeed the other therapists really don't know this method, I can tell you why they missed it: **First,** they completely under-estimated the enormous quantity of pain stored in the nervous system. **Second,** they never understood that it is the tears that cure the illness, rather than the insights and connections. **Third,** they never learned to recognize and get past the hypnotic command. It is the first barrier. If you don't get past the hypnotic commands, your therapy won't even get started.

The study of mental illness is different than all other sciences. In the study of frogs, whales, and planets, you would rightly expect the professional to know more than the amateur. **But in studying the sick mind, there is only one person who can see exactly what is going on...and it is not the therapist. It's the patient.** Only the patient has a front row seat. While he is piecing together a traumatic scene, and tears are running down his cheeks, the only person who truly understands what's going on is the patient. The therapist is getting a second hand description.

We mistakenly assume that mentally ill people are not intelligent, and nothing could be further from the truth. Even patients with multiple personalities have been shown to have very high IQ scores. No doubt, their illness interferes with their perceptions of the world, but their perceptions of what happens inside their own head during therapy is more accurate than what the therapist thinks is happening.

If I have contributed anything to the study of mental illness, it is that, in spite of my own neurosis, I was blessed with a logical mind and a talent for observing and reporting accurately.

I used to think I had a special talent for finding blocked scenes, but recently it has occurred to me that perhaps anyone with a lot of trauma in his brain might find his scenes easily, because the scenes themselves would be exerting an enormous force, trying to come out by themselves. Wouldn't that be great, if the sicker patient was easier to cure?

In this chapter, I want to tell you about the 20 discoveries that are the foundation of The Therapy. We'll talk about Sigmund Freud, Carl Jung, L. Ron Hubbard, Arthur Janov, Jonathon Winson, and I'll explain briefly the great lessons I learned from each one.

SIGMUND FREUD

I'm not going to tell you Freud's life story. I think you know who he was. He's the guy who came up with the *Ego, Super-Ego,* and *Id,* and the *Oedipus Complex.* It's popular to poke fun at old Freud because he was perhaps too obsessed with sexual symbolism, and yet I think we owe him a great debt. Before he came along, we used to think that psychotic people were possessed by the devil. Freud popularized the idea that mental illness has it's roots in early childhood, and he made us aware of the subconscious mind.

Freud was responsible for two powerful discoveries that we use in The Therapy:[33]

Freud's Discovery Number 1:

Free association.

If you allow a patient to say everything that goes through his mind, eventually he'll solve some of his own problems. We call it "the talking cure."

Freud's Discovery Number 2:

"Dreams are the royal road to the subconscious."

When Freud said those great words, he was perhaps the first to recognize that sleeping and dreaming are the mechanism of neurosis.

CARL JUNG

Jung was Freud's student and later became the president of the International Psychoanalytical Association which Freud had founded. Eventually they had a difference of opinion and Jung split away from Freud.

Some of Jung's ideas bordered on the mystical. He believed that deep inside of us is a *collective psyche* that connects the human race together.

Jung is important because he corrected and refined some of Freud's ideas. Freud tended to explain neurosis in terms of childhood sexuality. Jung said it better in terms of the child's need for love. Freud assumed that dream symbols always had a fixed meaning, and he would often dictate to the patient what the dream meant. Jung improved on Freud's system by encouraging the patient to decide for himself what the dream meant.

I feel a personal kinship with Jung. I had experienced my *Super Conscious* and my *other half* before I ever learned about Jung. It was reassuring to find out that Jung had observed the *Super Conscious* and the *other half* 20 years before I was born. He used different words. He called them the *archtypal self* and the *anima*.

His best contribution to The Therapy is implied in the way he did therapy, rather than stated in his writings. I've taken the liberty to state it for him:[34]

Jung's Discovery:
Trust the patient's instincts.
Let the patient interpret the dream instead of dictating to the patient what it means.

L. RON HUBBARD

Freud and Jung knew only vaguely that neurosis was caused in early childhood, but Hubbard was a little more specific. He said that the illness is caused by "engrams" (traumatic scenes) stuck somewhere in the brain, and that we can cure the mind by finding the engrams and draining off the "charge," one engram at a time.

Hubbard's book, *Dianetics,* is difficult reading. He spends the first 200 pages talking about his philosophy on life before he explains his method. He further confuses the reader by creating his own technical language: "auditor" (therapist), "engram" (traumatic scene), "somatic" (pain). I get the feeling he was intentionally making his method sound technical, instead of making it easy to understand.

In his second book, *Dianetics 55,* he shifted away from discharging old traumas and became more interested in "exteriorizing"…in other words, traveling out of the body. His idea was that if you could leave your body, you could think without the limitations of a physical brain. He built a religion called *Scientology* around the concept of exteriorizing, and it became a world-wide organization.

He received a lot of bad publicity in the '60s and '70s. Some of his followers were perhaps overly enthusiastic. There were rumors of Watergate-style break-ins. One national magazine called it "The most dangerous cult in America."

I personally don't care if Hubbard slept in a coffin, had 8 girlfriends, and smoked feathers. There is no doubt that he was an unusual person who made his own rules, but he was also a genius. His first *Dianetics* book contains some history-making discoveries. His only mistake is that he didn't carry it far enough. He expected a cure in 25 to 100 hours. Like most other students of the mind, he underestimated the enormous quantity of pain inside the neurotic.

I am indebted to him for his concept of *discharge,* as though each traumatic scene has a quantity of electricity stored with it, and when the patient cries, he is removing (discharging) the electricity from that scene. It may not be technically or scientifically accurate, but it is an easy way for the layman to visualize what happens. Most likely the charge is stored as a chemical with electrical potential.

Several of his discoveries are absolutely basic to the methods contained in this book:[35]

Hubbard's Discovery Number 1:

Blocked memories are connected to specific words.

If you can find the right word,
and say it out loud, you'll start to cry.

Telling specific details will make you cry.
Using general words will prevent tears.

Hubbard's Discovery Number 2:

Watch your viewing screen.

The viewing screen, like dreams, is the
"royal road to the subconscious." It is the
number one tool of therapy.

Hubbard's Discovery Number 3:

If a patient tells a blocked scene over and over, he will find new details and tears each time through.

If the therapist keeps asking for an
"earlier beginning" the patient will find
many earlier scenes connected to the first scene.

Hubbard's Discovery Number 4:

Programmed command or hypnotic command

A programmed command is a word or phrase
stuck in a person's mind and having the power
of a command or a hypnotic suggestion.

Hubbard called the hypnotic command a "holder". Without that great discovery, some patients could not be cured because they could never get started.

For example, the phrase "I can't see" could program a person to have a blank viewing screen, and it could make therapy impossible. It could also cause physical vision problems. Hubbard undoubtedly learned about hypnotic commands from Josef Breuer and Jean-Martin Charcot, but he gave us a technique for discharging the command by repeating the phrase.

ARTHUR JANOV

I have nothing but praise for Arthur Janov and his Primal Therapy method. His book, *Primal Scream,* is easy to read and it is full of true case histories. It might be instructive to summarize for you how his method works:

The patient is isolated for one day before he meets his therapist. He is given no cigarettes, no TV, no beer, nothing to distract him from the old scenes that are trying to come out of him. When he finally meets his therapist, he is so nervous that he instinctively puts up his defenses by acting a role (intellectual, martyr, etc.). The therapist forcefully breaks through his artificial role and makes him stop acting, and then his old feelings come out full force, in 3D stereo, with sounds and smells from the original event. It is what I call a *complete reliving.* Janov calls it a *primal.* The therapy goes on for 6 months up to 2 years. Blocked memories continue to come up after the patient leaves the clinic.

Primal Therapy is faster and more thorough than my method, but it has a few disadvantages. It cannot be done at home without a professional therapist. I've tried it, and it doesn't work. The problem is that the therapist has to be mentally healthy. At the moment when the patient comes out of isolation, the therapist has to be alert enough to recognize phony games and forceful enough to make him stop acting. The only way the therapist can have this strength is if he is already cured.

Primal Therapy is done only in two places, Los Angeles and New York City. The fee is around $10,000 in 1994. Most normal people cannot afford the fee, and they can't afford to leave their jobs to travel to another state for up to 2 years.

While my method is not as fast as Primal Therapy, it has the advantages that it can be done at home, and the only cost is the price of the book. But if you have the resources to pay the fee and take time off from your job, I would strongly encourage you to go to Primal Therapy.

The most valuable ideas we have used from Arthur Janov are:[36]

Janov's Discovery Number 1:
The incredible quantity of pain.

Before Janov's discovery, nobody knew how much pain there was. No one knew where the end of therapy was. No one had ever really cured a neurotic, so there was no way to know how much crying was enough. Janov's hundreds of successful cases convinced him that the pain stored inside of one neurotic is "enough to power a small city."

Janov's Discovery Number 2:
Understanding does not cure the illness.

Only feeling the pain will cure the illness. Insights, understanding and connections come *after* the pain.

Janov's Discovery Number 3:
The traumatic scenes are trying to come up by themselves.

The patient has to do something all day long to keep the traumatic scene hidden. He must smoke, or work, or watch TV, or something to distract himself from the feeling that is coming up.

This is why The Therapy is natural. This is why the patient can trust his instincts. This is why the question doesn't have to be perfect, because the traumatic scene is trying to come up even without a question.

Janov's Discovery Number 4:

A nightmare is an old feeling trying to come up during sleep.

This is important because it would seem to verify the temporary file theory.

Janov's Discovery Number 5:

The nervous system has a built-in governor.

It is virtually impossible for a patient to experience more pain than he can handle comfortably.

Hubbard also touched on the idea of a governor when he said, "The mind is a self-protecting mechanism."

JONATHON WINSON

Professor Jonathon Winson, Associate Professor of Neuroscience at Rockefeller University, wrote a landmark book called *Brain and Psyche,* in which he tried to show that Freud's idea of the subconscious might actually have a physiological explanation. If a human had to store all of his experiences without processing, his head would be as big as a house. The evolutionary solution was to create a temporary storage place in the brain, and off-line processing at night time. The processing is experienced as a dream. For a more detailed explanation, see pages 81-84 and 184-187.

While Winson is not the only researcher who advocates the theory of dreaming as *off-line processing,* I am personally grateful to him for writing his wonderful book. It is the most thorough and documented book I have ever seen on the subject.

Professor Winson's contribution to The Therapy is:[37]

Winson's Discovery:
Dreaming is off-line processing.

This explains why traumatic scenes can get stuck in the temporary storage place, and why all neurotics have sleep problems. And it gives us physical evidence for Freud's statement "Dreams are the royal road to the subconscious."

THOMAS A. STONE

And now I'd like to add my own discoveries to the list. I feel just a little uncomfortable calling them "great discoveries." I suspect that other therapists have also discovered them, and perhaps not written them down. So let's just call them "discoveries," and let future generations decide whether or not they were "great."

Stone's Discovery Number 1:
The more you cry, the more your mind will heal itself.

Even crying in a movie will reduce the pile of pain.
It is not insights and understanding that cure
the neurotic. It's feeling the pain, getting it out
and over with.

Stone's Discovery Number 2:
Curing the brain is natural.
The mind is constantly trying to heal itself. Neurotics like to talk about the past because they're trying to resolve it. I found my first traumatic scene simply by isolating, because the scene was trying to come up by itself.

Stone's Discovery Number 3:
The spoonful theory.
The nervous system cannot let go of all the pain at once, but it will let go of a small portion (a spoonful). It may not be what you asked for, but it will reduce the pile of pain a little bit.

Stone's Discovery Number 4:
Three kinds of reliving.
There are three distinct forms of reliving, and all three can eventually cure the neurosis: *Complete reliving* is best, but also hardest. *Symbolic* or *similar story reliving* is the easiest way for the amateur. *Fragmented* or *reconstructed reliving* is slow, difficult work.

You must discharge a scene *symbolically* before your mind will let you see the scene in *fragmented* form.

Stone's Discovery Number 5:
Doing therapy alone.
You can do therapy alone with the movies, music, a blindfold and using the basic therapy procedure.

Stone's Discovery Number 6:

Doorways.

A doorway is an easy entrance,
a shortcut into the pain.

The best way I can explain doorways is by example. Whenever Nancy finds a color on her viewing screen, for example the color green, we can always find feeling by asking, "What is it about green." Whenever I find a movie star in a dream, for example, Michael Douglas, I can usually find discharge by asking, "What is it about Michael Douglas." It's almost as though the Super Conscious is intentionally giving us an easy entrance into the pain, so we won't have to dig so hard.

Stone's Discovery Number 7:

Every defense is a doorway.

For example, a programmed command interferes with
therapy, and yet when you recognize it, it becomes the
doorway into your pain.

I'd like to tell you how I first came upon this idea that every defense is a doorway. The professionals have told me that my logic is a defense against feeling, and yet I have ignored the pros and I have sunk into my logic. I have found buckets of tears by using my logic. Next, when we started work on Nancy's therapy, her "always" feeling was a defense. But after we recognized it, it became an easy doorway.

Janov tells the story of a homosexual patient in Primal Therapy. The therapist had instructed him to avoid any sexual contact during the therapy because it was a defense against the pain. One night the patient snuck out and found a homosexual partner. Trusting his instincts, he not only did the sexual act, but he went farther than that. He sunk into it more deeply than he ever had before. He wanted his partner to degrade and humiliate him, and in the process, he was able to primal about the old feeling that was hidden under the homosexual act. He remembered that his father had ignored him except when he was being punished. He had come to enjoy being degraded and humiliated because it was the only attention he ever got from his dad. He discovered this old pain by sinking into his "defense." His defense had become his doorway.

WHERE NO ONE HAS GONE BEFORE

In reality, Freud, Jung, Hubbard, Janov, and Winson have made hundreds of minor contributions to The Therapy, and I have made about 30 minor discoveries that are scattered in other chapters of this book. I have chosen to tell you about these 20 discoveries because they are the *foundations* of this book. They reflect several lifetimes of study and experience.

I believe strongly in them because they are simple, natural, common sense principles. In some cases they are self-evident.

I've written them down because I'm trying to equip you to go into the future. I don't have the final answers. I fully expect that you will take what you have learned and carry it farther. You may even disagree with me on some things. Freud made some mistakes, Hubbard was wrong about some things. As you learn more, you may discover that I've made a mistake or two. But as you go beyond the contents of this book, I hope you will refer back to these 20 basic discoveries, to double-check your new ideas.

COMPARING THE GREAT THERAPIES

I find it intriguing that The Therapy is in many ways opposite of Primal Therapy. The Therapy is gentle, while Primal Therapy requires firmness. The Therapy can be done by two neurotics, Primal Therapy requires a mentally healthy therapist. Primal Therapy aims for *total reliving*, while The Therapy uses *symbolic* and *fragmented reliving*. They are opposites and yet they both work. The differences between them give us a 3-dimensional view of how the mind works.

One way to understand this difference is to consider how you might repair a computer that has some blocked circuits. The Therapy would be like going through each computer chip with a magnifying glass, and cleaning out each blocked circuit one at a time. Primal Therapy would be like plugging the computer into 10,000 volts of electricity and blasting through the blockages all at once.

The Therapy says, "I realize your emotions are buried in old pain. Let's use what you have left, your intellect, to carefully discharge your blockages one at a time." Primal Therapy confronts the patient firmly and says, "Stop acting! Stop being an intellectual! Show me your real feelings"

Psychoanalysis, Dianetics, and The Therapy are all parts of one family. They all work on the prefrontal cortex, which is the part of the brain we use for thinking and planning. Most likely, the pain is not stored in the cortex. It is probably stored chemically someplace nearer to the brain stem, possibly the hippocampus.

Psychoanalysis, Dianetics and The Therapy would find the pain by finding just the right word or phrase that is connected to the pain. The right word or phrase might literally represent a specific nerve cell that stretches from the cortex down into the pile of pain somewhere near the brain stem.

Primal Therapy bypasses the prefrontal cortex, and goes right to the pile of pain. It stimulates the pain until it is forced to the surface, forced to complete an electrical circuit that began many years ago. And when the pain comes out, part of the electricity goes up that same nerve that is connected to the right word in the prefrontal cortex. And when that nerve is stimulated full force, the word comes out of the patient's mouth, more as a scream than a word, "Help!"

Psychoanalysis, Dianetics, and The Therapy are all similar. Each one evolved from and added to the one before it. Psychoanalysis gave us the subconscious, free association, and the use of dreams. It was on the right track, but it was too slow. Dianetics multiplied its speed by adding the process of asking questions and watching the viewing screen. Primal Therapy helped us to understand the cause of neurosis and the enormous quantity of pain, and it helped to clarify that feeling the pain, not just understanding, cure the illness.

The Therapy goes beyond all other therapies by adding some discoveries of it's own: the *obvious question,* the use of the *blindfold, progress dreams, doorways, doing therapy alone* with *movies* and *music,* the *spoonful theory,* and the *3 distinct kinds of reliving.*

The Power Of Isolation

When I first started looking for a self-cure for neurosis, I experimented with isolation because Janov had used it successfully in Primal Therapy.

In Janov's method, the patient isolates in a hotel room for one, two or three days before his first session…no TV, no books, no phone calls, nothing to do but think. Janov's theory, and I agree, is that the neurotic is constantly doing something to keep himself from noticing his old feelings. The neurotic must smoke, drink, chew gum, work, nibble, watch TV, theorize, or do something all day long.

Each neurotic has a different set of habits, and it is not always an obviously sick habit. It can be something as normal as reading or working. A person who has to read or work constantly might be doing it to control his pain.

The Therapy differs from Primal Therapy on this issue of isolation. In Primal Therapy the patient is supposed to *primal,* which means a *complete re-living* of a traumatic scene in 3-D stereo. Isolation is helpful to push the patient into feeling his pain.

In The Therapy, a total reliving is possible but rare. Most of the discharge will be indirect *symbolic reliving.* Isolation can stimulate too much pain and create defenses that the amateur therapist cannot break through. Still, isolation can be a useful tool, and so I'd like to tell you of my several experiments so you won't have to duplicate them.

In my first experiment, I isolated in my house for a day. I asked my wife and kids to sleep with a neighbor. After about 5 hours, I started to think about Karen. I cried a few tears, but nothing explosive. Even so, this was a minor success because it demonstrated that the old feelings were exerting a force of their own, and that's why we say that the question doesn't matter. Let me explain.

When I eventually tried Dianetics, the therapist ran me through a battery of questions for three hours while using an E-meter (an instrument similar to a lie detector) to measure my emotional response to the questions. The result of this scientific procedure was to reach the decision, "Let's start the therapy with this issue of Karen." She was right, of course, and I started crying immediately when I talked about the day that Karen had left. The therapist had helped me find the *mouth of the river.*

But we did not need the three hours of questions nor the E-meter to find it. I had found it myself accidentally, three years earlier during my first isolation experiment. The story of Karen was pushing itself to the surface all by itself, and that's why the question doesn't really matter. If you put on a blindfold, watch your picture screen and ask a broad question like, "What's the old feeling?" the *mouth of the river* will very likely present itself on your viewing screen.

In my second experiment, I isolated in a deserted farm house owned by a friend. Some people in the neighborhood thought I was a drifter, called the police, and I was very embarrassed when a group of ten "vigilantes" came knocking at the door. I explained my experiment, and they all went away laughing.

After two days, I had found no memories and no tears, and I began to suspect that isolation by itself was not enough. I was about to discover that the real power of Primal Therapy was isolation *plus* the anticipation of facing an unknown therapist.

In my third experiment, I hired Dr. Dunner, a psycho-analyst, to be the therapist. We scheduled a session for Monday morning, and I isolated in a nearby hotel room all day Saturday and Sunday. This combination of isolation and anticipation definitely worked! I had a terrifying nightmare that made me throw up. The nightmare was so thinly disguised that it was obviously a specific traumatic scene trying to come out of me.

When I got to Dr. Dunner's office, nothing significant happened because she did not know how, or had no interest in, pushing me into a primal. An experienced Primal therapist would have confronted and forced me to feel the pain, but Dr. Dunner used her usual psychoanalytic procedure. She just sat there and listened, and so nothing happened.

Even though I did not primal, I learned some valuable lessons. I had a glimpse of the enormous amount of pain that was stored inside of me, and I became convinced that a nightmare is an old scene trying to break through.

While both The Therapy and Primal Therapy can lead to a cure, there is a difference on this issue of isolation. In The Therapy, isolation can sometimes interfere with discharge. Let me explain:

When a patient isolates, a traumatic scene will come close to the surface, and the body will react by creating defenses. Smoking, eating and watching TV have been taken away from the patient, so he resorts to other defenses like yawning, giggling, theorizing and transferring feelings to the therapist or the monster under the bed. The Primal therapist must be skilled and forceful to break through these last ditch defenses and push the patient to a total reliving.

In The Therapy we don't expect a total reliving. We drain the pain out of a scene in *spoonfuls* by symbolic reliving. **Isolation works great if you plan to go all the way to a primal, but it can backfire if you only go halfway there.** It can cause the patient to put up so many defenses that you don't get any discharge at all...not even a symbolic discharge. The patient may experience a lot of terror, and end up with a bad headache...for nothing.

In fact, this is one reason why I know that headaches are old feelings coming up. Several times I have given myself a headache by isolation.

When Nancy and I started to develop our do-it-yourself therapy, we hoped to combine the best of Primal Therapy with the best of Dianetics and psychoanalysis. We had to reconsider the role of isolation, and we were especially interested in using isolation to break plateaus (See page 129).

The loudest most violent discharge I've ever experienced happened after a day of isolation. I isolated a day in my bedroom, then did therapy that night with no significant discharge. The next day I went to work and felt very strange all day. I felt light-headed, very calm, as if I were mildly drugged. That evening I laid down on the floor to do therapy. I put on the blindfold, and Nancy asked simply, "What's the feeling?"

Very soon some strange things started to happen. My words became slurred like a child learning to talk. My chest started to expand as though someone were pumping me full of air. My chest felt so big, I thought it would explode. My mouth was trying to say, "It's not words! It's not words!" I was experiencing feelings that could not be said as words. My effort to speak became a yell that got louder and louder and louder. Soon it was loud enough to wake up the neighbors. I yelled for 20 minutes and was vaguely aware that I was experiencing a scene that I had been working on in previous sessions. For 20 minutes, I was a baby, one year old, laying on my mom's bed with two pieces of glass stuck in the back of my head. It was very near a total reliving, and yet I don't think it was a primal. It was a compromise, a blend.

In spite of this one very obvious successful discharge, we've also done many isolations that did not lead to a discharge. In spite of our inconsistant results, we have arrived at a few usable conclusions:

1. Isolation in an effort to primal is a waste of energy without a trained Primal therapist. Most likely you'll experience terror and end up with a headache for nothing. If you want to try a total reliving, the best way to do it is to go to the Primal Institute.

2. In The Therapy, a day of isolation will probably not lead to an immediate discharge, although it may lead to discharge several days later. I suspect that the

isolation forces the feeling to the surface which forces you to put up defenses during the first session. Then during sleep, your brain does some rewiring to give you a controlled discharge the next day.

3. One big problem with isolation is the cost of a day away from work. If you're wealthy, you can get the job done quickly by going through Primal Therapy. But The Therapy is designed for people who can't afford to do that, and for most of us normal people, isolation is impractical because of cost.

4. A more affordable way to use isolation is to put on the blindfold and isolate one or two hours before you start a session. Even as little as 20 minutes isolation can be a big help. With a little luck, you'll find some feeling before the therapist arrives, and you might start crying when he asks his first question.

The question of whether to isolate will resolve itself quickly because the more you do the therapy, the more your mind will grow. You'll get interested in so many activities that pretty soon you won't have time to isolate, and you might not have any time for the therapy at all.

If you try isolation, and especially if you have some success with it, please write and tell us what you learn so we can include it in the second edition of this book.

Gagging

Early in my therapy, I felt a slight gagging feeling in the back of my throat. Janov had mentioned that his patients often use gagging as a last ditch *physical defense* just before they primal.

I suspected that the gagging was a signal that I was close to a total reliving, so I carefully re-read Janov's description, printed below, of how he pushed his patients into a primal:

"We do not discuss Primal theory or its validity, as many patients would like us to do. Each day an attempt is made to widen the hole in the defnese system until the patient can no longer defend himself. His first few days of therapy seem to parallel the first few years of the patient's life, before the occurrance of the primal scene that shut him down. He experiences isolated and discrete events in bits and pieces. As each fragment combines into a meaningful whole, the patient goes into a primal.

If the patient is being bright, humble, polite, obsequious, hostile, dramatic...whatever front he presents... it is forbidden in an effort to get him beyond the defense into the feeling. If the patient raises his knees or turns his head, he is made to lie straight. He may giggle or yawn as feelings arise, and this is immediately pointed out with impatience. He may try to change the subject, and that is stopped. Or he may literally swallow the feeling, as is true with many patients who swallow each time a feeling starts to come up. This is one reason we keep the mouth open.

As the patient discusses a new, early situation, we continue watching for signs of feeling. The voice may tremble slightly as if jostled by tension. We repeat the process of urging the patient to breathe and feel. This time, which may be an hour or two later, the patient is shaken. He won't know what the feeling is, just that he feels tense and "uptight"...that is tightened up against the feeling. I start the pulling and breathing process. The patient swears that he doesn't know what the feeling is. His throat becomes tight, and his chest feels as though there were a band around it. He begins gagging and retching. He says, "I'm going to throw up!" I inform him that it is a feeling and that he won't throw up. (No patient has actually vomited despite long periods of gagging.) I urge him to say the feeling even though the patient doesn't know what he is feeling. He will start to form a word only to begin thrashing about and writhing in pain. I urge him to let it out, and he will continue to try to say something. Finally, out it will come: a scream ..."Mommy, help!"[38]

I've said many times in this book that you will not likely have any success doing Primal Therapy at home, although it is not impossible. I for one have stopped trying, mainly because the gentler *symbolic reliving* works pretty well for me. And yet the gagging feeling was persistent. It was happening by itself, and so whenever I felt the gagging sensation, I would lay down on the floor, open my mouth and breathe deeply. I tried it on 20 different occasions with the same result. The gagging would turn into a few quick yells, but no scream and no reliving. Each time I tried it the yells got louder and louder. Finally, on one occasion, the yell was so loud and strong that I felt like it was tearing my throat out.

I never did primal that way, and I found no connections, but the physical strain of this powerful yell convinced me that Janov was telling the truth. Before your nervous system will let go of a total reliving, your body will put up a line of last minute *physical defenses:* swallowing, shallow breathing, physically holding yourself, yawning, giggling and gagging.

I haven't had the gagging feeling for a long time. I believe the gagging occurred early in therapy because I had a very big pile of pain, and my system was unbalanced. Since then I have discharged so many scenes and reduced my pile, and now I assume my nervous system is nicely balanced.

Looking back, it seems to me that *my gagging stopped about the time that my progress dreams started.* That statement has a clear meaning for me. I was gagging because early in therapy I was unbalancing everything. Then my Super Conscious started helping me. He gave me doorways and progress dreams. Together we have kept the whole system balanced and that's why I no longer gag. Pretty wierd.

Heart Attacks and Sleep Apnea

Many heart attacks happen during the night, and I've always wondered why. It's one of those issues, like headaches and schizophrenia, where the medical profession says, "We don't know for sure what causes it."

One possible explanation is that heart attacks are at least partially caused by blocked memories. If you've ever had a nightmare, you know how much fear and panic you can feel at night time. I am not saying that nightmares cause heart attacks, but rather that the nightmare demonstates the incredible power of the blocked memories.

When you are asleep, your brain has a serious dilemma. It must open the temporary file to process it's contents, without loosing control of the blocked memories. It's a delicate task, a little like trying to reach into a bee hive to remove the honey without disturbing the bees.

Janov has suggested that nightmares happen because we have lowered defenses at night.[39] I suspect that the problem is not lack of defenses. The real problem is that at night time, your brain has an impossible task, to open up the temporary file and simultaneously keep it closed.

How does your nervous system solve the problem? It undoubtedly does more than one thing. If you get close to an old feeling, your brain will simply wake you up and you would have insomnia. Also your brain might adjust the quantity of neurotransmitters. It might increase or decrease the sensitivity of some receptors. We have already talked about how your brain might indent the sleep switch, so the inner part does not make contact.

Another adjustment has to do with oxygen and it might explain night time and early morning heart attacks. Janov has pointed out that neurotics do not breathe deeply. They tend to hold their breath as a way of holding in feeling.[40] During therapy, Janov forces his patients to breathe more deeply as a way to start feeling again.[41]

But why does shallow breathing help us to control our feelings. It could be a symbolic symptom, or perhaps a hypnotic command. It is also possible that the nervous system is purposely trying to reduce the amount of oxygen in the blood, for the same reason that it might reduce the quantity of a neurotransmitter...to control a chemical reaction, and to prevent an explosion of old pain.

If neurotics tends to hold their breath in the daytime, they might do the same thing at night time. It's called *sleep apnea*. It means the neurotic stops breathing for 10 or 15 seconds, and sometimes up to 60 seconds, resulting in very low levels of oxygen in the blood. The low oxygen can cause abnormal heart beat irregularities and even death by heart attack.[42]

It's another one of these issues that will take a billion dollars to prove. I wanted to tell you about it because it is the reason why we discourage people with a pre-existing heart condition or sleep apnea from doing The Therapy. (See cautions at the beginning of the book.)

The sad truth is that you're at risk either way. In theory, The Therapy might stir up old pain and contribute to your sleep apnea. But if you don't do The Therapy, your old blocked pain might contribute to a heart attack anyway.

Research on Tears

Crying is one of those subjects, like yawning and headaches, that is not completely understood by scientists. One researcher, biochemist William H. Frey, II, Director of Dry Eye and Tear Research Center at the St. Paul-Ramsey Medical Center, has made some startling discoveries in recent years.[43]

There are three kinds of tears: *cleansing* tears that continually wash the eye, *irritant* tears produced in response to smoke, dust and other irritants, and finally *emotional* tears. I bet you've already guessed that we are mainly interested in emotional tears.

If you cut the facial nerves that seem to control tears, the *cleansing* tears and *irritant* tears will stop. But the *emotional* tears will keep coming. It appears that the emotional tears work on a separate system.

Emotional tears have a different chemical make-up than the other two. They contain more proteins and other chemical substances that the body uses during stress. Frey has suggested that *emotional* tears might be a part of the body's waste-disposal-system. If you consider that a neurotic probably stores his blocked memories physically in the form of chemicals, then it is easy to imagine the possibility that when a neurotic cries, those blocked chemicals are released out of the brain through tears. I can tell you from experience of hundreds of hours of bawling that the chemicals might also be released through nasal fluids.

FOOTNOTES CHAPTER 10

1. Jonathan Winson, *Brain & Psyche,* pp. 72-75.
2. L. Ron Hubbard, *Dianetics,* pp. 63-69.
3. Dr. David Cheek, "UCLA Neurosciences Lecture," *Primal Man,* p. 263.
4. Jonathan Winson, *Brain & Psyche,* pp. 53-59.
5. In 1951 Kleitnan and Aserinsky demonstrated that dreams can be measured in humans and in mammals because of changes in EEG and because of REM (Rapid Eye Movement) during dreams.
6. This discovery is based on an experimental operation by Dr. William Scoville in which he removed most of the hippocampus and amygdala from a patient he called H.M., at Hartford Hospital, Dept. of Neurosurgery, Hartford, Conn., 1953.
7. Jonathan Winson, *Brain & Psyche,* pp. 181-190.
8. Gershon and Rieder, "Major Disorders of Mind and Brain," *Scientific American,* Sept. 1992, pp. 127-129.
9. James Clash, "Relief for Migraine Sufferers," *Forbes,* p. 126.
10. Janov and Holden, *Primal Man,* pp. 407-409, pp. 174-175.
11. Dr. Donald Mendor, *The Myth of Neuropsychiatry,* p. 25.
12. Vitamins A, B6, D, and niacin can have side effects in extremely high doses. Niacin can cause skin to flush red and feel hot for 15 minutes. It is temporary and harmless. Minerals can cause problems in metalic form but are believed to be safe in organic form. Lead

and other heavy metals can be removed from blood by vitamin C. Also individual vitamins can be toxic if you have pre-existing illness.

Most toxicity can be avoided by taking a full spectrum multi vitamin-mineral supplement. It can be ineffective or dangerous to just take one vitamin or one mineral without all of the others.

13. Durk Pearson and Sandy Shaw, *Life Extension,* pp. 125-136, pp. 167-195.
14. Same.
15. Same.
16. Durk Pearson and Sandy Shaw, *Life Extension,* p. 135.
17. Janov and Holden, *Primal Man,* p. 288.
18. Durk Pearson and Sandy Shaw, *Life Extension,* pp. 125-136, pp. 167-195.
19. Same.
20. Same.
21. Same.
22. Same.
23. Linus Pauling, *How to Live Longer and Feel Better,* p. 17.
24. Linus Pauling, pp. 53-59. Also Pearson and Shaw, p. 425.
25. Linus Pauling, *How to Live Longer and Feel Better,* pp. 243-263.
26. Same.
27. L. Ron Hubbrad, *Dianetics,* p. 444
28. Dr. Joel Wallach, *Let's Play Doctor,* p. 50.
29. Linus Pauling, *How to Live Longer and Feel Better,* pp. 243-263.
30. For most vitamins, our ancestors would have gotten about 3 times the RDA. But for vitamin C, they got about 2.3 grams or forty times the RDA. Linus Pauling, *How To Live Longer and Feel Better.*
31. Linus Pauling, *How to Live Longer and Feel Better.* Read the whole book.
32. Dr. Joel Wallach, *Dead Doctors Don't Lie,* speech given in Kansas City, 1994.

33. Sigmund Freud, *The Interpretation of Dreams,* p. 135, p. 647.
34. James Hall, *Jung: Interpreting Your Dreams,* cassette. Also Jonathon Winson, *Brain & Psyche,* pp. 142-146.
35. L. Ron Hubbard, *Dianetics.*
36. Arthur Janov, *Primal Scream.* Read the whole book.
37. Dr. Jonathon Winson, *Brain & Psyche.* Read the whole book.
38. Arthur Janov, *Primal Scream,* p. 83.
39. Same, p. 264.
40. Same, pp. 260-271.
41. Same, p. 82.
42. Kristie Willert, APR, "When Your Dreams Are Nightmares," *Health Newsletter,* Des Moines General Hospital.
43. Samual A. Schreiner, "Why Do We Cry?", *Readers Digest,* pp. 141-144, Feb., 1987.

11

Meet The Family

TOM. I wasn't aware of any emotional problems before I got married, but during the first week after the wedding, I became morbidly depressed, almost suicidal. It was the worst week in my life...*at least it was the worst week I was able to recall.*

Before being married, I had many symptoms that should have been obvious: headaches, shyness, difficulty falling asleep; but I had no idea what neurosis was. The only symptom that was really a problem for me was my difficulty with reading. It would sometimes take me a whole hour to dig through a single page. I once took a remedial reading class and I was the slowest reader in the class full of other slow readers. I made it through college by majoring in two subjects that required little reading, mathematics and art.

Our marriage was unhappy from the very first day and our sex life was miserable. Eventually we found our way to a marriage counselor. After 9 months of weekly sessions, our counselor informed us, "I would like to continue working with Nancy, but I think that Tom should see a psychoanalyst." I was insulted. I remember thinking, "There's nothing wrong with me! My wife Nancy is the one who's sick!"

The counselor referred me to a doctor named Ada Dunner. She was a skilled psychoanalyst and she had a lot of wisdom. I went to weekly sessions for about a year, and I learned the power of *free-association*, which means that the patient should say everything that goes through his mind, no matter how silly, rude, embarrassing, or irrelevant. It is the number one tool of psychoanalysis.

In all the sessions with Dr. Dunner, I cried briefly only once, and I didn't find even one blocked memory, and yet I learned one important lesson that would change my life forever: I discovered that it wasn't just my wife who was sick. It might be me. **I discovered that I was neurotic.**

I still remember the moment. I was talking in normal free-association style and all of a sudden I said something that surprised me. I said, "Do you like me?"

I did not like Dr. Dunner. She was old and wrinkled and fat. So why would I care if she liked me. It was as though someone else had said it…someone inside of me…someone I had never met before. The Tom Stone that I was aware of "didn't give a damn what she thought." It was my first *pop-in*. It was my first clue that there was a hidden part of me.

About 3 years later, I was watching the Johnny Carson Show, and Arthur Janov was the special guest. Janov said that he had discovered a cure for neurosis. I immediately ran out and bought his book, *The Primal Scream*. His book taught me a second big lesson: that neurosis is caused by painful childhood events that you can't remember, events usually before the age of 8.

Janov's Primal Therapy is based on the theory that a neurotic must do something all day long to keep his memories blocked. He must smoke or drink or watch TV or get into mischief or make jokes or argue or be a workaholic… anything to distract his mind from the blocked memories trying to come up. His method is simple but tough: isolate the neurotic in a room for one day so he can't do those things, and the blocked memories will be forced to the surface. It works a hundred times faster than psychoanalysis.

I was not able to go to Primal Therapy because it required $6000 cash and six months in California away from my job. Even though I could not afford to go, I became a Primal Therapy enthusiast. I subscribed to their quarterly journal, and I tried experiments on my own, hoping to find a way to cure my own neurosis at home.

On one occasion, I experimented with isolation and hired Dr. Dunner to play the role of Primal Therapist. I arranged to isolate all day Saturday and Sunday, and then have a session with her on Monday morning.

The experiment was a partial success and also a failure. The isolation did bring me close to a blocked scene. I had the most terrifying nightmare I've ever had. It scared me so much that I threw up. Nightmares are blocked memories trying to come up, so they must be disguised to stop the blocked memory. The disguise of this nightmare was paper thin, and it's meaning was frighteningly clear.

In Janov's language, I was very close to a primal, which means a *total reliving* of a blocked scene. In a primal the patient is not just piecing together a puzzle, but rather he's experiencing the whole event in 3-dimensional stereo. He's actually there laying in his baby bed while Mom and Dad are drunk and arguing. He can even smell the liquor. And as the patient relives the scene, he bawls and screams out the feeling that he's been holding back since early childhood.

I was very close to primalling, but I didn't. Dr. Dunner did not know how to be a Primal Therapist. She did not know how to push me over the edge, but how could she know? I realize now that I was asking too much of her.

The experience convinced me more than ever that I was carrying around a lot of blocked pain. I wanted to find a way to cure my own illness without the help of a professional counselor, because as wonderful as they all were, I had never met a professional therapist who knew how, or had any interest in, finding blocked memories.

Several years later I met a young man named Brett, and he told me about Dianetics, which is a therapy method developed by Hubbard. Hubbard was a very strange fellow of questionable reputation and a lot of bad publicity, but his first therapy book contains some useful ideas. I read the book cover to cover. It claimed to produce the same result as Primal Therapy, but the method was totally different, with no isolation, no primalling.

Janov's book was simple and self-evident. Hubbard's book was complex and confusing. Hubbard had developed his own technical language. He called it "auditing" instead of "therapy." I didn't believe the book. It sounded like nonsense, and yet I wanted to try it because it held the potential of a cure *at home using an amateur therapist.*

Brett helped me find an experienced therapist who lived in Omaha named Julie. For ten weeks in a row I commuted from Des Moines, and I did therapy all day Saturday and Sunday.

Julie was amazed at how fast I whizzed through the process. I was finding scene after scene of blocked memories, and I was bawling my eyes out. She said that I was the easiest subject she had ever worked with and my insights were amazing. She said that her other patients were "like pulling teeth" to get them to remember anything.

I was very excited about my progress. I was actually seeing symptoms disappear. My headaches went away, my sleep improved, and my energy started to multiply.

As much as Julie helped me, we eventually had to confront our conflicting beliefs. I had been schooled in Primal Therapy which taught that if you **get all the pain out,** symptoms disappear. She had been taught that beyond 25 to 100 hours she should stop working on childhood scenes and change to a different procedure, a procedure I can best describe as "working on skills of the spirit" instead of blocked pain.

When she suggested changing the procedure, I became suspicious. My common sense told me that "If something is working, why change it?" Julie and Brett both told me that if I continue to dig out the childhood scenes, I would get more and more negative.

Julie gave me some research that suggested (assuming I read it right) that I might be incurable from their viewpoint. I was very confused. Julie had brought me so far. But what she was saying seemed illogical. It seemed self-evident to me that if reliving *some* blocked scenes would make *some* symptoms go away, then reliving *all* of them would probably make *all* of my symptoms go away.

Eventually I stopped going to Julie. We are still friends and I try to call her once a year. She had given me a wonderful start. I continued to use some of Julie's methods at home with Nancy as my therapist.

About this time, Nancy wanted to start therapy, and I became her therapist. We developed our own procedure that combined what we had learned from Julie with what we knew of Primal Therapy and psychoanalysis.

We worked every evening and continued to find more pain. I can easily understand now where Julie and Brett got their ideas. As more and more pain came up, I began to experience *death feelings*. For six months I was dull and emotionless. I was obsessed with death. I actually spent my lunch hours driving through a grave yard. It was my favorite place. That probably sounds morbid to some people. I was reliving a time when I had almost died.

The biggest problem Nancy and I had as we were doing therapy was that we didn't know where the end was...we didn't know if there was an end. At times I feared that Julie and Brett were right. It did seem like I was getting more negative. But we continued the sessions. We found more memories, more bawling. At last the day came when we could see the light at the end of the tunnel. My *death feelings* were over, and they have not returned. More and more symptoms disappeared. My energy continued to improve. My mind was growing and expanding. I began to read and study. I joined several self-improvement groups. I was 30 years behind the rest of the world and I had a lot of catching up to do.

Throughout all of this therapy, I kept notes religiously, and if you try this method I recommend that you keep notes. It's the only way to know for sure that you're making progress. It's been so long since I've had a headache or a nightmare that I sometimes wonder if I ever did. The only way to know for sure is to look at my past notes.

In my search for a way to cure myself, I have been intrigued by the differences between Primal Therapy and Dianetics. They claim to produce the same result, yet in many ways they are opposites. Dianetics is gentle, Primal Therapy is rough. Dianetics is like reprogramming a computer, one word at a time. Primal Therapy is like turning up the voltage and forcing all the disconnected wires to reconnect at once.

It is the comparison of these two opposite therapies that has given me a sort of 3-dimensional view of neurosis and how to cure it. The method in this book can be viewed as a combination of these two opposite therapies. Psychoanalysis is also part of the mix, but I view Dianetics as an extension of Psychoanalysis.

As the author of this book, I have had some occasion to doubt myself, and you would be within your rights to ask some questions. I'm reminded of the old joke from Mutt & Jeff comic strip: Jeff was under arrest for disorderly conduct, and he was pleading his case before the judge. "Well, Your Honor, I must admit, I've been acting a little crazy lately. I guess I'm guilty." With that the judge declared, "Guilty! Take him away! Next case!" Jeff protested, "Wait a minute, Your Honor. Why did you find me guilty?" to which the judge answered, "I thought I heard you admit that you've been acting crazy." Then Jeff said, " Yes, Your Honor, but are you going to take the word of a crazy man?"

Who is Thomas Stone? If he is or was neurotic, how can you trust his findings? Does he have a college degree in psychology? What are his credentials?

The whole concept of credentials is a little misleading. Orville Wright had no credentials when he invented the airplane. If he lived today, the police would arrest him for flying without a license.

In very old fields of study, credentials make sense. In architecture, for example, a college degree is and should be required. The study of architecture is 2000 years old. 95% of the knowledge is proven fact and only 5% is open for debate.

In the study of neurosis, the numbers are reversed. 5% is proven fact and 95% is open for debate. Compared to other sciences, the study of neurosis is very young, less than 100 years old. They've just begun to scratch the surface. The total lack of factual knowledge is evidenced by the wide variety of competing therapies. There are over 250 different methods practiced in the United States today.

It is difficult to develop an objective, factual, science of the mind because it is impossible to observe accurately what is going on when the illness is caused, and difficult to observe what happens when it is cured. There is only one person who can observe the cause and the cure first hand, and it's not the therapist. It's the patient. Only the patient has a front row seat. The therapist hears everything second hand.

Frankly, I'm convinced that all neurotics have an accurate power of observation within their own mind. **Mentally ill people aren't stupid. Even people with multiple personalities have been shown to be very intelligent.**

Who is Thomas Stone? Thomas Stone is a neurotic with a gift for accurate observation and reporting. I have been given a wonderful talent. Julie said l was the easiest patient she ever worked on, and I know what she meant. My mind was digging through the blocked scenes faster and more naturally than anything I've ever done in my life.

The Therapy that Nancy and I have developed is more effective than anything I have seen in the professional community. Nancy went to a professional marriage counselor and a professional psychiatrist, with no results to speak of. No tears, no blocked memories, no symptoms cured, yet she has made wonderful progress using The Therapy.

Our method is based on discoveries from psychoanalysis, Primal Therapy and Dianetics...plus many of my own. These discoveries came to me as hunches and intuition, almost as if the book were being written through me instead of by me.

I cannot prove anything in this book. It is not for me to say that everything in the book is true. I leave that to future scientists. I expect millions of people will eventually read this book. If they will try these methods, if they will cry and remember blocked scenes, if they will see their symptoms disappear, they will be the proof that this book is true.

All I can do is write it down the way it has been given to me from whatever power is guiding my hand. I follow the talent inside of me, and trust future generations to properly interpret what I have written.

Many of Sigmund Freud's discoveries seem a little silly by today's standards. Like all observers of the mind (including myself) his findings were prejudiced by his own unique emotional problems, and so today he is considered a little inaccurate. And yet how quickly we forget that before he came along, we used to think that mentally ill people were possessed by the devil and we would burn them at the stake.

The human race learns very slowly. Many of our lessons are learned at great cost over several generations. Architecture, medicine, dentistry, astronomy, physics, food processing, have all developed from thousands of years of accumulated trial and error. And the study of neurosis is no different. It is the youngest and perhaps the most important of all sciences. Try to imagine what society might be like, what kind of achievements would be possible if every person in the society were perfectly mentally healthy, no emotional problems, no addictions, no learning disabilities. Imagine every one with a photographic memory and the ability to master any goal that he set for himself.

In 1993 as I write these words, my favorite television series is Star Trek. Some people view that show as a fantasy, a fairy tale. But to me Star Trek is a vision of what is to come for mankind, and I suspect that Gene Roddenberry, the creator of the series, was trying to tell us something.

NANCY. I'm not sure what I can add to this book except my testimonial. Tom is much more knowledgeable than I on the subject of neurosis. He has studied the subject for 20 years.

The changes in Tom have been many. He has become much more affectionate, more giving, more open-minded, he reads better, and he's less forgetful. He used to have no sense of time. He was always late but is much more prompt now. He likes people better and also likes animals better. In fact, he has made our outdoor cat an indoor cat. She loves to cuddle up beside him and take a nap. He's more aware and appreciative of his surroundings, notices the sunshine, the fall leaves and the clouds in the sky. One of my favorite changes in him is the fact that he doesn't procrastinate any more. In the past, if I asked him to fix or do something around the house or yard, it could take him months to get it done. Now he says, "let's do it now." It's almost too fast for me. I may be preparing him for the weekend and he's ready to get it done right now.

When Tom and I first went to a marriage counselor I did not understand the concept of neurosis. I always knew that there was something missing in the way I was raised. My mother was a workaholic and my father an alcoholic with a bad temper. I never remembered any physical touching, hugs, holding, setting on laps, any kisses, never any complimentary words. I never heard the words "I love you" in my parents' home. I had no idea the damage that was being done to me.

The general attitude of my parents was that "children were to be seen and not heard." I hated that phrase. It was as if I had no rights, I wasn't allowed to express myself. I had to hold everything inside. I was afraid a lot and there was never anyone to comfort me or take the fear away. I always suffered through the fear alone. I became extremely introverted.

I had seen Tom become more and more interested in his mental health by going to the counselor, then the psychiatrist. After starting The Therapy he began to grow rapidly. As I saw the changes in him I realized that I would have to grow also or I would be left behind emotionally, then we would have another set of problems that could destroy our marriage. One day I asked our daughter to help me do The Therapy. That broke the ice. Soon I was Tom's patient as well as his therapist.

Tom seemed to be a natural at doing The Therapy but it was a bit more difficult for me to get started. I would talk about present day problems a lot. It was hard for me to get back into my childhood. I was so shy and embarrassed about everything that I know I held back during the therapy sessions. I was afraid of showing my real feelings, of being open and vulnerable. After all, I was never allowed to express myself as a child and wasn't loved. Could I show the real inner me to Tom and have him love me? Ironically, that is what did bring us closer. We have heard each others' pain, fears, doubts and insecurities resulting from our childhood traumas. We've witnessed each other struggling to get ahold of the fragments of the blocked scenes. We have cried buckets of tears together and it has brought us closer and closer through the years. We have become best friends. After all, isn't a best friend someone you can share everything with? And shouldn't your partner in life be your best friend?

My childhood days were repetitious. We hardly ever went anywhere or did anything other than work. My father had daily temper tantrums so I tried to stay away from him. The days were always the same so I had a hard time finding details of scenes. Actually, we discovered that "always the same" was a programmed command.

There were some violent scenes I remembered when my father was drunk. I would awake in the middle of the night to the noise of my parents fighting. There were times when it was so bad that my father broke furniture. One year he knocked over the Christmas tree and threw things everywhere. It was during therapy that I remembered *how* afraid I had been.

My mom had been sick a lot while I was young. She would suddenly be taken away and I was given no explanation. I had blocked this out and through The Therapy realized that I thought she was never coming back. I had always cried in movie scenes where people were saying good-bye or returning home after being gone a long time, and I hadn't understood why until I did the therapy.

Everyone's old feelings and blocked memories are different. They were created in different ways. Even people with good childhoods can have old feelings. For example, being left in a hospital by yourself or having your parent leave home for awhile can leave a child feeling abandoned. Having a friend or relative die or leave and not being allowed to grieve. As you can well imagine everyone's therapy will be somewhat different. But I believe that anyone can use this method to find the tears that will begin to relieve their pain.

I still have some blocked memories and I have some that are not complete but I have come far enough to have improved my life a great deal.

When I went to the marriage counselor I didn't learn anything new. She was nice and comforting. I cried very little and only about present time problems. The 50 minute sessions were restrictive. I would barely be getting into the session and the time would be up and I'd have to wait a week to start all over again. The psychiatrist was worse. The only time he would speak was to say "come in and lie down" and "time's up." I had questions about the process but he would be perfectly silent and refuse to answer me. I soon thought I'd be better off talking to a wall.

When I started The Therapy with Tom it was slow at first. I had held everything inside me for a long time and had certain periods of my life blocked. After a therapy session I would feel tired and sluggish. Crying often left me with a headache. It would sometimes take me 2 days to rebalance and feel normal again. I did the therapy intensively for about 2 years. I then started to do it whenever I felt it necessary. It could be once a month or once every 6 months. It takes a lot of time at first so you get to the point where you're glad to be able to spend some time on other things. I still have old feelings come up sometimes. I don't know if we'll ever know exactly where the end is. The process is so much easier and quicker now so if an old feeling does keep nagging at me I can do 2 or 3 sessions and feel okay again.

The benefits I have gotten out of The Therapy are many. I am more positive, more supportive of others, less critical, resentful and jealous. I am more patient and hardly ever get irritated. If I ever do feel irritable, I know that it is an old feeling inside me and has nothing to do with the situation or people at hand. I read faster and comprehend what I read much better. Also, my memory has improved. I struggled in high school and college with reading, did poorly on tests and always got just average grades. I went back to our community college a few years ago and got a second degree. I graduated with honors with a 3.94 grade point average. I was amazed at how much easier it was than before. I did well on tests, in fact the younger students would give me a hard time because my test scores would make the grading curve higher.

I'm not shy anymore. I am friendlier, I have a better sense of humor and am more giving. But best of all is that

I have a much, much better relationship with Tom and our three children.

Through doing The Therapy I believe I've become a better parent. I also believe that one of my purposes in life was to stop the cycle of bad parenting. Tom and I were not perfect parents but we knew we had to do better than our parents. We have taught our children the importance of being the best parents possible. They all will be better parents than we were. And we could not have done this without The Therapy.

If you read this book and don't want to do The Therapy that's okay. But I hope you at least learn the importance of being a better parent. A child's psyche is very delicate. A child needs to know he is always loved. He needs to express himself, to be able to feel his pain and fears, and to know the parent is there to comfort him. It takes a lot of patience and understanding to raise a child but it is the most important job you will ever do. The child needs limits and discipline but the discipline needs to be given in a kind and loving manner. He needs to be programmed with positiveness and support so that he will grow up to be the best he can be and not held back by a neurotic mind.

An excellent book or tape I would recommend is "Children of Trauma" by Jane Middleton-Moz. She describes many situations of trauma that effect children and she tells of three steps that will help the child deal with the trauma so they are not scarred for life.

One last comment I would like to make is that if you do decide to do this therapy, **be committed.** This process takes work and dedication on the part of both the patient and the therapist. It can be very slow and it can make you feel worse at times. It should be done on a regular schedule, about every 2 to 3 days. There will be times when you wonder if you should have ever started. Once you open the "can of worms," you can't go back. And so you'll continue on not knowing what's ahead or where the end is. But one thing is for sure, once you've gone far enough you will be so glad that you had the courage to do it. You can be a happier and more content person. Your relationships will be stronger and you will know that it was all worth while.

BETH. I decided to do the therapy because I was depressed and my life was going nowhere. I wasn't happy from day to day and I didn't have any proper direction. I felt miserable most of the time. I knew I needed to do something. Mom and Dad were already doing The Therapy so I asked Dad to help me do it too. My husband and I were living about 150 miles from home, so Dad sent us a few hand-written pages to tell us how to do it. There was no book at that time.

The therapy was the first step for me. It freed me. It cleaned out all the bullshit so that I could go on and learn new things. I'm still quite sensitive emotionally, however, The Therapy got most of my old feelings and negative images of the past out of my way, so that I could go on. Now, I am happy day-to-day. I'm not depressed at all any more. I have direction in my life. I love my life now. I'm not afraid of the future. I used to be really afraid and confused all the time. I don't feel afraid and confused at all. My health is better.

I smoked marijuana through my teen years and early adult years. Pot kept me unbalanced, made me much more sensitive to the way people felt and how they felt about me, and it made my eating problems and depression worse. Its hard to say, if it wasn't for the pot making me more miserable, maybe I wouldn't have been miserable enough to try the therapy. And if it wasn't for the pot, maybe I wouldn't have been so hypersensitive to my own feelings and thoughts. Maybe it helped my therapy, I don't know. Maybe it made it harder. After doing therapy, I found the courage and strength to quit smoking pot. **I did it,** not The Therapy or anyone else. **I am now strong** enough to take the steps to create the life I deserve.

I remember when I used to sit every night and get stoned and then I would become so lazy that I wouldn't even get up to go to the bathroom, get a blanket if I was cold or change the channel. I would just sit there. During therapy I realized that, gosh, I'm responsible, I owe myself my comfort. And it was really stupid to just sit there and be cold. I owed it to my body to get up and get myself a blanket. That's how lazy and depressed I was.

I used to have tension in my shoulder every single day. Now I don't. I still do when I am having a stressful day but it's not a daily thing anymore. It's very rare now. I used to have eating problems, intestinal cramping, spastic colon, heartburn, esophagus reflux very bad, and a very poor appetite. I don't know how much of that was due to smoking pot. I know that played a part in it also. But, I don't have eating problems at all now. I don't have mood swings. I used to be happy one day, depressed the next day. I basically feel steady and balanced all the time.

I also used to be very obsessive about men and it was extremely miserable, painful and torturous. Now my obsessions have decreased, almost completely gone.

My nightmares have decreased. My nightmares used to be about things that were not within my control and now whenever I have a bad dream I always conquer the evil thing that is trying to get me. It's like now **I have the control.** I have control of my life now where my life used to be out of my control. The change in my dreams shows a big difference in the way that I handle things now.

It was really scary for me at times. Three years was a long time to do therapy, being miserable and crying all the time. I didn't know if it was going to end. That was basically my only problem with The Therapy, not knowing if I would ever feel better. I was depressed and all alone. Mom and dad were never scared like me during therapy.

My husband helped a little at first but he really didn't know anything about The Therapy. He couldn't read the book because it wasn't written yet. I used to phone my Dad long distance and do therapy over the phone for an hour. But in between talking to Dad, I had some pretty scary times. One of the biggest things I want to say in this book is that even if you feel you are at your lowest, feel suicidal or worthless, or like there is no reason to keep going, you should always keep going because **it will get better!!!** You always have to hang on to that fact.

Around the time that I was at my very lowest, my most scared, this lady walked into my office one day at work. I was suppose to interview her and she ended up interviewing me for about 45 minutes. She told me about when she was depressed and she used to scream and cry every day for a couple of years. She told me how horrible it felt and how much she has her life together now. She reassured me that things really would get better. She was like an angel that came to me to give me that message. So I want people to know that even though the therapy is hard, scary and lonely, for Mom, Dad and myself, it really helped us, we all really did get better. Sometimes things get worse before they get better.

My therapy went differently than Dad and Mom's. It gave me a release for my cooped up feelings that I had held in for years and it definitely cleared me out. I never had much luck with my picture screen. That's what is so great about The Therapy, it can fit each different person. I can't say that I was neurotic or screwed up but I definitely had some old feelings. I definitely had some things to let out. Don't feel like you are doing it wrong or it's not working if something doesn't go the way it went for us. That's what's so great about The Therapy. I think it will automatically start working for each person.

I still have problems, I still have old feelings, I still get my feelings hurt, etc. However, now **I have the courage and strength to change what I need to, and to *do* what I need to, with my life.** I no longer have fears, confusion, depression, addictions, lack of interest and lack of direction, etc., blocking me and holding me back. It's like I feel all "cleaned out." I have the power and control in my life now.

The Therapy has changed both my parents. Dad still amazes me. He's much more loving, outgoing and happy, much more natural, cheerful, and full of life. All through my childhood he seemed dull, dead inside, and sad. I remember when I was a kid, I used to see him like a sad little boy. I cried about that a lot in my therapy. But I don't see him that way now. He seems strong and positive, happy and true to himself. Mom is very accepting now, a lot less tense, a lot more open-minded, outgoing, and she's in control of her life. It definitely helped both my parents.

The Therapy is a way out. **It is a way to help you to change your own life.** I haven't read the whole book because it's not finished yet. But the chapters I have read are put together very well and I think it's a wonderful thing. I think it can help a lot of people. It sure did help us.

I guess that's all I need to say. I want people to know that they can certainly call or write to me anytime. I think it's important that people can get ahold of us because going through such a major change in your life can be hard, lonely and scary. Somebody may be doing The Therapy on their own with no therapist, nobody else that really understands.

DAVID. As a child, I remember my father talking about neurosis, and how it affected his life in many ways. At that time I didn't understand but as I grew older I realized how it affects me and many people around me.

I haven't done therapy yet, though I think about it alot. I guess I'm a little scared and unsure.

I'm 25 years old and just starting to realize I need a solution to my problems. After seeing the changes in my family as a result of The Therapy, I believe this to be the most logical solution.

My parents started therapy years ago and I've seen many changes in them. My Mother changed more than my Dad. She is stronger, more open-minded and understanding than ever. My Dad improved his reading skills, he is less forgetful. He is more decisive. He's more emotional. He even likes animals, though he hadn't in the past.

Every day I deal with my own neurotic problems. A beautiful girl walks by and I'd like to talk to her, but my nerves take over and I turn away. I let people take advantage of me because I'm afraid of standing up for myself. I have addictions that I want to quit but can't seem to control.

I would like to change some of these things in myself. I hope to in the near future.

I also hope this therapy method will help millions of people, and help solve many problems for future generations.

Appendix **A**

The Questions

In this appendix, we will give you a list of 76 questions to help you get started. This may seem like a lot to learn, and yet you will learn them naturally when you understand the reasons behind them.

If you can understand why the questions are asked, you'll learn them quickly, and you will find yourself rewording them so they feel more natural for you. You will even create new questions of your own, and that's what I want you to do. We are all different, and sometimes changing one subtle word can make an enormous improvement in the effect of a question. If you do therapy in another language, you'll have to create your own questions.

To make things even simpler, you don't have to use all of the 76 questions. You can do therapy for weeks and months, with just one question. The question you will use the most is "What's the feeling?" It is a shortened way of asking "What is the one feeling that is trying to come up by itself?"

■ **STARTING QUESTIONS.** At the beginning of therapy the patient may be distracted without knowing it. He may claim to be ready but in reality he is hungry, or sleepy, or mad at his boss, or worried about the therapist telling secrets, or nervous about people in the next room. The purpose of the starting questions is to discover and eliminate those distractions.

Another purpose is to look at those distractions because they may actually be old feelings trying to surface. For example, if the patient is mad at his boss, and if he talks about it for a while, he may clarify a specific feeling, "My boss never notices my work." Then he may find tears when he remembers, "My Dad never noticed."

Here are the starting questions:

> How do you feel? Any strange body feelings?
> Is there something on your mind?
> Anything you'd like to talk about?
> Do you have a present time problem?
> Have you had a recent misunderstanding?
> Do you have negative feelings about this therapy?
> What question would you like me to ask?
> What is the feeling ?

■ **CORE QUESTIONS.** These questions get right to the core of the neurosis. In effect they all ask the same question in different ways. They all ask "What happened to you when you were little?" That basic core question rarely gets a direct answer, and yet the entire therapy is the answer to the question. After a year of therapy you may have uncovered 15 traumatic scenes. You may have found them by using the indirect questions. The discharge may have come in small spoonfuls. But you did get an answer.

The core questions are important because they shake the wires, loosen the log jam, rattle the drawer full of junk, and they tell the Super Conscious that you're aiming for a total cure, and you need him to "get to work on it." My favorite core questions are:

> Can you remember the most unhappy day in
>   your life?
> Why did you have to split?
> Why did you stop feeling?
> What is the one feeling that is trying to come up?
> What is the feeling?
> What is the old feeling?
> What do you want more than anything in
>   the world?
> What happened to you when you were little?

Why did you have to stop being yourself?
Why can't you scream?
Why can't you finish the therapy?
What was the worst physical pain in your
    childhood?
What was the worst emotional pain in your
    childhood?
Did someone leave you?
Did someone die?

■ **INDIRECT (OR "SCAN") QUESTIONS.** I think it was Freud who first discovered what he called "transference." A simple example of transference is when you feel anger at your boss so you kick the cat. That's a simple example, but not a real good one. You may not really understand transference until you experience it in your therapy.

Transference means that when an old feeling starts to surface, for example, a feeling that "Dad never noticed me," you will feel the "not noticed," but you won't be aware that the feeling is about Dad. You'll have the feeling, but no one to aim it at. So you might feel it toward your spouse. Your spouse will try to convince you that he does indeed notice you. But no amount of talk will convince you. This is transference. Neurotics do it constantly. It happens automatically and unconsciously. The neurotic is unaware that he is doing it.

It takes a great intelligence to spot transference in yourself because it just plain feels exactly like your spouse never notices you. Neurotics transfer feeling onto their spouse, kids, boss, fellow workers, politicians, neighbors, football teams, pets, and hammers. Perhaps the easiest transfer you can see in yourself is to think of a movie that makes you cry, for example, *West Side Story*. When you see Tony die in Maria's arms you feel that painful loss...but you weren't in love with Tony. You are really crying about someone you lost, some one you loved a long, long time ago, but you can't remember who it was. You may have lost someone when you were 3 years old, and you have *transferred* the feeling to Tony and Maria.

Since 90% of all old feelings will be felt *indirectly* and *symbolically* before the memory can be viewed, and since 90% of old feelings will be *transferred* onto the wrong object, indirect questions can be very useful when the core questions seem to get no results. Go down the list and ask each question. Most of them may have no effect. Don't panic, just go to the next question. Sooner or later you'll find one question on the list that will spark the patient's interest, and he will become talkative. The very fact that he is talking fast will tell you that the question has sparked an old feeling.

This is a designed systematic list. It is a checklist. It is designed to touch on every person or object that could possibly be the object of a transfer. This is one time when the patient should not decide the question. The patient may object to one of these questions and five minutes later he will be bawling about the very question he did not want to use.

Indirect questions are helpful for a patient who has difficulty with free association. If the patient has nothing to say, ask all of the questions on this list. Sooner or later you'll find a question that will make him talk freely.

Here is our list of INDIRECT QUESTIONS. I also call them "SCAN" questions because they scan all the possible objects of transferred feeling. I might also call them "TRANSFERANCE" questions. All three names are descriptive. This is a carefully designed list. I don't recommend changing it very much:

> What's the feeling?
> Tell me about your dream.
> Is there a movie that makes you cry?
> Is there a song that makes you cry?…book?…story?
> Is there something you don't understand
> about yourself?
> What do you want more than anything in
> the world?
> Is there someone (or some group) that irritates
> you?
> Is there someone you'd like to be closer to?

> Is there someone you can't communicate with?
> Is there someone who believes differently from you?
> Is there a problem you can't solve, no matter how hard you try?
> Is there something you'd like to say to your Mom?
> Is there something you'd like to say to your Dad?
> Is there something you'd like to say to your Sister? Brother? Aunt? Uncle?

These next questions are also part of the INDIRECT or SCAN list, but since they can embarrass the patient before he is ready to bare his soul, you should instruct him that it is okay to not answer them:

> Do you have a secret you're afraid to tell me?
> Have you recently been almost caught in your secret?
> Do you have a sexual fantasy?
> Other than sex, is there another feeling in your sexual fantasy?
> Do you have a negative feeling about the therapist?

■ **PROBING OR FOCUSING QUESTIONS.** The *starting questions, core questions,* and *indirect* or *scan questions* are all asked at a time when we don't really know what feeling is coming up. Their job is to *shake the wires,* to look at all possible places that old feelings might hide, and try to find a pop-in.

Once the pop-in shows itself, the game has changed. Let's suppose that while answering the scan question, the patient has a pop-in, for example, "a woman in a black dress." If it pops-in to the viewing screen just once, I'd ignore it. But if it pops-in a second and third time, I'd consider the possibility that it is the first piece of a blocked scene. You've found a leak in the dam. It is at this point that you use PROBING and FOCUSING questions.

Like tuning in a TV set, or focusing a camera, you don't do it until you've found the right channel. Starting, core, and scan questions can be asked without a lot of skill, but PROBING and FOCUSING questions should be asked carefully, gently, as though you are talking to someone who is busy solving a calculus problem. You don't want to intrude. You don't want to interrupt. The patient may need your silence while he is trying to get hold of this vague, fuzzy, ghost that we call a pop-in.

This is where asking questions becomes an art. You, as a therapist, must be sensitive enough, tuned in to the patient enough, to decide whether your probing question will interrupt a delicate fragile thought, or will it be just the perfect gentle nudge that helps the patient explode. Listen to your patient. She can tell you when a question feels right. When in doubt, silence and gentleness is always safe.

If the pop-in is, for example, about a woman in a black dress, you ask:

> What is it about the woman in the black dress?
> Tell me about the woman in the black dress?
> Do you see any other pictures?
> Tell me what happened.
> Go to the beginning and tell me the whole story.

Typically, when a blocked memory starts to surface, the patient may say "This is silly. I feel like I'm making this up." These doubts are actually a sign of health. You must encourage the patient to keep looking at the unbelievable story as it unfolds:

> Go ahead. You're doing good.
> If you feel like you're guessing, that's OK.
> Go ahead, make a guess.

The Therapist should never make a guess. Let me say that again. **The Therapist should never make a guess,** because he could be planting ideas in the patient's head. It is safe for the *patient* to make a guess because his guess will be based only on his pictures and his feelings.

If the patient pauses for a long time, you might say:

> Continue.
> Is there more?
> What's going on in there?
> What's the feeling?
> What question would you like me to ask?

When the patient begins to cry, you can see it by watching his lips and nostrils. If he seems to be holding back his tears, don't point out that he is holding back. That will just interrupt him. Say in a gentle whisper:

> What are the tears for?
> What's the feeling?

If the patient has just spent a long time talking about present time, if for example, he talks 30 minutes about his boss, encourage him to look into the past by asking:

> Does your boss remind you of anyone earlier?

The patient may avoid feeling by talking about his boss in *general, vague terms.* If you help him to get specific, he is more likely to find old pain. Ask him if there is one specific word to describe his boss. He may answer, for example, with the word "unfair" or "arrogant." Then you can lead him into a specific old feeling by asking:

> Was there someone earlier who was *unfair?*
> Was there someone earlier who was *arrogant?*

Sometimes the patient will have a lot of feeling connected to a single word. You can unleash the tears by asking for a definition.

> What does *arrogant* mean to you?

■ **QUESTIONS FOR FINDING BLOCKED MEMORIES IN DREAMS.** Dreams are discussed in Chapter 4. Here are some questions you can use with dreams:

> Tell me the whole dream.

Was there a feeling in the dream?
Was there a famous or special person in the dream?
Look at each piece of the dream and tell me what it
reminds you of.

■ **PROGRAMMED (OR HYPNOTIC) COMMAND
QUESTIONS.** These questions require explanation and are
discussed more thoroughly in Chapter 5. They are important
in the first several sessions when a patient can't get started. If
a patient starts easily, you may never need these questions:

What do you see on your viewing screen?
Are you having problems with your viewing
screen?
Is there a word or phrase that is interfering with
your viewing screen?
Is there a word or phrase that you use all the time?
Do you have a hypnotic command interfering with
therapy?

If the patient has a word or phrase that he repeats habit-
ually, for example "You know," you should instruct the
patient to:

Repeat the phrase "You know," over and over and
watch your viewing screen.
If that doesn't work, then repeat the *opposite,*
"I don't know" over and over and watch your
viewing screen.

■ **QUESTIONS TO DIG OUT A BLOCKED SCENE.** These
questions are explained thoroughly in Chapter 3:

Can you remember the most unhappy day in
your life?
Move to the beginning of the scene and tell me
when you're there.
Now run through the entire scene to the end.
Is there an earlier beginning?

Move to the earlier beginning and tell me when you're there.

Now run through the entire scene again.

■ **SYMPTOM QUESTIONS.** Sometimes a physical symptom can be a pop-in. In other words, the symptom can be a message from your subconscious. A backache can mean that you have carried a heavy burden of blocked pain. A buzzing in your mouth can be the blocked need to suck milk from your mother's breast. An aching back, a sore muscle, a rash, a buzzing feeling in your mouth, might be your body trying to tell you something. If you have an aching back, ask the question, "Why does your back hurt?" If you have a skin rash, ask "Why is your skin sore?" or "What is it about the rash?"

CAUTION: Obviously, backaches, rashes, etc. can also be completely physical and unrelated to blocked memories.

Messages From The Super Conscious

Nothing is more burdensome than trying to understand someone else's dreams and symbols. I nearly died of boredom when I read Freud's classic "Irma Dream" because I knew in my heart that no one would truly understand it except Freud himself. That's why I have intentionally placed my few significant dreams in an appendix where the normal reader will not bother to look.

This brief appendix is purely for future scientists who might wish to delve deeper than the average reader. These few symbols and dreams are significant because they represent *messages from my Super Conscious.* Depending on how open-minded you are, my Super Conscious could be considered as a source of scientific information or a figment of my imagination. I personally view Him as a living being who knows more about brain function than I do.

"WHY CAN'T YOU PRIMAL?"

When Nancy asked the question "Why can't you primal," this is the picture that appeared on my picture screen, and I knew its meaning instantly. When I was 5, 6, and 7 years old I loved to play with clay. I enjoyed rolling it into the shape of a snake, or a long rope. It would always be pointed at both ends. Sometimes I would cut the snake with a stick or a knife.

The Super Conscious sent me this picture of my clay snake in sections as a way of telling me that the neurotic pain is like my long clay snake. It is also like a long pointed turd wedging it's way out of the opening of the anus. The pointed ends are like a wedge, meaning that once the tip wedges its way into the opening it will widen the opening and then it can't be stopped.

The Super Conscious was telling me that once the pain starts coming out of me full force, there will be no way to stop it. It is safer to cut the pain into sections before we open the door.

THE YELLOW HOUSE PROGRESS REPORT DREAM

In all of my progress dreams, a hill is the symbol for therapy. Therapy is like a hill because it is hard to go up to the top (stage 1) but it will be easier to go down the other side (stage 2). At the top of the hill is a yellow house, and inside the house is an old woman with a broken arm.

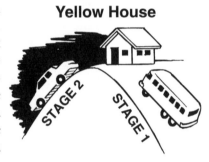

Yellow House

The story goes like this: As I go up the hill I am trying to steer a bus while sitting in the back seat. My visibility is so bad that I cannot stay on the road. This means that the first stage of therapy is sloppy and uncontrolled because I don't know what is coming next. But when I reach the top of the hill, the old lady with the broken arm gives me a road map to guide me on my way down the far side of the hill.

As I go down the other side, it is dark and scary, meaning that I am closer to real feelings, but I feel safe because I am inside a very solid car, and I have a road map to guide me. This means that stage 2 will be frightening yet safer because I will already be familiar with each scene. In stage 1 I will have already experienced my 25 blocked scenes. Stage 1 will be like a *road map* for stage 2.

There is an additional meaning of the two stages. This meaning might be critical to any scientists who are looking for a *total cure*. It means that I must go through each scene *twice*. The first time I experience each scene as *symbolic* or *fragmented* reliving. The second time I will experience a *total reliving* of each scene, but the intensity will be reduced because I've already drained off a large percentage of the pain.

The *yellow house* and the *old lady with the broken arm* later proved to be predictions of scenes to come later. They are at the top of the hill because they are pivotal. In other words, when I experience the yellow house scene, I will be simultaneously ending the symbolic reliving of stage one and entering the total reliving of stage 2. The *yellow house scene* came to me many months after the progress dream. I was lost in Chicago for 6 terrifying hours and the police found me in a yellow house. The scene about the *old lady* did not come up until 2 years after the progress dream. The *old lady* was my Grandma. She had lived next door in a garage that my Dad had remodeled into an apartment.

It is significant that the *yellow house scene* and the *old lady scene* came to the surface many months *after* the *progress dream*. Apparently, my progress dreams have predictive power. But this is not magic or clairvoyance. It simply means that the Super Conscious has access to information that I don't have from the other side of the blockage.

THE YELLOW TRUCK PROGRESS DREAM

In my dream a yellow semi-truck is speeding up the hill. When I free-associated about the truck, I remembered a time when I used to work in a retail store. Every day we would unload at least one 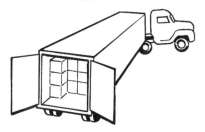 truck behind the store. There were two men that helped me unload the truck, and they reminded me of my two brothers, Dick and Bill.

I immediately knew the meaning of the dream: My blocked scenes are like the boxes in the truck. Each scene is packaged separately from the other scenes so I can discharge them one at a time. The truck was originally loaded in chronological order, and we will have to unload it in the opposite order...reverse chronological order.

Again for the scientists looking for a *total cure,* this dream adds to the meaning of the previous progress dream. It means that during stage 2, when I totally relive my blocked scenes, the scenes will be felt in reverse chronological order. For example, age 13 first, then 12, then 11, and so on.

The Certified Therapist

Throughout history it seems that every large organization eventually loses sight of the original intentions its founders. For that reason I would like to make a clear statement to those who may own the Cure By Crying Institute and copyrights after I die.

The Therapy belongs to the common man and woman. It is a tool that low income people can use to lift themselves up out of poverty and create more productive lives for themselves. It would be a crime against the common people to require 4 years of school, large fees or state licensing for such a simple process. The only requirement, as far as I am concerned is that both the patient and the therapist must read the book. There is a tape version of the book for slow readers. I don't object to certification from the Cure By Crying Institute as long as the common man is still allowed to do The Therapy without a certificate.

This simple requirement that the patient read the book (or tapes) will prevent every conceivable abuse. If the therapist does something wrong, the patient will spot it.

Obviously the do-it-yourself therapist will make a few mistakes, but the most incompetent therapist could not harm the patient. The nervous system has a built-in "governor" (see pages 8-10) that makes it impossible to remember or to feel more pain than you can handle. The very worst thing that can happen with an incompetent therapist is nothing... no tears...no scenes...no memories...and a big waste of time. That's the worst!

The uncertified therapist will work for trade. No money need change hands, though frankly I don't object to money changing hands. All that is required is two neurotics willing to help each other. It can be two friends, roommates, sisters or brothers, husband and wife. When Nancy and I did it, we alternated days. On Monday, Wednesday and Friday, I was the patient and she was the therapist. On Tuesday, Thursday and Saturday, she was the patient and I was the therapist. We traded time instead of money.

The therapy is done in the privacy of your own home. There are no chemicals, no drugs and no way that innocent bystanders can get hurt. The only tools are questions, answers, and intelligence.

It would truly be a crime against the human race to require a college degree or state licensing for such a natural process. It would be like requiring a license to go for a walk, or to contemplate nature.

It pains me to imagine where I would be today if I were not allowed to use The Therapy because I failed to meet college requirements. I'd still have a rash on my face, I'd have headaches, nightmares and sleepless nights. I'd still be a slow reader. I'd still have a miserable marriage and I would proba-bly have raised 3 neurotic kids who would go out and raise more neurotic kids.

MONEY ENTERS THE PICTURE

During the year while I was writing this book, I would often sit in a restaurant sipping coffee, while working on a chapter, with papers and pens all over the table. Frequently a person at the next table would ask what I was doing, and I'd tell them. It happened many times, and I've told strangers about the book.

To my surprise about 9 out of 10 of these people would say, "I'd like to read that book when you're done." Then they would tell me about their own emotional difficulty and that nothing they had tried so far had solved it, or they'd tell me about a son or daughter who needed help. It appears to me that the majority of families in the United States has at least one member with a serious emotional problem.

I have no doubt that there is an enormous demand for The Therapy. I can easily imagine that someone may wish to use it as a way to make money. In fact, I can imagine a day when there are thousands of therapists charging a fee for their services.

Once money comes into the picture, certification may become a serious issue, and I may not be here to tell you my wishes, so I'm going to tell you now.

I do not object to eventually having educational requirements, as long as there is also a provision that the amateur therapist can freely use The Therapy without a certification. It is my fond wish that low income people who cannot afford a therapist will always be able to use this method.

I do not object if professional psychiatrists and counselors wish to use The Therapy. It would not surprise me if some therapists are already using similar methods, but just call it by a different name. We don't own the method. It belongs to the world. It has existed for 40 years in the writings of Freud, Janov, Hubbard, and many others. All I have done is to organize it, and say it clearly without all the voo-doo language, so that common people can use it.

If a professional therapist wishes to use The Therapy, his only requirement is to read the book all the way through. He does not need my permission, nor certification other than a certificate from his own professional association.

There may be times when a professional therapist wishes to be certified for his own prestige and credentials. If we decide to certify therapists, the most obvious requirement would be not schooling, but rather to go through The Therapy as a patient. Then he would experience first-hand the bawling, programmed commands, doorways and pop-ins, finding scenes, and all the rest.

A schooling requirement is less important because The Therapy will greatly increase the person's ability to read and learn. School does not make a person smarter. Everyone is smart. Everyone is a potential genius. The Therapy will unblock the brain power that is already there.

You're probably tired of hearing me say it, but even if we have certified therapists, I insist that you also allow amateurs to use The Therapy freely. The professional can take pride in saying, "I'm certified." The amateur can say honestly, "I've read the book and I have permission to do The Therapy, even though I am not certified."

PROTECTING OUR GOOD NAME

One valid reason for certification is to protect a name that has financial value. Let's say for example that one day there are 100,000 therapists using The Therapy. If 5,000 are certified per year, each one pays a fee of several thousand dollars to become certified, then the Institute could have annual sales in the millions just for certifying therapists. The name would be valuable to the Institute and to the thousands of therapists.

Let's imagine what would happen if one unscrupulous therapist got into the news for molesting children, or having an affair with patients, or using his clinic as an outlet for drugs. He would tarnish a name that has taken years to create.

We may be tempted to use certification as a way to check a person's honesty and integrity before certification. This is valid thinking, as long as you realize that there is no paper test that can measure honesty, and there is no 4-year college degree that can teach integrity.

A personal interview is of no value because some of the most evil people in the world are great performers and willing to say anything. The most valid way to check a person's integrity is as old as the hills. We check their past record, IN PERSON! Find out where he has worked and how long. Talk to his supervisors and find out the quality of his relationships. Was he a hard worker? Thorough? Dependable? Most importantly, did he have good relationships with other people?

It is a bad sign if a person changed jobs (or wives) every 3 weeks. It is a good sign if he has a history of finishing what he starts.

We in the therapy business must believe that people *can change*. People do quit drugs. People can stop stealing...but that does not mean that we have to certify them.

In the case of someone who has a horrible past record, who has turned their life around by using The Therapy, here is how we should certify them: We create a status between certified and uncertified. Perhaps call it an "apprenticeship" or a "probation."

Then if that therapist does something bad that gets into the news, we can be interviewed publicly and say "We have not certified Mr. Jones yet. He is in our apprenticeship program. We were aware of his past drug problem, and we were willing to give him the benefit of the doubt. That's why he is an apprentice instead of a fully certified therapist."

And thus, the name is protected.

HOW TO TEST THE CANDIDATE

Many years ago, I was a member of a club of public speakers. A man named Jerry was the *worst* speaker in the club. His speeches were slow, boring, and lacked emotion. To my surprise, he was awarded "Speaker of the Year" for the entire state, because he had passed all of the paperwork requirements, perfect attendance, etc. But the paper testing did not measure the one thing that mattered, speaking.

I tell you this as an example of what often happens to big, old organizations. The really *talented, creative* people who start the organization move on to bigger and better projects or they die of old age. The less talented people stay for 30 years and ultimately, they run things. They're not bad people, but their understanding of the *original creative process* is reduced to a bunch of written *rules and procedures* that get more and more out of date every year. In the words of the great Peter Drucker, "Every knowledge eventually becomes the wrong knowledge." Ultimately, these less creative people lose sight of the goal of the organization. They consider paperwork and legalities to be more important than getting results.

If I were to write a letter to the people who might one day control the Cure-By-Crying Institute, here is what I would say:

"Please don't forget your goal is to cure neurosis. Being a therapist is a creative talent. It is an art more than a science. It requires skills that will not show up in a paper test: patience, honesty, persistence, sensitivity, warmth, the ability to listen without judging, and a little bit of intuition.

4 years or 40 years of college will not increase those qualities. And I don't think there is a paper test that can measure them. A better way to train therapists is to put them through The Therapy. As their mental health improves, they will grow in patience, persistence, sensitivity, warmth and intuition.

A one-page form may be useful to be sure you have their name and address correct, and other essential information, but it will not measure their skills. A better way to test would be an internship or apprenticeship where an experienced therapist could watch and observe the younger therapist.

There is a danger that the older therapist could himself be a paper pusher who values rules and regulations more than results. So to be fair to the younger therapist, I would suggest that 3 different experienced therapists should observe him in action for several hours each. If 2 of the 3 think he is qualified, he should be certified.

Another valid method of testing would be to personally interview the candidate's patient to find if he/she was helped by the candidate. It would not be valid to do this by mail or phone. It would be easy for an unscrupulous candidate to ask his best friend to write a fake letter, and again a bureaucratic old therapist could misjudge the patient. I would suggest again that 3 older therapists interview the patient to determine if the neurosis has been improved. And if 2 of the 3 say yes, the therapist should be certified."

STATE LICENSING

As I write these pages in 1994, it would be legal for you or I to do The Therapy for pay in many states, as long as we don't call ourselves by the wrong title. In Iowa, we can legally call ourselves "therapists" or "counselors" or "blocked memory therapists," but we cannot use the term, "Mental Health Counselor." That particular term requires a masters degree, and 2,000 hours of internship.

In my state in 1992, the various therapy associations lobbied in the legislature because they wanted to be licensed as badly as I wish to avoid it…but why? Why would professional therapists want to be licensed? Why would they want to pay the fee, and do extra paper work? Why would they invite government regulation?

The most obvious answer is money. They want legally acceptable credentials so they could receive payments from insurance settlements and government programs like Medicare. Perhaps they also felt that the credentials might give them more respect in the court room and in the news room.

On the surface, it would appear to be a good thing that therapists can be paid by insurance and government, but there is a danger whenever you let yourself be owned by someone who does not understand your work. Every good businessman knows that it is dangerous to have a silent partner own more than half of your business, because he will eventually force you into some bad decisions.

I suspect this is where the doctors got off track. They get so much money from insurance companies and Medicare that medical decisions are no longer made by doctors, but rather by politicians and accountants. A doctor today will often close his eyes to his own good judgement and recommend surgery because the insurance will pay for surgery, but it will not pay for prevention.

Every psychiatrist knows deep in his heart that his patients need to feel the old childhood pain. Yet he'll put his patients on drugs because the insurance company will pay for drugs but will not pay for a hundred hours of talking therapy.

This book and this therapy is committed to the principle that should have been obvious 50 years ago. If you want to cure the patient, he must remember and cry about his childhood traumas. I'm afraid that if your income depends on insurance companies and politicians, they will eventually talk you out of that commitment. So my advice is this: Do the therapy for free, or do it for whatever the patient can pay you. Do it for sweet corn and tomatoes. As long as you own yourself, you will be likely to do what is good for the patient.

HOW TO PREVENT GOVERNMENT REGULATION

There are some valid "public safety" reasons for government licensing, but none of them apply to The Therapy.

A car should be licensed because a car can hurt innocent bystanders. A meat market should be licensed to avoid food poisoning. A doctor should be licensed because he can kill people with surgery and drugs.

In The Therapy, there are no innocent bystanders to be hurt, no food to be poisoned, no surgery, no chemicals, and no drugs. The requirement that the patient must read the book will prevent the naiive from being mislead.

In The Therapy, the patient does the work. The patient cures himself. If anyone should be licensed, it's the patient rather than the therapist. But I hope you can see how rediculous that would be to require a person to have a license to look into his own mind. Only the most oppressive and mindless government could conceive of such an idea.

Governments tend to get involved when there is a conflict, when someone is hurt, or imagined to be hurt. If we can avoid conflicts, there will be no reason for a fair and reasonable government to notice us. And that is what we want, to handle our affairs with so much integrity that there are no conflicts and no need for government involvement.

If you are in conflict with psychiatrists and other therapists, they may react by suing you or by using their political power to require licensing. It is better politically and financially to team up with other therapists. It is a foolish businessman who tries to "fight" his competition. It is wiser to love your competitors and form a brotherhood with them.

Years ago auto dealers learned that they sell more cars when they locate next door to other dealers. They create traffic for each other, refer specialized business to each other, and they learn from each other. Sometimes they even share advertising costs, "Come see the 8 auto dealers in downtown Wichita."

The same is true in the therapy business. It is a good policy to never say an unkind word about other therapies. Give them your respect. You can learn from them, and they from you. Instead of fighting them, let them buy our books and tapes, and perhaps a certification fee. And we might consider buying their book. Don't be so arrogent as to imagine that our method is perfect. It is just a beginning. There is much more to be learned.

Be careful about your prices. A high price invites bad publicity and criticism. Why not sell a million books and certificates at a fair price instead of a thousand at a high price.

Some people believe that America is great because of free enterprise, but the age of true free enterprise ended around 1870. I believe that our greatness lies in our ability to BALANCE free enterprise with socialism. Europe and Russia went too far with socialism and that's why they had trouble in the 80's. America stayed strong because we balanced socialism and free markets. And you should do the same, sell your service at a reasonable profit and sell as much as you can, but also consider the good of the common man and the future of our planet. If you can balance profit with social needs, you'll have a business that will last a thousand years. And if you consider the needs of the people, there will be little reason for government to get involved in your business.

LAWSUITS

A few lawsuits are normal for any successful venture but a lot of lawsuits might open the door to government involvement.

Let's imagine the worst possible scenerio. Let's say a drug addicted teenager, high school drop-out, reads the book and decides to do therapy. After several sessions he commits suicide. The father becomes aware of the book and believes that The Therapy caused the suicide so he decides to sue the Institute.

At this moment, if you are the president of Cure-By-Crying Institute, you might decide that to prevent future lawsuits, every therapist must have a college degree in psychology and must pass a stringent paper test.

Please, I beg you, stick to your guns! The patient must read the book (or tapes). The amateur therapist must read the book (or tapes). The professional can be certified if he goes through an apprenticeship program. Otherwise, no requirement.

Take my word for it. Requiring a college degree or a complex test would not have prevented the suicide, nor the lawsuit. But it might prevent millions of low-income people from curing themselves.

If you remember to balance profit with society's needs, to always consider what is good for the common man, in all of your business decisions, you will have no problem with the judge or the jury. Ask the judge and jury to read the book and especially this chapter. Point out that the book is full of cautions and warnings to protect vulnerable people from damage.

It's the people who quit high school that need The Therapy. Why do you suppose they dropped out in the first place? Perhaps because of emotional problems, lack of energy, depression. If high school drop-outs and drug addicts do The Therapy, we should be proud of it, shout it from the roof tops.

One final word on business advice and on avoiding legal trouble. The secret to making money and avoiding lawsuits is to be a giver, not a taker. Not that you should work for free, but rather you must always put your needs last and the needs of other people first. If you always do what is good for society, then free enterprise and socialism begin to blend together. No one can sue you and make it stick if you think of other people first. And, the funny thing is, when you think of others first, in the end, you'll make more money.

Index

E

Echidna, 185-187
Edwin, Norum, Schrumpf study
of vitamin B12, 197
Ego, Super-ego and Id, 203
E-meter, 53, 216
Ending the session, 117-118
Ending The Therapy, 143
Engrams, 104
Enormous quantity of pain, 61,
123, 201, 208
Exploding patient, 138-140
Exteriorizing, 178, 205

F

Faith healing, 17
Fatigue, lack of energy, 11, 197
Fear, 117, 139-140, 167-169
FDA, 199
Fields, Sally, 170
First session, Chapter 5, pp.
103-122,
How to instruct the patient,
109-111
Flow, 48-49, 120, 131
Fool's reliving, 32-33
Four bushes, 112-115
Franklin, Benjamin, 161
Fragmented reliving (same as
reconstructed reliving),
27-29, 169
Free association, 46, 227,
Definition, 48-49
From dreams, 89-90
Freud and, 203
Instructing patient, 110-111
Patient can't, 130-131

Free radicals, 199
Freud, 25, 81, 91, 119
Discovery of subconscious,
181-186
Great discoveries 202-203

G

Gagging, 146, 168, 219-221
Genetic, 173-178
Governor, 9-10, 138-139, 176
Great discoveries, 201-213
Greeks, 198
Grouper, 107
Growth hormone, 196
Guessing, 70
Fragmented reliving, 28-29
Therapist must not, 74-76, 122
Gun dream, 99

H

Hallucinations, 176
Harrel, Dr. Ruth, 197
Headaches, 11, 18, 191-200
Hearing voices, 170-173
Heart disease, 9, 98, 198
Warning, 10
Sleep apnea, 221-223
Heavy sleep, 87-88
Heroes, 160-162
Heroin, 139
Hilgard, Ernest, 17
Hill, Napoleon, 173
Hippocampus, 174, 00000
Hoffer and Osmond study of
vitamin B3, 197
Holder, 107
Holocaust, 163

THE PRINCIPLES

Audio
Cassettes

"Tom has a talent for simplifying complex material. He get's a chapter down to a page, then a page down to a sentence. And when he gets it down to a sentence, it's so pure and simple." *Matthew Spivie*

THE REALITY TAPES by Thomas A. Stone

The cheapest way to buy The Reality Tapes is to order the whole set for $260.00. You'll be paying $10 per hour. You may order tapes individually for $15 per hour. All prices include shipping. The whole set includes:

- History of the World, 4 hrs.
- Religion and Morality, 4 hrs.
- Economics-vs-Politics, 3 hrs.
- Why Wars Start, 1 hr.
- World Trends, 2 hrs.
- How to Solve Money Problems, 1 hr.
- How to Find an Opportunity that Fits Your Talents, 4 hrs.
- How to Borrow Money, 1 hr.
- Secrets of the Millionaires, 1 hr.
- Taking Bull out of Bookkeeping, 1 hr.
- Getting Things Done, 1 hr.
- How to Sell More Stuff, 1 hr.
- Taking Bull out of Selling, 1 hr.
- How Mental Blocks Keep You From Making Money, 1 hr.

COMING IN 1996, NEW TAPES by Thomas A. Stone

- Taking the Bull Out of Investing
- How To Know What Is True
- Managing Your Car
- Sexual Reality For Men
- Sexual Reality For Women

THE JAMES E. TOLLESON TAPES............................$200

I told you about Mr. Tolleson on page 161. Mr. Tolleson will verbally turn you upside down and dump all the junk out of your head. Then he'll teach you how to think the way you did when you were a little kid, before you got messed up. Price includes shipping.

DEAD DOCTORS DON'T LIE by Dr. Joel Wallach $15

Dr. Wallach has been nominated for a Nobel Prize. This tape is a wonderful explanation of the importance of minerals in the body. Price includes shipping.

CHILDREN OF TRAUMA by Jane Middleton-Moz $15

This wonderful lecture helps us to see how we traumatize our children, and suggests a better way to help them during trauma. Price includes shipping.

HOW TO ORDER. The prices above may be out-of-date by the time you order your tapes. So please call our office to get the current prices. 1-800-410-CURE (that's 410-2873). Send check or money order payable to:

CURE BY CRYING, 4316 ½ S.W. 9th, Des Moines, Iowa 50315